THE ECONOMY OF ABUNDANCE

BY
STUART CHASE

330.973
C487e

NEW YORK
THE MACMILLAN COMPANY
1934

Copyright, 1934, by STUART CHASE

All rights reserved—no part of this book may be reproduced in any form without permission in writing from the publisher, except by a reviewer who wishes to quote brief passages in connection with a review written for inclusion in magazine or newspaper.

Set up and electrotyped. Published March, 1934.

34313

PRINTED IN THE UNITED STATES OF AMERICA
NORWOOD PRESS LINOTYPE, INC.
NORWOOD, MASS., U.S.A.

7/7/34 B. & T. (Carnegie) 1.88

We have learned that history is something that takes no notice whatever of our expectations.

OSWALD SPENGLER

The consistency of modern technique is tough and demanding. No doubt it will have its way.

REXFORD G. TUGWELL

The vital point in business practice is the vendibility of the output, its convertibility into money values, not its serviceability for the needs of mankind.

THORSTEIN VEBLEN

CONTENTS

CHAPTER I

FORTY TO ONE

Suppose that the thirteen million people living in the United States in 1830 had awakened on the morning of January 1, 1831, with forty times the physical energy they had gone to bed with the night before. An active picture meets the mind's eye; a very active picture. A lumberman can fell forty times as many trees in a week, a housewife sweep forty times as many square feet of floor; forty barns can be built in the time hitherto required for one—and forty chests, and forty chairs. Porters can transport forty times their accustomed load in a day; weavers ply their shuttles forty times as fast—if the shuttles can brook the strain; and children raise forty times their normal rumpus.

Assuming no increase in the invention of labor-saving devices—and where would be the point with such an exuberance of labor available—what might we logically expect in the way of economic changes in a culture essentially handicraft? From an economy of scarcity, with barely enough to go around, the young republic would almost immediately enter an economy of abundance. The food supply could be increased, not forty-fold, due to the lack of tools and cleared land, but perhaps five-fold, in a remarkably short time; whereas to double it would probably provide a plethora for all. Every family could have a fine house,

1

filled with fine handmade colonial furniture; every man could have a fine coat, one for every day in the week; and every woman a chest of linen as big as a box stall. . . . Fine horses and fine carriages, books, flat silver, tapestries, gardens, great public buildings, medical attention, education.

The new energy would get through to everybody. It would flower at once into goods for the ultimate consumer. Workshops must be enlarged, tools added to, new houses, roads, capitols, libraries, theaters, hospitals, built. In a fairly simple economy such as that of 1830, the standard of living for the whole community could not fail to mount enormously within a relatively short time.[1] Indeed, a very high standard in terms of the forthright and durable articles of the day could be achieved with only a fraction of the energy delivered. Rather than forty-fold, perhaps five-fold, or even less, would be enough to achieve the standard, so rapid and direct was the conversion into consumers' goods at that time. Hours of labor could be cut to two or three a day, and still the citizens would have to take to climbing mountains or organizing expeditions to the unknown west, or playing the most strenuous variety of games, or writing long epic poems, or painting miles of murals like Diego Rivera, or even dispensing with work animals, to spend their surplus vitality.

Today, in the United States, we have precisely this equivalent of energy per capita. It is not in our muscles, but in our delivered power resources.

---

[1] 1830 was not a pure handicraft society. Prime movers were just coming in, but their frailty is demonstrated by the historic thirteen-mile race on August 25, 1830, in Baltimore, between Tom Thumb, the first locomotive built in the country, and a horse and carriage. The horse won.

Observe that it is not a potential total of installed horsepower, but actual coal, oil and natural gas burned, and water turbines turned. If we counted *capacity* to deliver work, the ratio would be greater than forty-fold.[2] This energy is given, and has been used, every foot-pound of it. Yet the average standard of living, while including more commodities and services than that of 1830, is still below the margin of health and decency; millions are acutely undernourished, miserably housed, deplorably clothed, while economic insecurity clutches at almost every heart.

Energy, the capacity to do work, is here, a living, demonstrable reality, but it has not got through to the wayfaring man as expressed in his standard of living; the essential work has not been done.[3] Even in 1929, with an average wage of only $1300, it obviously had not been done. The furnaces roar, the turbines whirl, the compression chambers stiffen to the shock of the explosion, but life is a more uncertain business than it was a century ago, and that happiness which Mr. Jefferson bade us pursue is as remote as when he wrote the Declaration of Independence.

The capacity to produce goods, furthermore, is not measured by raw energy alone. Also important

[2] Walter N. Polakov, writing in the *New Republic,* January 4, 1933, gives the average working hours for all central power stations as 2800 a year. The total number of hours in a year are 8760, so the ratio of use to full capacity is only about 32 percent.

[3] According to Professor A. B. Lamb of Harvard, the maximum potential energy of high handicraft cultures, including manpower, work animals, windmills, water wheels, etc., is about 4,000 kilogram calories per capita per day. This is our 1830 base. In 1929, the energy in coal, oil, natural gas, and waterpower actually consumed was 156,000 kilogram calories per capita per day. Adding the original 4,000, we get a total of 160,000, which is forty times greater than in 1830.

is the skill of the mechanism which takes the energy and shapes the product. To use a homely illustration: I can mow about an acre of pasture in a ten-hour day. My neighbor, a farmer all his life, can mow two acres in an equal time, with a smaller expenditure of energy. His muscles are trained to the scythe, where mine are not. Similarly, in the field of mechanical operations, engineers have devised increasingly skilful methods of utilizing a given quantity of energy. For the twenty years from 1909 to 1929, for example, F. G. Tryon in *Recent Social Trends* computes an increase of 66 percent in kilowatt hours secured from every ton of coal used for the generation of electric power, and a 47 percent increase in railroad haulage per ton of fuel burned.

But multiplying energy, however efficient its application, cannot proportionately multiply standards of living in industrial societies. Such societies are subject to extreme specialization, and great quantities of energy are required to link the specialized processes together, especially in the form of transportation. The United States has been justly called an "experiment in transportation." Whereas in 1830, the forges of Connecticut obtained iron ore almost in their back-yards, and delivered horseshoes and hinges to the man across the street, the steel mills of the 1930's haul iron ore by boat and rail from northern Minnesota, coke from Pennsylvania, manganese from Russia, and sell rails, girders, sheet steel and tin plate from Florida to Oregon. Most of the sheet steel goes to Detroit to be made into motor cars, which in turn are shipped to every corner of the nation. It takes energy to mine these raw materials—including the coal which is potential energy itself—to fabricate them in scores of interlocking processes, and to haul both the partly finished, and the completed article, all about the map.

So in the best ordered of societies devoted to technology, output for the consumer could not increase so rapidly as total energy. A philosopher would, however, expect to see living standards increase directly with energy delivered, but at a somewhat slower rate. Swinging his dispassionate eye upon the United States of America, he finds a forty-fold increase in energy per capita and a standard of living which, in terms of material wellbeing, is still deplorably low.

How great is the unavoidable loss due to specialization and to absorption in the process of transforming raw energy into useful heat and work? Even if we assume that this fraction is as large as 75 percent, which would seem generous, a forty-fold increase in energy would result in a ten-fold increase in living standards. But the actual increase in material wellbeing of 1930 over 1830 is probably not more than two-fold.[4] Ninety-five percent of our energy is doing us no good.

Something is wrong here; something very wrong indeed. The experiment in transportation could never account for such a difference. Where has the balance of delivered energy gone? This is no academic question. Somebody has robbed us of that which is more vital than gold. A ton of coal can perform as much mechanical work as 1,000 men. "The energy basis," says E. W. Zimmerman, "is truly the foundation of civilization. It determines the choice of materials which can be utilized; it sets a definite limit to the size of performance; it governs the degree of mobility,

[4] See Chapter IV for a description of pre-machine standards in America.

and in general controls the arts, and through them shapes the institutions—material and non-material. . . . It may be said that, in its widest sense on its material side, history is the story of man's increasing ability to control energy." [5]

Observing a hypothetic community specifically designed, in the words of Buckminster Fuller, "to get the most for the least," and then observing the real America of today, it is reasonably clear what direction the vanished energy has taken. It has disappeared down fifteen paths, as follows:

1. In the construction of factories, railroads, skyscrapers, stores, warehouses, oil wells, mines, in excess of prudent requirement and use. Capacity enormously exceeds output.

2. In constructing the plant in uneconomic locations, involving wasteful crosshauling of both raw materials and finished product.

3. In building Megalopolis, the machine age city. Upwards of 30 percent of all energy delivered to it must be used solely for the purpose of preventing citizens from expiring of congestion.

4. In reclaiming and irrigating agricultural lands for crops which never should be grown—not for "market" reasons, but because they cannot be consumed. If we ate all that our reclaimed acres could grow, we should be seized with national stomach ache.

5. In maintaining plant projects 1, 2, 3 and 4 above. Excess capacity demands its upkeep.

6. In cutting forests beyond prudent needs and requirements, and fighting fire in the resulting slash.

7. In the operation of competitive establishments—duplicate haulage, selling forces, branches, advertising

[5] *World Resources and Industries.*

outlays, administrative and clerical forces. The waste here is predominantly human, but no little energy is required to transport and supply the competing corps.

8. In a monumental obsolescence rate. The building and tearing down of plants, houses, machines, equipment of all kind. Much of this is due to shoddy construction, much to the salesman's demand for a high replacement rate.

9. In energy delivered to the financial structure: bank buildings, telephones, telegrams, cables, radios, airplanes, crack express trains, elevators, tickers, Wall Street "extras." There are about 1,000,000 persons in this sector at the present time to be supplied and energized.

10. In style changes—goaded by salesmanship rather than human nature. Energy losses are fantastic in this department, as any textile mill executive can tell you. A factory's output for weeks may be rendered worthless because the designers guessed wrong.

11. In competitive small scale farming and its mechanized equipment—tractors used only a few hours in the year, for instance.

12. In overproduction—actual goods spoiled, burnt and dumped. We are not allowed to add this to our standard of living, much as we might like to.

13. In exports for which no exchange in imports is accepted. A favorite pastime of generous Uncle Sam. Goods *for* foreigners, but no goods *from* foreigners. The spirit, of course, is charming, but gifts on this scale require large blocks of energy.

14. In pleasure motoring. This is perhaps the greatest single consumer of the new energy. Obviously it is not all waste. Some of it comes under the head

of death and destruction, with 30,000 citizens killed on the roads; some under the head of escape from intolerable cities, intolerable homes, and intolerable monotony; some under the head of putting one's neighbor's eye out, and some under the head of genuine pleasure and use. With all due allowances, the last item bulks large, and so adds to material wellbeing, and a genuinely higher standard of living. What this fraction may be, no sensible statistician would dare to compute.

15. Finally in the factor of conversion loss—probably the only item which is strictly unavoidable. About 15 percent of all electric power generated is lost in transmission to the ultimate consumer. A locomotive turns only some five percent of the potential energy of the coal it burns into actual mechanical work. (A turbine does much better.) The same holds true for the human engine, however. The potential energy of the food we eat suffers large losses before the residue appears as muscular work. We must also remember that a great fraction, approaching half of all modern energy, is devoted to heat, not to mechanical work. The steel industry is a ravenous consumer of energy in the form of heat for its furnaces. Energy so utilized is not necessarily wasted; it is cardinal in the technological process, but one must beware of considering the forty-fold increase as being all devoted to mechanical motion.

Adding these fifteen categories together, a reasonably complete story appears of where energy has been dissipated, and why so little gets through to the ultimate consumer. It is perfectly obvious that his wants and desires have never been central in the picture. The plant has been built with other ends in view; a crazy patchwork, magnificent in bulk, superb in some of its detail, but not designed for securing the most for the least.

The modern standard of living comprises no more food than that of 1830, though the variety is greater, the balance somewhat better dietetically. Living quarters are more crowded, but with better heating facilities, and with a marked improvement in water supply and sanitation. Conveniences and labor-saving devices in the home are impressive—electric power, telephones, radios, refrigerators. Nine farmhouses out of ten, however, are still without electric power connection. Clothing is flimsier and less durable, but perhaps more comfortable and certainly more hygienic, except for shoes. Schools are greatly improved, and reading matter omnipresent—with the reservation that most of it is not worth reading. Health services are often magnificent; but two persons in five, according to the Committee on the Costs of Medical Care, are unable financially to avail themselves thereof, while mental diseases are on the increase. Facilities for recreation have expanded greatly, primarily as commercial enterprises. Sociologists are inclined to doubt, however, whether play is as rewarding to the individual as it was in simpler cultures.

Riding through North Carolina not long ago, I saw a bright blue motor car, resplendent with chromium fittings, in the yard of a dilapidated shack constructed of rough logs and plastered with red mud. The car and the hut belonged to the same share cropper. It struck me as a not unreasonable summary of the net gain in living standards since 1830. Measured in tonnage and variety, the wayfaring man has undoubtedly improved his position, but in fundamental wellbeing, I hold to the conviction that doubling the standard is a fair estimate.

These immense new powers have run to immense new wastes. Our very junk piles would have ransomed a king in the middle ages, with their stores of metal and findings. The state of New York undoubtedly contains more fabricated "wealth" than did all Europe in 1400 A.D. But, for all its due capitalization, it is not wealth in terms of human use and enjoyment. It is largely misplaced energy crystallized in stone and steel. The United States was a poor country in 1830 and is a poor country today in terms of the human calculus.

Ten definitions

The Economy of Abundance is self defined. It means an economic condition where an abundance of material goods can be produced for the entire population of a given community, a condition never obtaining anywhere until within the last few years.

Behind this obvious definition, however, lurk a series of more subtle connotations. The smooth optimism of the phrase is seriously disturbed when, for instance, we set technological abundance into a background of prevailing financial habits. These habits were laid down in an Economy of Scarcity, and clash bitterly with the facts of plenty. Abundance is not alone a promise to mankind, it is a savage threat to the real or supposed interests of special and powerful groups of men everywhere. Let us select a series of these more realistic definitions, including both promises and threats. Abundance may be defined as:

1. A condition where the bulk of economic work

is performed not by men, but by inanimate energy, drawn from coal, oil and water power. Such a condition was reached in the United States towards the close of the nineteenth century, *circa* 1880.

2. A point at which living standards per capita reach an average which is, at least potentially, twice as high as ever obtained under scarcity conditions. Reached *circa* 1900.

3. A point at which the curve of invention, following, as it does, a geometric increase, becomes the dominating factor in economic life—precisely as the Nile was the dominating factor in the economic life of Egypt. *Circa* 1870.

4. A point at which the scientific method supersedes the use and wont of the craftsman in the production of most material goods. *Circa* 1900.

5. A point where output per man hour becomes so great that total productive labor must thereafter decline, even as output grows. A point at which labor ceases to be a measure of output—as it always has been in preceding ages. *Circa* 1920.

6. A point at which overproduction carries a more serious threat to the financial system than shortage. *Circa* 1880.

7. A point at which specialization has destroyed all practicable local self-sufficiency and made economic insecurity for all classes latent, growing, and ultimately intolerable, given no change in financial methods. *Circa* 1900, with the closing of the American frontier.

8. A point at which consumption becomes a greater problem than production. *Circa* 1920. "Our economy," says F. L. Ackerman, "is so set up that it produces goods at a higher rate than it produces income with which to purchase them."

9. A point at which the industrial plant is, substantially, constructed, requiring relatively smaller
outlays for capital goods in the future, and where
pecuniary savings are not only unnecessary in their
old volume, but seriously embarrassing. *Circa* 1925.

10. A point where, due to the pressure of the technical arts, costs, prices, interest rates, debts, begin a
descent with zero as their objective. *Circa* 1920.
(Hidden for a time by the credit inflation of the
New Era.)

The Economy of Abundance is a composite of all
these definitions. The date of its appearance on the
American scene varies as one definition or another is
chosen. A simple average of all ten dates gives the
year 1902. The concept has more substance when
taken in the light of the first five definitions, which
deal with physical facts. In view, however, of the
practical problems now confronting not only America,
but all industrial nations, the last five definitions, dealing as they do with financial institutions, are significant. It is interesting to note that the dates of the
first group average earlier than those of the last.
Abundance was in operation for some years as a
physical reality, before it began seriously to obstruct
the financial mechanism.

Before proceeding to a categorical analysis of the
effects of Abundance upon prevailing institutions,
financial and otherwise, let us cast an inventory of
what energy and the technical arts might do in the
way of living standards, using the existing plant.
How abundantly could we live, if the powers of
Abundance were permitted freely to function in our
behalf? We might or might not be ten times better

off in a pure technical Utopia; how much better off might we be tomorrow? Engineers have been presenting us with hopeful promises for years. What is the best they can do for us without starting from the beginning and building the plant anew? Of all the questions which the Economy of Abundance has raised, this is one of the most relevant.

CHAPTER II

IS THERE ENOUGH TO GO ROUND?

THE technocrats promised every family on the continent of North America $20,000 a year, and a sixteen-hour work week. This is perhaps the peak of promises based on an abundance economy. Charles P. Steinmetz saw a two-hour working day on the horizon —he was the scientist who made giant power possible —but he stipulated no family budget total beyond "necessities and comforts."

"All engineers know," says Ralph E. Flanders, former president of the American Society of Mechanical Engineers, "that if an engineer-dictator over industry could be appointed and given complete control over raw materials, machinery and trained labor, he could flood, bury and smother the people under an avalanche of gods and services such as no Utopian dreamer in his busiest slumbers ever imagined."

Wolman and Peck in *Recent Social Trends* tell us: "Advances in the application of science and engineering in industry have radically transformed our conceptions of the inevitable scarcity of material goods and of the niggardliness of nature by expanding, apparently without limit, the possibilities of increased production."

Fred Henderson, in his *Economic Consequences of Power Production,* is more specific: "Without any further increase in our knowledge of power and of

14

technical processes, or of our available materials, we could multiply production ten times over if the needs of the world were permitted to express themselves in effective demand. . . . It would not be a question of an eight-hour day or a six-day week, but more probably of a six-months working year—which is already the rule for university dons."

Buckminster Fuller is still more definite. Modern man, he calculates, is 630 times more able than was Adam. Eliminating wasteful forms of work, four million Americans laboring fifty-two seven-hour days in the year (364 working hours, an average of one per day) "could keep up with every survival need"—meaning basic necessities for the whole population.

Walter N. Polakov announces that "fifty weeks, four days, six hours is enough"—a twenty-four hour week and two weeks' vacation—and presents the following equation:

Output $= T \times E \times R$.

Where T equals time, E equals the number of employees, R equals the rate of work. New drafts of energy and technical skill are constantly increasing R. Therefore, in the same time, with the same number of employees, output must increase with R. Conversely, for the same output, T or E, or both, must decline. As industrial methods improve, total hours are reduced for an equivalent output. Whether unemployment or leisure will result depends on non-technical factors.

Harold Rugg in *The Great Technology* estimates a possible minimum living standard between ten- and twenty-fold greater than the minimums of 1929, on a sixteen- to twenty-hour work-week.

The All American Technological Society, headed

by General W. I. Westerveldt, recently announced:
"We find that between ten and twelve million men
and women, engaged in the various technological
activities of our productive and distributive system,
produce and distribute all the raw materials and
finished commodities required by a population of 125
millions." That is, about ten percent of the population
can now take care of the material needs of all. This
ratio, says the Society, promises to be rapidly reduced, due to "technical improvements of great consequence now looming on the industrial horizon."

Rexford G. Tugwell writes: "Our industry sup-
ports a larger population, furnishes it more generously
with goods, and requires the expenditure of less effort
[human effort] than was ever true at any other time
or place. But at the same time if the present scale of
operations were expanded, if the last vestiges of competition were abolished, and if we worked to a plan
which encompassed our total resources and required
of each industrial group its utmost capacity, we should
be able to multiply many times even our present possibilities."

"It is an open secret," said Thorstein Veblen in
1919, "that with a reasonably free hand the production experts could readily increase the ordinary
output of industry by several fold—variously estimated at some 300 to 1200 percent."

Sir Arthur Salter in his recent monograph on
mechanization announced:

We have now, for the first time in human history, all the
material resources and the human skill needed to provide both
the necessities and comforts of life to the whole of the world's
population; to support, indeed, a population several times as
great at standards very much higher than any hitherto known;

and to give to every man not only material wealth but the leisure and opportunity which he needs to realize the full potentialities of his nature and enjoy the full heritage of the civilization in which he lives.

"With existing plant and power, and natural resources, labor and managerial knowledge," remarks J. A. Hobson, "the world could produce at least twice as much wealth per capita as it is actually producing, without undue strain upon human energy."

One can continue to cite such evidence indefinitely. Fortunately, A. M. Newman has been collecting it for years and saves us the trouble by the following summary: "Among them [such estimates] a substantial agreement is found that by better use of the mechanical facilities at our disposal we could produce many times our present supply of goods at considerably less effort." The five-hour day tends to be the maximum estimate in Mr. Newman's collection.[1]

This is all very fine and cheerful; but examination of the estimates shows wide variation in possible performance, while the basis of calculation is reasonably cloudy. One wishes that the speculators would get together more, define their terms, delimit their territories, and check their figures. I for one doubt profoundly if the whole world should be comprehended in any of these optimistic calculations. The energy, materials and technical training required effectively to raise the living standards of the populations—"teeming" is, I believe, the word—of China and India, present a problem which staggers me, if not the cheery calculators. To give Chinese and Indians, for instance, as many automobiles per capita as Americans now drive would mean 140 million

[1] *Enough for Everybody.*

cars. At only 5000 miles each per year, and twenty miles to the gallon of gasoline, this fleet would demand thirty-five billion gallons of gasoline, which alone would take far more than the whole world production of petroleum in recent years. As future reserves are severely limited, the happy Chinaman would be lucky if he drove his new car as much as two years before junking it forever.

Almost a decade ago I wrote a book, well supplied with figures, which sought to analyze the waste of manpower in the United States, based primarily on the Census of Occupations for the year 1920.[2] The final summary ran as follows:

Manpower wasted in useless and vicious goods and services	8,000,000
Manpower idle on a given working day, including preventable sickness and accidents	6,000,000
Manpower wasted in inefficient production	4,000,000
Manpower wasted in distribution	2,500,000
Total, a minimum of	20,500,000
Against a potential working population of	40,000,000

On the basis of these calculations, an Industrial General Staff could presumably double the then standard of living. A good deal of water has gone through the turbines since the figures were prepared. In 1920 transmission lines were few, automatic factories almost unheard of, technological unemployment an unknown phrase. Since that year, the industrial plant has had upwards of 100 billions of new capital investment added to it. Management methods as well as machines have been greatly improved. Again, energy consumption has streamed ahead as a more relevant index of

[2] *The Tragedy of Waste.*

productivity than manpower. The above estimate stands in urgent need of revision, and the direction can only be upward. The ratio of waste, if cast in terms of energy, is greater now; and *per contra,* standards of living, were waste eliminated, could be more than doubled.

Suppose Mr. Roosevelt, or Mr. Flanders, or who you please were given power to appoint an Industrial General Staff, and to establish immediately the highest standard of living possible with the existing plant. How many hours of labor a day would it take, and what would be the minimum family income? Nobody knows. No authoritative study has ever been published. Dr. Harlow S. Person of the Taylor Society believes that "if equipment were utilized to capacity we could double the quantity of physical goods produced in a working day." This is a common estimate, based on the known fact that industrial capacity as a whole is about twice normal market demand.

The plant

Let us take an aërial view of the plant as it stands, with the invaluable assistance of Robert R. Doane.[3]

THE PHYSICAL WEALTH OF AMERICA

1,000,000,000 acres of farm land
  500,000,000 acres of forests
  100,000,000 acres of coal, iron, copper and mineral land
   34,000,000 acres of rivers and lakes
  100,000,000 acres of urban territory in various stages of development
     316,000 oil wells
   6,500,000 farms
  185,000,000 horses, mules, cows, sheep and swine

[3] *New Outlook,* April, 1933.

500,000,000	chickens, turkeys, ducks and other domestic fowl
16,000	cities and towns
37,000,000	buildings—factories, warehouses, power plants, stores, schools, libraries, churches, theaters, hospitals, homes
127,000,000	major machines—locomotives, turbines, motor cars, tractors, trucks, lathes, looms, etc.
700,000,000	installed horsepower, plus
2,000,000	miles of rural roads
750,000	miles of surfaced highways
250,000	miles of railroads
59,000	miles of navigable waterways
736,000	miles of pipe lines
160,000	miles of electric transmission lines
88,000,000	miles of telephone, telegraph and cable lines

These figures are impressive. America possesses a magnificent plant in the aggregate. Where is another nation with such natural resources, installed horsepower, bulk machinery, network of transportation and communication lines? Scanning the table, and remembering that only 125,000,000 citizens are heirs to this wealth, it seems incredible that any should be in want. Yet perhaps half of them are in comparative want as I write. The reason is not far to seek. We shall pause for a moment to examine it, for the distinction which it covers is cardinal for this book.

Vendibility and serviceability

The United States has not hitherto regarded itself as a social group composed of men, women and children who need food, clothing and other things. It has never had a national economy or, at least up to March, 1933, any but the most casual interest in the material welfare of the group. As Veblen said:

Industry is carried on for the sake of business, and not conversely; and the progress and activity of industry are conditioned by the outlook of the market, which means the presumptive chance of business profits. . . . Serviceability, industrial advisability is not the decisive point. The decisive point is business expediency and business pressure. . . . The vital factor is the vendibility of the output, its convertibility into money values, not its serviceability for the needs of mankind.[4]

The great plant with its imposing assets has hitherto been placed in one frame of reference: that of business, finance and saleability. What is it worth, in dollars? It was "worth" perhaps 400 billions in 1929 and 200 billions today, which, you say, is obvious nonsense; for the land has not sunk into the sea, the fowls are still squawking in the barnyard, and the machines are more powerful than ever. Wait, my friend! You are *changing the frame of reference* from vendibility to serviceability. In terms of dollars —and dollars are the counters in the game the citizens have hitherto played—the United States, after four years of depression, is a jewel in a pawn shop, worth fifty cents on the dollar.

God and geology laid down the natural resources, without capital valuation; but the operating plant has been constructed primarily in the vendibility frame, to sell either its output or itself at a pecuniary profit. Its vendibility has been measured and remeasured on the ledgers of banks, the balance sheets of great corporations, the tickers of stock exchanges. Its serviceability is unmeasured and unknown.

"Competitive business," says James Rorty, "is war. Advertising is a means by which one business competes against another business in the same field,

---

[4] *The Theory of Business Enterprise.*

or against all business, for a larger share of the consumer's dollar. . . . The pother about ethics, about
'truth in advertising' is now and always has been
too silly to waste time over. Judgments of ethical
values are inapplicable under the circumstances. Good
advertising is advertising which promotes the sale of
a maximum number of goods at a maximum profit for
a minimum of expense. Bad advertising is advertising
which doesn't sell, or costs too much. Judged by
these criteria, good advertising is testimonial advertising, mendacious advertising, fear-and-emulation advertising, tabloid balloon-technique advertising, effective advertising which enables the advertiser to pay
dividends to the widows and orphans who have invested their all in the stocks of the company." [5] A
flatter and honester statement of the principle of
vendibility would be difficult to find.

Engineers, economists, politicians, journalists, even
business men, constantly speak of America as though
it were one great household, devoted to improving its
material condition. "We produce so much, and we
consume so much. . . . The national income is thus
and so. . . . We divide the product so and so and
our average income is blank." Stuff and nonsense; the
frame of reference has been unwarrantably shifted.
There is no national family, no national plant, no
national income, in any collective sense. The development of American industry cannot be understood in
such terms—terms which assume a controlling intelligence. Five million business men, more or less, make
certain decisions, corporate or individual, which affect
directly forty million wage and salary workers, and
indirectly the entire population.

[5] *The Nation*, December 20, 1933.

As a byproduct of this individualistic behavior, certain goods are produced, certain inventions made, certain buildings and machines constructed, certain services rendered. One speaks of the paradox of plenty. Who has plenty? *We* have too much: *we* have overproduced. But there is no *we*. There are only you and I. Have you too much? I am sure I have not. A few rich families have too much—or had in 1929. But most American families—say 98 percent of them—did not have too much in 1929, or any other year. And where is the paradox, so long as money, not goods, is the object of production?

Certain corporations have too much copper, rubber, merchandise, on hand. They heave and strain but cannot get rid of it. Certain farmers have too much wheat, cotton, tobacco, in storage. Certain factories have more square feet of floor space and more machines than they can use. Certain skyscrapers have offices which cannot be rented. Coal mines, oil wells, filling stations, railroad tracks, are indifferently busy. Obviously, in good times and bad, there are more capital goods than can be utilized, and more consumers' goods than can profitably be sold. But *we* do not own or control them. *We* should be glad to use them, but that requires purchasing power, and *we* cannot obtain more purchasing power without disallowing a great many pecuniary claims, and indeed disrupting and remaking the whole financial structure.

The Roosevelt Administration (February, 1934) cannot make up its mind whether it wants to restore vendibility—popularly known as Recovery—or inaugurate a new economic system based on serviceability. Obviously, until this choice is made, the conflict will be reflected in zig-zag administrative performance.

An inventor comes to you with a new aluminum alloy, talking behind his hand. He produces samples, diagrams, cost figures. You ask to see the patent papers. They are in order. The thing looks good; remarkably good. Who else knows about it? Nobody knows about it. Splendid. Not a word to a soul. Old Johnson would give his eye teeth to get in on this. Not a word to him. But there are Jackson and Josephson, good men both. With money. Jackson has the ear of the First National, moreover. Good. Now for a lawyer. We must move quietly, quickly and safely.

So you put up your money, and Jackson and Josephson put up theirs, and the First National puts up its money—on a first mortgage. Contracts are executed, ground is broken, a factory is built. It is built in your town because you live in the town; or it is built in the next town because "labor conditions are better," which means that laborers are willing to work longer hours for less pay. (The whole distinction I seek to make lies in this phrase. "Better" labor conditions from the point of view of vendibility mean poorer labor conditions from the point of view of serviceability.) You are not building that factory to give your neighbors higher standards of living. The idea never crosses your mind—until possibly your advertising agent suggests that a "service appeal" might increase sales. You and Jackson and Josephson and the First National are building that factory to make money.

This little story illustrates how all the factories and all the railroads and all the power developments and all the commercial buildings in America have been constructed. Only government and a few charitable foundations have built with use standards predominant. To them we might add those who build their own houses and clear their own acres without benefit of contractors. The contractor's main business, of course, is to make not houses but money. He will contract to build a skyscraper on the top of Mount McKinley, or an opera house on the Dry Tortugas, if there is money in it. Witness what he did in Florida in the days of her front-foot glory. The energy and materials thrown away in a few years were probably sufficient to maintain the population of Florida in opulence for a generation. Living standards were not the idea; money was the idea, and waste was the result.

The United States Department of Agriculture has drafted a bill to revise the Pure Food and Drugs Act, with the purpose of protecting the people of America, especially the poor and unsophisticated, against substances proven to be either useless, fantastically expensive, grossly misrepresented, noxious, habit-forming, or deadly. In Washington recently I saw six testimonials from innocents who thought they had been cured of diabetes by a quack remedy, and side by side with the letters, the six death certificates of the same persons, dated a few months later. This fair and strictly serviceable proposal to prevent mass injury, fraud and murder has been met by a veritable avalanche of abuse, obfuscation and indignation. Three great industries are roaring defiance, threatening to deprive congressmen of their seats, newspapers and magazines of their advertising, the administration of support for its recovery program. The drug and cosmetic trades have no more interest in rendering a service to the community than a blind man has in the cinema. The proposed bill threatens sources of income.

Vendible values might be lowered. Nothing else matters.

Indeed it is almost impossible to conceive of any genuine service to be extended to the American people which will not instantly be attacked and vilified by some or another vested interest. The Tennessee Valley Authority proposes to reduce the price of electricity to home owners and farmers, and the whole power industry rises up in arms. Certain architects and manufacturers design pre-fabricated houses, cheaper, cleaner, tighter, more efficient and comfortable than anything previously known, and bankers, insurance companies, mortgage holders, real estate speculators, plumbers, masons, carpenters, electricians, rise up in arms. A devastating insect plague descends upon the cotton crop, and a statue is erected to the boll weevil. Cotton is grown not for use, but for sale, and plagues promote the scarcity, and hence the vendibility of cotton, or almost any other crop.

Considering the history of the American plant, and the motive of its construction, one is perhaps surprised that it is capable of throwing off even the meager standard of living it does. Left entirely to enterprisers it could hardly have reached its present level. Fortunately, enterprisers have not had the entire direction. Engineers must be consulted when railroads are built and profitable inventions exploited. Engineers must deal in the terms of energy and the laws of physics. There has resulted a century-long struggle between the money-making wishes of business, and the orderly conceptions of engineers.[6] Utter confusion has thus been held in check to a degree, and the plant constructed with at least a left-handed re-

[6] See Horace Taylor: *Making Goods and Making Money.*

gard for orderly considerations. It had to be, or it would fall down.

Again, vendibility has been in violent conflict with an abundance economy. When goods are relatively scarce, the price for them is relatively high, and the margin of profit relatively great. Technology reduces costs and threatens price structures, thus throwing the interests of money-makers at right angles to the needs and desires of consumers, who want low prices.

When a nation exports more than it imports it is said to have a "favorable balance of trade." Favorable to whom; to the people of the nation? Not at all. Favorable to the profit and loss accounts of exporters. Obviously the nation is not served by sending out more goods than it receives, but the contrary. From the point of view of serviceability, it constitutes an unfavorable balance.

The past is past. We cannot go back to 1830, and build the plant over again on a serviceability basis, as a city lays out its water supply system, as a housewife prepares a meal. In casting an inventory, I must perforce try to measure a thing in terms other than those which have governed it heretofore. Competently to assess real serviceability would require a group of engineers, economists and statisticians working for many months. There are, however, certain known facts, and particularly certain qualitative considerations, which may make a rough chain-and-compass line by one lone student not too presumptuous.

CHAPTER III

THE frame of reference in this chapter is straight serviceability, with an Industrial General Staff in control. It is assumed that business considerations are non-existent; vested interests unknown. The major elements in a material living standard are food, clothing, shelter, educational facilities, health services, recreation. Energy consumption is common to them all, and should head any contemporary survey. Let us consider the elements, one by one.

Energy

With the present supply of energy the General Staff would have no trouble. As explained in Chapter I, energy consumption is forty times what it was in this country in 1830 for every man, woman and child. The plant already possesses the naked power for throwing off a tremendous increase in living standards, provided other factors, such as raw materials and labor, could be arranged for, and certain debilitating wastes eliminated. Not an additional ton of coal or oil would need to be burned, not another power house constructed—though it would be well to finish Boulder Dam and Muscle Shoals. Certain gaps in the nation-wide transmission grid should be filled.

Food

Coming to tangible goods, it is certain that adequate food supplies are available. Where earlier cultures spent from 80 to 90 percent of their total energy for the production of food, American spends only ten percent, according to Bassett Jones. If the General Staff managed agriculture as one great, coöperative industry, it could, without adding materially to present equipment, provide a succulent and balanced diet for every family, with considerably less energy than is now expended, and with less land. How? By allowing the poor, marginal soils to return to forest, and concentrating on the rich soils, employing somewhat more intensive cultivation. O. W. Willcox, agro-biologist, after careful study makes the claim that if only 80 percent of possible yields were achieved by means of water and fertilizer, *50 million acres* would grow all the wheat, corn, oats, barley, rye, cotton, potatoes and sugar now produced on 350 million acres.[1]

Indeed, technology permits expansion of food supply either way: by making intensive cultivation easier, or by extensive cultivation of certain poorer soils where tractors run readily. Zimmerman points out that mechanized agriculture widens the choice of crops, reduces minimum time required for field operations, and permits farming on land which under a scarcity economy *could not support a population.* Dry farming in the wheat belt is a case in point. The pressure of food supply on population is chronic in an abundance economy.

Food is probably the most inelastic of all human wants. It does not proliferate into luxury consumption with the readiness of housing or clothing. The per capita tonnage today is undoubtedly *less* than it was a hundred years ago, although the diet is better bal-

[1] Letter to Senator Robert F. Wagner, January 26, 1933. Copy sent to the author with yield calculations.

anced. Population will probably decline after 1950, according to recent calculations, which means that the demand for food will decline. Furthermore, under high energy conditions, many people live in heated houses, and work in heated shops, offices and factories. They do not need the bulky, heat-giving food of their ancestors. Thus, however you look at it, there is, or could easily be, more than enough food to go around on a serviceability basis.

The General Staff would have to change the crop schedules to give a better balanced diet. We are still eating too much cereal, sugar and lard, and not sufficient "protective" foods, like fruits, vegetables and especially milk.[2] Dr. O. E. Baker says that a man can be fed for a year on two and a half acres of hay stoked into a milk cow, but requires eleven acres of fodder to keep alive on beefsteaks. Such are the calculations with which the General Staff must be vitally concerned. The Staff could not provide us with coffee, tea or certain tropical fruits. If these were to remain in our diet, surpluses should be grown, or manufactured, to exchange for them.

To get the most food for the least energy, great mechanized farms are clearly indicated. Russia, with the scourge of scarcity still near, promptly set them up. We shall probably come to them for some crops, but the General Staff could readily insure the food supply without them by budgeting physical requirements, eliminating marginal farms,[3] allocating present equipment to the better soils, acting as a single distributive agency for all food output. We could be fed

[2] See Emily White Stevens. *New Republic,* October 25, 1933.
[3] President Roosevelt is now proposing a huge program for buying up marginal lands (December, 1933).

well—there is not the slightest question about it; and it could be done almost immediately with little capital expenditure. The food supply needs neither more energy nor more machines, for the moment. *It needs planning.*

Clothing

Clothing, like food, presents no real problem from the point of view of adequate quantity. Style factors, however, which are not serious in foodstuffs, are something else again. Always in considering national budgets—and they keep me awake of nights—I have in the forefront of my mind a picture of a Georgia Negro and his family on a one-mule cotton patch. Is this family to be adequately fed, clothed, sheltered, educated and entertained? If it is not, the calculations are irrelevant. We could undoubtedly clothe this family, and all other families, from our present supplies of raw materials, textile mills, and garment shops. Rayon, and perhaps ramie, might displace silk, but the excess capacity of rayon factories—excess in terms of vendibility—is large. Furthermore, rayon, being a synthetic fiber, is better adapted to automatic machine production than silk, wool or cotton. We have a huge surplus of cotton and, with centralized planning, plenty of wool and leather. But to give the Georgia Negro and his wife all the latest in fancy fabrics and style changes, would tax the clothing industry beyond its present capacity.

Here are a few of the figures on which I base my confidence as to clothing. Preparing their case for the cotton code of the National Industrial Recovery Act in the summer of 1933, a special committee of the textile manufacturers reported thirty million spindles and 582,500 looms in place. On a three-shift basis, this standing equipment "would care for more than twice normal consumption requirements." Normal consumption is inadequate consumption on a service basis, but twice normal is probably more than adequate for all varieties of cotton goods. In 1927, the capacity of the woolen industry was reported by the Wool Institute as three times the output. Ethelbert Stewart, of the United States Department of Labor, calculated the capacity of the shoe industry in 1927 at 730 million pairs against consumption of 330 million.[4] This capacity has since increased. He figured that 260 shoe plants, out of the 1329 then in the country, could supply the whole market demand at the time.

Nor should the General Staff overlook the very important point laid down by F. A. Westbrook in a case study: "The layout of the plant [the Belknap Manufacturing Company] was so carefully planned that it was possible to double production by adding machinery but without changing the location of any machines originally installed."[5] Under modern methods, production can be increased drastically without equivalent increase in investment. The same roof, power connection, floor layout, are sufficient.

Shelter

Moving on to the third great staple, shelter, a problem of the first magnitude confronts us. One can say flatly that American industry is not now organized and cannot be organized, short of extensive readjustments covering a number of years, adequately

[4] New York *Telegram,* July 24, 1928.
[5] *Industrial Management in this Machine Age.*

to house the people of this country. At a conservative estimate, two-thirds of all American families are inadequately if not indecently housed, according to the researches of Edith Elmer Wood and others. The condition obtains in the slums and cubicle apartments of great cities, in the peeling bungalows of suburbia, in the shacks and shanties of the coal towns, in the leaky, cold, unplumbed farmhouses of the great open spaces, in the mud plastered cabins of southern share croppers, in the desolate hovels of the hill billies. The editors of *Fortune* declare:

Authoritative estimates put something up to 90 percent of farmhouses, 80 percent of village homes, and 35 percent of town homes beyond the pale for lack of a sanitary toilet within the house, and almost as many for lack of running water. To these inadequate homes must be added homes inadequate for lack of light and air (say a third of the homes in the greater cities), homes inadequate for reasons of overcrowding, toilets in common, dampness, etc. The total most certainly exceeds half the homes of the country.[6]

If to this we add homes without bathrooms and central heating—certainly necessities in any adequate standard—the ratio of subnormal housing jumps to at least two-thirds of all. This means that of thirty million families, twenty million need new homes, or extensive capital improvements in old homes. William F. Ogburn finds that in 1930 the average value of all non-farm family houses was $5,000; 13 percent of such families lived in homes valued at less than $1,500 —the kind you can put your foot through. In that year, one in every eight families paid less than $10 a

[6] *Housing America,* by the editors of *Fortune.* On page 23, twenty million new houses are called for to meet health and decency standards —fifteen million in the towns; five million farm homes.

month rent. Only one family in fifty paid as much as $100 a month.[7]

To put eighty million people into decent, tight, heated houses and apartments, with electric lights and running water, quarters otherwise however modest, would place a burden on lumber mills, brickyards, cement factories, glass works, paint shops and railroads which they have never met; which is beyond the capacity of most of these industries, save over a long period.

The only way out of this time dilemma lies in the pre-fabricated house. Housing, save for bathrooms, electric lights, central heating, and a few gadgets, has changed little in two hundred years. Most of my neighbors in Connecticut, even summer city folks, live in houses built a century ago or more. If city people cannot buy a house as old as that, they build a copy of it. Yet they do not drive about in chaises of 1830, or eat the same heavy food, or wear the same load of homespun clothes. The world rushes by, leaving housing—save in big cities—essentially unchanged, a clumsy, costly, often lovable, handmade article.

Suppose the General Staff brought it up to date by mass production, so that one secured as much housing, for a given cost of energy and materials, as one now secures motor car transportation. This would operate enormously to decrease the cost of new houses if it were done on a sufficiently large scale. One would order from the factory standard parts, which could be assembled in a great variety of wholes. In a day or two a trained service squad would lay down the cement base and bolt the parts together thereon.

[7] The New York *Times,* August 27, 1933.

Between the order and the completed home, ready to live in, days would elapse instead of months, as under traditional conditions.

Pre-fabricated houses, furthermore, can be taken down as easily as they are erected, and thus provide *mobile* shelter. We are going to need mobile shelter increasingly in the years before us. Technological change is shifting industries and with them occupations. It is almost folly today for a working man to own his own home. How long is his job going to last, and where is a new job to be found? The Economy of Abundance has forced us to be a migrating people. We are on the march. Under a General Staff we should still be on the march—with the important exception that a planned job would be found at the end of the journey. Gypsies take their tents. We must take our houses. If we followed Buckminster Fuller's suggestion, those of us who did not live in city apartments would rent our fabricated houses from a central service company, and when we had to move from the Boston district to Denver, let us say, the old house would go back to the Boston warehouse—ready for shipment to somebody else in Boston —and a new house, with changes if we wished them, would be ordered from the Denver warehouse of the same organization.

This may sound wild and strange. It is probably the only way to secure decent, attractive homes for all Americans in the calculable future, at a low cost. It is not a job to be done in a year, or two or three. New factories must be built, new distribution methods worked out, a colossal tonnage moved. For a time, energy resources might be almost taxed. I suspect it would be a ten-year job; at two million homes a year.

But for traditional housing, with its greater tonnage, its hand fitting, its craftsman methods—to say nothing of its immobility—the period would be twice as long. We conclude, then, that the General Staff could not provide us with adequate shelter short of a long, intensive construction program covering at least a decade. Well fed and well clothed, most of us must continue to live in the houses already built, with such plumbing, roofing, electrical and other improvements as fall under the head of patching up, rather than of genuine reconstruction.

Education

Could the last child in America secure a good education on the basis of the present plant? Some critics gloomily assure us that no child in America now secures a good education. They may be right, but our concern here is with buildings, textbooks, and teachers. So defined, I think we can point with considerable pride to our educational plant. Unlike the factory plant it was built primarily for serviceability. It is unquestionably the finest single body of buildings in the republic. Above the dull, ugly quarters of the most ramshackle town, rise the trim and spacious walls of the new high school. Even as a church dominates a Mexican community, a school building dominates an American. Employing Mr. Wirt's platoon system, which keeps the entire school plant continuously engaged, we could undoubtedly accommodate every urban child, with comparatively little additional construction. He could be supplied with teachers, perhaps not the best of teachers at first, but conscientious American teachers, without an undue strain on the normal schools. Textbooks, supplies, transportation busses, would be simple.

The National Conference on Financing of Education has already laid down a blue print for the General Staff to follow.[8] The 150,000 one-room schools (little red ones) still existing should be junked in favor of "central school plants," built under the federal public works program. The present school district map should be obliterated in favor of a new map in which rural units would have about 1500 pupils, urban units 10,000 pupils. The average school district is now only twenty-three square miles in area and requires but seven teachers. Enlarge the areas, centralize the plant, specialize the curriculum, use busses for transportation. Admittedly this is quantity production in education, but it strikes me as inherently sensible as well as efficient.

The conference insists that the national government must come actively to the support of local education. This is probably inevitable, as the mobility of high energy conditions obliterates political boundaries laid down in stagecoach days. The fact that we now have four million persons in the country totally illiterate, and eight million more "whose knowledge of reading and writing is so small that they are near illiterates," is a national problem, as well as one for Saugus County.[9] The illiteracy the General Staff could liquidate through new schools, and classes for adult education. Incidentally this would open up tens of thousands of new jobs for teachers and for college graduates. The Civil Works Administration is already moving to the task.

[8] Report submitted September 10, 1933, after two weeks' conference at Columbia University.
[9] Louis McHenry Howe, secretary to President Roosevelt, in the New York *Times,* November 20, 1933.

Health

The money we have been spending for doctors, hospitals, nurses and drugs is enough, under more rational methods of distributing and paying for medical service, to provide adequate care for all of us who need it, with adequate return for those who render the service. Yet the Committee on the Costs of Medical Care, from whose five-year researches that conclusion is drawn, finds that during the course of a year, two out of five of us receive no individual medical care of any kind. We cannot use what we already have in the way of health resources. "Physicians, on the whole, are unoccupied between one-third and one-half of their working time; one-third of the hospital beds are empty most of the year; thousands of nurses seek employment, but in vain. Meanwhile millions suffer and tens of thousands die from ailments which might be cured or alleviated by medical aid." The committee presents the following table, which the General Staff, if it knows its business, should be quick to seize upon:

	Actual number in 1930	Number needed to provide full service for all Americans
Physicians	144,000	174,000
Dentists	68,000	219,000
Nurses—visiting	19,000	54,000
Nurses—hospital and home	118,000	216,000
Hospital beds	956,000	1,422,000

The personnel increases are considerable, and a certain time would be needed to train the required staff. But what a splendid opportunity this would open for thousands of college undergraduates who have no careers whatever before them under the present economic system. The General Staff would undoubtedly

follow the recommendations of the Committee on the Costs of Medical Care, in respect to group medicine. Under vendibility it is to a doctor's financial advantage to keep people sick. I have been sitting in dentists' chairs on and off for thirty years, and I have yet to hear a dentist volunteer any information as to how I could sit in them less. Doctors and dentists have beautiful codes of ethics dedicated to serviceability, but it is almost impossible to live up to them. The General Staff would make it easy, and I think all but the fee-splitters would be happier men, and do sounder work.

Recreation

Recreation is perhaps more complicated than health but not much more. It is a larger economic field. The automobile industry has already come close to providing a car for every family in the country on the average (thirty million families, twenty-three million pasenger cars). With a capacity of eight million cars a year it would be no trick at all to keep everyone supplied. Indeed the trick would be to keep them from being oversupplied, considering existing highway and parking facilities. Radios for all are easy—factory capacity is in excess of fifteen million sets a year. Parks and playgrounds could be extended without difficulty —once the land value obstacle was taken firmly in hand—as could sporting goods and equipment. Mr. Roosevelt is even now employing 300,000 young men to prepare the national forests for, among other things, great recreation centers. The movies already reach the entire population, statistically, every two weeks—but they do not reach me.

If the General Staff placed its accent upon first-hand

participation rather than upon watching other people play, one can readily prove that the American people could secure a rewarding quota of play at far less cost in energy, materials and labor, than now obtains. The present normal bill for recreation has been estimated at ten to twenty billions of dollars a year, depending on the items comprehended. It is, due to commercialization and excessive mechanization, far too much. Recreation has been taken well-nigh bodily into the province of vendibility, where it emphatically does not belong. Play is by definition not a business proposition. The General Staff should put it back where it belongs, at a huge saving in cost. Incidentally, we should have more fun.

Well, what remains? Religion, art, philosophy, spiritual values? Fiddlesticks. Only fools make budgets for religion, art and philosophy. It has been found, down the aisles of history, that when a given community perfects a technique which allows it to eat with some peace of mind, art, philosophy, scientific curiosity, invariably make their appearance. Egyptian civilization was based on adequate supplies of wheat, Mayan civilization on maize. Ours is the first civilization to be based on inanimate energy. Religion is beyond me altogether in terms of this inventory. Bertrand Russell asserts that the intensity of religious belief among fishermen varies inversely with the size of their vessels. I doubt if economic security will destroy religion, but it may change its form. Doubtless much could be done by the General Staff in centralizing, coordinating, rationalizing, the very large and extremely ill-distributed religious plant we now possess. But if the Staff takes my advice, it will not waste five minutes

on the job. Religion in terms of cubic feet, excess capacity, and balanced load, is a denial of its spirit.

This preliminary survey makes it clear that the existing plant, with its thirty-seven million buildings, its 127 million major machines, its ninety-two million miles of transport lanes, and the rest, is capable of providing adequate food, clothing, education, health services, and recreation, serviced by boundless energy, to all the 125 millions of *us*. Wars we may fear, love we may fear, and the bitter conflicts of our own half-tamed natures, but destitution for ourselves and our dependents we need no longer fear.

An adequate standard of health and security could be set in operation almost immediately without profound physical adjustments, whatever might be the profundity of the mental adjustments. More rural school buildings, recreation centers, sanitary engineering projects, research laboratories, would be required, and some rearrangement of the agricultural output. A larger medical and educational personnel must be trained. The General Staff could not, however, provide adequate shelter for the nation short of a decade. In other departments, every family could be provided for; every sick person; every old person; every child. The standard would be higher than 90 percent of all families actually received in 1929. The Georgia Negro would be five to ten times better off.

The average work week would be thirty hours as a maximum, and might well be less. This estimate is arrived at as follows: In the industrial boomlet of the summer of 1933, government figures indicated that sixty workers, on a shorter work week, were producing as much as a hundred workers did in the "normal" period, 1923 to 1925. If all workers in 1933 were

given employment, they could, theoretically, produce this normal output in a twenty-six hour week.[10]

The total tonnage of goods produced would, I believe, tend to be rather under than over the tonnage of 1929, with far more consumers' goods, and far less capital goods than were produced in that year. Five percent of American families would, on an equal division, receive less in the way of physical quantity, and fewer luxury services than they did in 1929, although in terms of genuine serviceability many of the group would receive more. The very rich would be behind their present style, but they are only a handful and their style does not matter. If equality were not to be the rule, rather merit or ability, the mass standard would drop somewhat, though it would still remain far above the 1929 average, allowing a sliding scale of standards over this base.

Admitting that the General Staff could do thus well by us immediately, how much better can it do in the future? It can build us houses. That will help. It can slowly reorganize and rationalize the plant. That will help. I doubt, however, if we can go more than thrice above a good healthy minimum—which in turn would be far better than 1929—because of certain rigid limitations in the present plant itself.

Limitations

To begin with, the transportation load fixes a maximum, unless railroads, highways, waterways, pipe lines, transmission lines, are to be drastically replanned and relocated. B. E. Hutchinson estimates that the present railroad system is "fully capable of handling about

---

[10] For details of this calculation, see an article by the author in *Current History,* November, 1933.

twice the normal volume of traffic now moving by all means of available transportation." [11] In other words, it could at full capacity move say two million carloads a week, as against the 1929 performance of 800,000 cars. Trucks, waterways and pipe lines could be utilized to add to the total. Present transportation capacity might allow three times the 1929 tonnage flow, but hardly more. I suspect that if all traffic bottle-necks, such as the approaches to Manhattan Island, were given due consideration, the possible expansion might be less, even with crosshauling saved. If all plants in New York City, moreover, were given the opportunity to operate with throttle wide open, could they get their raw materials in, or their finished products out? It would provide a splendid jam for a time, in the best of circumstances.

Again, while American factories have a theoretical capacity probably twice their normal output, they have never operated at capacity as a group, and we cannot be sure that raw materials are available to supply them at capacity. We know that a substantial fraction of total output is now on an automatic or semi-automatic basis, using relatively little direct labor; that a larger fraction is on a mass production basis akin to motor car manufacture and assembly, where many men are on the belt; and that a remaining large fraction is still produced by older methods involving much skilled hand labor. The size of these three fractions has not to my knowledge been determined. Is the skilled labor available to operate the third fraction at capacity? Nobody knows.

In a brilliant quantitative analysis of the history of

[11] Pamphlet: *The Automobile's Challenge to America's Transportation Policy.*

American production, Bassett Jones has laid down certain growth curves which must be given emphatic consideration when estimating potential production.[12] Like population, production has entered a declining growth phase. The rates began to slacken for many commodities about 1910. The curves are heading for an ultimate plateau, due primarily to the exhaustion of non-replaceable raw materials like iron, coal, copper, oil. Sooner or later the world must run short of these prime necessities. Oil appears to be a matter of a few years. Unless substitutes are developed, or resources conserved by better methods of exploitation and utilization, we must be chary of predicting vast increases in physical production.

The cotton textile manufacturers' committee quoted earlier in respect to the number of spindles and looms in place, makes a significant contribution to the theory of limitations: "This mechanical capacity is at present considerably limited by existing housing facilities at the plants." In other words, if textile mills tried to operate at capacity, they could not do so for lack of means to shelter the additional working force. A limitation of this character is temporary, of course, but must be considered.

A definite ceiling to possible living standards is furnished by the transportation load, the availability of raw materials, skilled labor, present housing facilities for workers, the inevitable decline of certain natural resources, and the fact that not all of industry is organized for mass production. Excessive optimism is distinctly out of place when these limitations are given due weight. Sunshiny predictions as to a ten- or twenty-fold increase are downright nonsense. To

[12] *Debt and Production.*

secure any such levels, the plant must be redesigned, relocated and rebuilt, and a whole new science of substitute commodities developed. My guess is a threefold maximum, and I base it primarily on the transportation limitation. Within these limits, however, the General Staff can still work out enormous economies for application to the budget of the wayfaring man. Let us make them explicit.

It can demand more durable goods and proscribe useless and vicious commodities. By doubling the life of a motor car, piece of furniture, pair of socks, razor blade, towel, carpet, electric heater, tennis racket, or what you will, the quantity of goods for distribution theoretically doubles without much increase in cost. Nearly all articles for consumers are now made under the compulsion of rapid replacement. This course is logical and inevitable in an economic system dominated by vendibility. When business enterprise is replaced by central planning, quick replacement becomes illogical and scandalously wasteful, even as it was to the craftsman of 1830. By means of standards, specifications and the use of somewhat more energy—remember there is plenty of energy to spare—the quality of most American goods can be greatly improved. Automobiles can run 300,000 miles (taxicabs already do), razor blades last a lifetime, certain fabrics never wear out. On this program a given amount of raw material can go two or three times as far as at present. This not only increases living standards, but conserves natural resources at the same time.

"Hardly anything," says F. J. Schlink, "tested by Consumers' Research shows signs of the perfect diffusion of the technical arts through industry. Many of the electrical appliances of today are as poorly and unsafely constructed as though the public utilities power network were a development of but yesterday. Some electric fans are found to be so poorly made that the early Singer sewing machines of the sixties partake of the quality of scientific instruments by comparison. Household electrical appliances are among the least badly contrived of all consumers' commodities. Compared with the products of the shirt trade or the laundry industry, electrical goods seem the result of matchless skill. Compared with what engineers can do, and what they do actually perform when the president of the Bell Telephone system wants a first-class phonograph or radio set for his own use, these appliances are as primitive as the blacksmith's forge. Electric clocks that hum and wheeze too loudly to be used in a sleeping room; toasters that burn the bread on one edge and leave it pale brown at the other; table grills that when touched by the wet hands give a slight or considerable shock; electric water heaters that are burned out on the slightest misuse . . . are but examples out of thousands that we have collected by observation and experiment." [13]

The General Staff can release all patents and suppressed inventions for operation as fast as circumstances permit. The obsolescence rate must not be raised too rapidly. Many useful inventions are now locked up because they might hurt somebody's vested interest. Under the assumptions of this chapter, there are no vested interests to hurt. I give you, in passing, the new electric house furnace, and the new arched hollow brick. Both must struggle desperately for life, in the courts and out of them, under the present system. Both can immediately be put to work in a society

[13] *The Economic Forum*, Fall, 1933.

dedicated to serviceability, with healthy royalties to the inventor, as in Russia.

An unknown but manifestly great saving is possible by liquidating present restrictions on output by workers. S. B. Mathewson has explored this dark territory, and come to some surprising conclusions.[14] He finds an exceedingly widespread and ingrained institution. Efforts of management to speed up production in recent years have been repeatedly offset by the ingenuity of workers in collectively lying down on the job. Conscious of the omnipresent threat of technological unemployment, they have taken to quiet and effective sabotage as naturally as a turtle draws within his shell when danger threatens. Who shall complain of this tropism? If, however, the threat of economic insecurity is removed, and a job, or a high living standard guaranteed, we may expect to see a dramatic increase in output per man hour in those establishments or services where energy has not displaced human labor.

Finally, let us not forget the growing importance of services as against goods under modern conditions. Energy releases labor. The service industries require labor, and not much else. The General Staff is thus enabled by conserving labor on the goods front to throw it into the service front—and to raise standards by virtue of more doctors, nurses, dentists, hospital attendants, clinic operators, research workers, statisticians, teachers, foresters, playground attendants, highway workers, traffic directors, mural painters, librarians, actors, dancers, entertainers, linemen, repairmen, servicers of home equipment, and so on. In this department the limitations of transportation load

[14] *Restrictions of Output among Unorganized Workers.*

and of physical production do not apply. While the General Staff may not be able to push goods for personal consumption beyond certain rigorous margins, it has a free hand to push these collective and cultural services as high as available manpower warrants. It is here that a straight per family budget calculated in tonnage or in dollars becomes almost meaningless. Such services belong to no family, but to the whole community, and they are civilization itself.

The above four factors, added to the more obvious economies of a functional control, would, I believe, operate in perhaps a decade to produce an average standard of living at least three times higher than a simple health and decency budget. If you must have a money total—though I warn you it means almost nothing—$6,000 worth of consumers' goods a year at 1929 prices, plus the collective and cultural services which absolutely defy pecuniary appraisal. You will live much more comfortably and derive more satisfaction out of life than did most families in 1929 on $10,000 a year. I see no reason why the thirty-hour average work week should be exceeded, even with the budget pushed to its upper limit.

The above estimates are admittedly crude, and in the nature of pioneering work. Nobody, to my knowledge, has ever passed this way before. If they have value, and I believe they have, it is for their qualitative rather than their quantitative findings. I have tried to set forth the major factors which must be considered; factors which too frequently are disregarded in the usual optimistic estimates. We must be sure, initially, which we are discussing, a Utopian plant, or the present one; we must remember the appalling difficulty of housing—which everybody seems to forget; we must be mindful of limitations like the transportation load; we must be careful to distinguish between goods and services, between consumers' goods and capital goods; we must think primarily in terms of connected energy rather than in manpower and work weeks.

Also, unless one is prepared to face a long, hard transition period involving the complete reconstruction of the plant, it is cruel to submit hifalutin estimates promising to make everybody rich. If this study is worth anything, it shows that the General Staff cannot make everybody rich. It can make everybody in America economically secure, well supplied with mass production comforts, reasonably happy, let us hope, but not rich as a stockbroker counts material riches. You cannot lift the Georgia Negro so far as that with present equipment. Even with Utopian equipment, the ten-fold increase indicated in the first chapter must fall short of the stockbroker's dream—and, in bull markets, his actual realization.

We might maintain a small class of glittering spenders as a sort of national display, if you please, much as a municipality keeps a zoo. It could be as numerous as actually obtained in 1929—say one family in 1300. To supply this gay menagerie with the gilded cages to which it is accustomed would be no trick at all—a mere drop in the total flow of consumers' goods. The rich often set us a very bad example, true, but in high energy cultures, their bill for luxuries is a postage stamp. I doubt, however, if the menagerie should be retained.

In this inventory I have sought to indicate what Americans—all of them—might reasonably expect from an Economy of Abundance in the immediate future; when and if the frame of reference swings from vendibility to serviceability. It is probable that the plant of Europe, outside of Russia and the Balkans, under one general staff, could do almost as well. Russia, in that she is building a new plant from the ground up on a strict serviceability basis, may, when it is built, do even better.

CHAPTER IV

THE ECONOMY OF SCARCITY

Two men are lost on a great desert. One has a full bottle of water, the other a bottle quarter filled. As they move wearily onward, hoping for an oasis, justice demands that they pool the water supply and share it equally. Failure to do so will undoubtedly result in a fight. Now let us transport these two men to a row-boat on Lake Superior. Again they are lost, and again one has a full bottle of water, and one a bottle a quarter full. The full bottle man refuses to share and a battle ensues. Maniacs! There is plenty of fresh water over the side of the boat.[1]

The desert is the Economy of Scarcity; the lake, the Economy of Abundance. The choice between sharing or fighting is chronic in the former, pointless in the latter. Today, throughout western civilization, men in boats are fighting, or preparing to fight, for fresh water. They do not know they are in boats; they think they are still on camels. The lake, as we have seen in the foregoing chapter, is not limitless, but nobody need go thirsty.

Logically, the boatmen appear quite mad. Psychologically their dementia is explicable. The fact that they *live* in the Economy of Abundance, and think and behave in the tradition of Scarcity, is understand-

[1] Adapted from Gorham B. Munson.

able. Even where inanimate energy obtains to insure every survival need, the actual stuff, in the form of consumers' goods, has not got through to the wayfaring man in sufficient volume to give him any assurance that old concepts can be discarded. His new house is foreclosed; his automobile replevined. Even if he knows he is in a boat, dipping water over the side might be punished as mutiny.

All his early conditioning has been in terms of scarcity. The received wisdom of his elders, the philosophies he has imbibed, whether radical or conservative, the books he has read, the sermons he has listened to, the laws he has obeyed, the constitutions he has honored, the moralities he has observed, all have been grounded solidly in scarcity. The philosophy of the desert has been universal. All his going institutions are subservient to it, property concepts are derived from it, political democracy was nourished by it, liberalism grew up in it, free competition was the essence of it, business principles are inexplicable without it, the *Saturday Evening Post* is a serialized scarcity bible. No. We must not judge the men in the boats too harshly nor too hastily.

The typical organization of past civilizations has been a mass of poor peasants, or slaves, tilling the soil. The small surplus per capita above their survival needs was taken by landowner, noble, priest, warlord or king. The overlord fed himself and his retainers, together with a group of craftsmen manufacturing comforts and luxuries. The peasant looked from his wooden plow to the man on horseback in scarlet cloak and envied him; sometimes rose in bitter anger against him. Yet if the whole surplus had remained with the peasants, their standards of living would have risen but little, so relatively small were the ruling class and its body of retainers.

Nourished on this slender margin of food and fuel, civilization maintained artists, poets, statesmen, cathedral builders, scientists, philosophers, as well as overlord, clergy and army. "Dividing up" would have crushed it. J. B. S. Haldane well says that in scarcity, civilization and socialism are incompatible. Here we see the class struggle, the exploiters and the exploited, naked and clear. Yet it was hopeless, the surplus was too pitifully small. Now, in the west, for the first time in history, the surplus is great beyond all previous imaginings. But again, "dividing up" is not the answer. How shall one divide up the Empire State Building, the *Leviathan,* the United States Steel Corporation, or the Pennsylvania Railroad? We may revolt in our row-boats, true, but it must be a different procedure from revolt in the desert.

CONNECTICUT IN 1760

One can reach out in almost any direction for a concrete case exhibiting the Economy of Scarcity: Mexico, the South Seas, China, India, today; yesterday, Egypt, Greece, Rome, Yucatan, Florence, Elizabethan England. As this book is primarily about America, I shall take an American case, even if it is not quite so typical as the more usual lord and peasant community. The life of the Shelton family of Stratford, Connecticut, as carefully portrayed in historical documents collected by a descendant, gives us an accurate picture of what the Economy of Scarcity was like in these United States, 150 years ago.[2] We need this picture as a background for the discussion to follow.

[2] Jane de Forest Shelton: *The Salt-Box House.*

Daniel Shelton came to Stratford, at the mouth of the Housatonic River, in 1686 and applied for permission to build a dock and a warehouse. He died in 1728, leaving nine children. Thaddeus, the third son, inherited 260 acres of primeval land on the edge of town, together with Cuffee, an African slave. Only a rough Indian trail led to the property, but Thaddeus and his wife invaded the wilderness, built a house, cleared the land and grew wheat, rye, flax, barley, corn and clover.

Here young Daniel was born, grandson of the settler. He was taught first by his mother, and then attended the district school. He toiled over Ward's *The Young Mathematician's Guide, in five Parts, Arithmetick Vulgar and Decimal with all the Useful Rules, and a General Method of Extracting the Roots of All Single Powers.* He also learned, perhaps aided by pith ball and string, that "Electricity consists of fine, invisible Effluvia supposed to be of an unctuous and oily nature, which are excited by Attrition." Phonetic spelling was strictly in order, and *cichon* for kitchen, was as readily understandable as *Injun* for Indian.

Daniel not only picked up at home the techniques of farming and craft work but, as the squire's son, he was inducted into business. Large landowners were not mere farmers. They made loans of seed and grain, hired out their slaves and their "five cattle team"— two yokes of oxen and a horse. From time to time they took a flier in West Indian shipping—rum, molasses and tobacco. Accounts were kept on the cellar door, and subsequently transferred to long narrow ledgers. . . . Credit the blacksmith with shoeing horses and oxen, making door hinges, "puling a tuth" [tooth], "up-seting a axe;" charge him with bushels of turnips, corn and wheat. From time to time a balance was struck, together with "resete in full for all acompts from the Beginning of the World to this day."

In 1758, Daniel married Mary of Stratford village, a girl of seventeen. Thaddeus built the couple a house near his own, and Mary's dower furnished it. It was a noble house. The stone chimney was twelve feet square at the base, and the whole structure swung upon it. The oak sills were a foot square, good for two centuries of wear and tear. The sides were sheathed with planks, two inches thick, that ran twenty feet vertically from sills to eaves, and were set in place with wooden pegs. Bricks were not to be had; the central obelisk was native rock, cemented with shell lime mortar from Long Island Sound. All lumber was locally cut and milled, most of it hand hewn.

The whole community assisted in raising the ridge-pole, indeed it could not have been put in place without the aid of the neighbors. As they worked, they refreshed themselves with cider, "winkum" or apple-jack, and "raising cake," furnished by the host. From the house, a long ell led to the great barns. Two wells were dug: one inside the house with wheel and rope, one outside with long pole well sweep. The kitchen was the heart of the house, and the fireplace, nine feet by five, was the heart of the kitchen. Four-foot back logs were dragged by a horse to the very hearth, to burn for a week or more. From October to May, the fire never went out; there were no matches. It was lighted in the fall by flintlock and powder. It is difficult to exaggerate the importance of fire—and the fear of conflagration—in these old New England homes;

and it is interesting to remember that fire is a form of energy consumption.

Thaddeus deeded the new house to Daniel and the lands around it: "Know all men by these presents . . . for the love and affection I bear my son . . . a certain tract of land . . . at a crotched walnut tree with a stone laid on the crotch, running easterly to a group of chestnut spires, then south to a pepperidge tree . . . to him and his heirs forever."

Mary's dower provided homemade linen, iron pots and kettles, wooden ware, chairs, dressers, tables, a few imported textiles from England and Holland, specially commissioned of a sea-captain acquaintance at the beginning of her engagement; a silver tankard and cream pot from the shop of Paul Revere's father in Boston. The groom, according to custom, provided the beds, though not the bedding, a tall grandfather clock, a desk with a secret compartment, the great bible with silver clasps, and blank pages for records of births, marriages and deaths. Nine children were to have their names inscribed in this bible. As the second was being baptized, a breathless courier on horseback arrived from the Hudson Valley, crying the news of the fall of Quebec, a week or more after the event.

The house and the land about it supplied the family with food, fuel and clothing. The cash sale of a small surplus paid for a few imported necessities and comforts. Hogs and beeves, some twelve animals a year, were slaughtered, and bacon and sides preserved in the smoke house. Leather was tanned on the premises, and a cobbler's bench set up. From time to time a journeyman shoemaker came and lived in the house as a guest while he made shoes for all the family, including the slaves. So came the tailor, the cooper, the cartmaker and the weaver. Flax was grown, and spun by the women of the house. Wool was carded from Daniel's sheep. After the cloth was woven, it was sent to the village fulling mill to be dressed. Linen was bleached at home; the coarser tow made clothes for the slaves.

A huge woodpile fed the house's heart, its size denoting prosperity and industry. In the yard stood the great caboose kettle of iron, for rendering animal foods, and for soap making. Lye came from the wood ashes of the hearth. Cider and beer were brewed at home; a barrel of cider made three gallons of "winkum," of which the village distiller took one gallon for his labor. Floors were covered with white sea sand, in the parlor brushed into elaborate patterns by brooms made of cornhusks and twigs. There was a dye pot for homemade dyes. Work clothes were of linsey-woolsey—two threads of linen and one of wool; with leather breeches for master and man. Boots were unknown.

Potatoes were rare, chocolate and coffee almost unheard of, tea a great luxury for company only. It was served in cups no bigger than liqueur glasses. The bill of fare included Indian pudding (from corn), turkey, goose, pork, mutton, salt beef, eggs, wild birds, rabbits, pies, baked apples, apple dumplings, fritters, milk, butter and cheese (made in the butt'ry in the summer), molasses (imported), gingerbread, dough-nuts, cookies, seed cakes, a few vegetables, mostly roots. Oranges were a rare delicacy, suitable for holi-day presents. To handle the great stone oven was a highly skilled task, which only Mandy, the black cook, was competent to fulfill.

Goosequill pens were made with a penknife. In a

neighbor's house there was no clock, and the housewife timed the boiling of her eggs by singing hymns. At the end of the sixth verse, out came Samuel's; the seventh verse, Obadiah's, the ninth verse, Abigail's. . . . Hour after hour, Mary would sit spinning two threads, one with each hand, a foot keeping the flax-wheel moving, and a baby sleeping on her lap. "Everything was at hand and of use; nothing was wasted or destroyed. Idleness on the part of master or mistress, child or slave, was disreputable."

Yet the tempo of life was unhurried. Manners were cultivated; little girls curtseyed and little boys bowed, to strangers on the road. The bolts on the great front door were never shot while the family was at home. Whoever entered was given welcome: drink, food and shelter. Tea, "winkum" or cordials were forthcoming before the guest was seated.

Nomadic culture still survived in extensive hunting and fishing operations. The blunderbuss stood in the shed ready for wild turkeys. Quail, partridge and squirrel were trapped. Deer were decoyed by salt deposits. Wild pigeons were caught in a springpole net. The finding of a wild honey tree marked a festival. In the summer the entire family migrated to camp out for a few days on the white beaches of Long Island Sound, and to dig clams and oysters. The spring run of shad and salmon in the Housatonic was a great event. Stations were assigned to each family along the river bank. Nets and seines made by candle light of winter evenings were flung out. On moonlight nights, the haul for a family might be as high as 1200 fish. It was promptly salted down. The folkways permitted no seining on Saturdays and Sundays; two days a week the fish passed freely upstream to spawn. In lake fishing,

Daniel was ever on the lookout for "scouring-rush," a water weed heavy in silicon, to be gathered and dried for cleaning pots and pans.

Boys were always whittling—traps, wooden spoons, netting-needles for the seines, checkers for evening games, homemade sleds. They were expert, too, at making long whiplashes from woodchuck skins. Many games were played, but the equipment was all produced at home. Dolls were unknown, except "rag-babies" made from linen waste.

Books were few; travel extremely limited. A trip to New York, if winds were unfavorable, might take as long as ten days. The church or meeting-house was the cultural center, and vast and profound were the theological discussions. The parson must watch his discourse, for every member of his audience was a bible scholar, and touchy on fine points of doctrine. As late as 1800, the salary of the Episcopal rector of Stratford was "£100 in lawful money and forty loads of wood."

Candles or pipes were lit by a coal held in stout tongs; the candles, of course, were homemade. Thin sticks were whittled to use as lighters; paper was too scarce. Sometimes, when the central fire went out, coals were carried from a neighbor's as much as a mile away—but this did not happen in Daniel's well-regulated household. During the Revolution even the few imports were mostly unobtainable. Pins were not to be had for love or money. Molasses jumped to $20 a gallon, and Daniel turned to making his own from cornstalks. Tea and paper vanished; the boys wrote their school lessons on birchbark.

No carriage was seen in these hills until 1820, travel was always by foot or horseback, Mary upon a pillion.

The first gig frightened the horses and mules, as the first automobile frightened them a century later. Doctors were few, and each house had its closet of "simples" and remedies, many gathered in the local woods. In the spring, the children all stood in line for a dose of garlic and rum. Smallpox was the curse of the community. In 1777, 600 people were ill of it in the town of Stratford alone.

In 1786 the first newspaper came to town—*The New Haven Gazette and Connecticut Magazine.* In due time it carried an advertisement: "In despite of Deism, Tom Paine and the Devil, the following very valuable book is offered for sale: *The Pious Christian.*" Fashions moved slowly; quality was what counted; and Mary did the family haircutting.

Daniel and Mary lived to be over eighty, and were buried from the parlor of the house they had built. A married daughter lived out her life in it; and her daughter after her. When the last Mary died, the house stood deserted; frost and wind eating at its stone heart. At the turn of the nineteenth century, the heart failed. This hand-built house had lived 130 years, and many like it live longer. Rafters and eaves and walls followed the great chimney to ruin. Perhaps one may still see the lilac bushes by the mossy cellar stones.

In this account of a New England family the gains and losses of the Economy of Scarcity are vividly brought to our attention. We see the kind of world in which American economic customs, behavior and philosophies were molded. Those of us who are indigenous New Englanders feel a clutch at the heart as we read of this world; our grandfathers made it real to us when we were children; in eddies off the cement highway we can find it feebly functioning even today. It is all but dead, but its death agony has been long. Like the stone chimney, it was built four-square.

Central in the picture is hard work, both as a stark necessity and as a moral obligation. The shirker was an outcast, eating in the sweat of another's brow. Be it observed that this compulsion to work devolved upon master as well as upon man, and upon children from the time they could walk. Play, however, in its proper place was not frowned upon, and the harsh tyranny of time serving and clock watching, so prevalent to-day, was absent. Unemployment and overproduction were, of course, unknown. Unknown, too, was the idea of quantity production; that a large volume could be produced at a smaller cost per unit.

Almost equally striking is the extent of self-sufficiency. Perhaps 75 percent of all economic goods and services were derived from the household itself; another 20 percent from the village with its blacksmith, fulling mill, craftsmen and journeymen, leaving only some five percent from the world outside— molasses, tobacco, spices, silver tankards, bibles and Holland lace. Specialization of work as between women, men, slaves, farmers, craftsmen, traders, professional people, was in evidence; but the community of Stratford, comprising perhaps 2,000 persons, was almost a self-sustaining unit. If the rest of the Colonies were destroyed over night, it could continue to function. Today, if the town of Stratford stood alone on the continent, its citizens could hardly exist a month. The rupturing of the thousand veins which tie them in to a vast continental economy, if not a world economy, would leave them dazed, helpless and undone. We note, further, the tiny orbit in which people moved under scarcity conditions. To go to New York, seventy miles away, was as much of a trip as it is for us to go to San Francisco; and more hazardous. Energy was not available to fling citizens all over the planet.

The society was one of function. Money played a small part in economic life. Things were made by the user to use, hence the better they were made the longer he could use them, and the longer the period before he must expend effort in replacing them. When he bought or exchanged, it was largely with his neighbors. Producer met consumer face to face. In such circumstances *caveat vendor* necessarily replaced the modern rule of *caveat emptor;* the seller, not the buyer, must beware in scarcity communities.[3] Quality was a desideratum; fashion came second, if at all. Mary bought her English and Dutch fine textiles to last a lifetime. *Per contra,* waste was as abhorrent as wilful idleness. String, paper, old metal, pins, buttons, findings, all were carefully saved. Material thrift was indigenous, and laid the basis for pecuniary thrift.

Energy and effort passed directly into consumers' goods; into food, shelter, fuel, clothing. The resulting standard of living was low when measured against modern conveniences, but reasonably plentiful in its essentials. Daniels and Marys and Mandys do not live to be eighty and ninety if they are not well fed and warmed and clothed. The diet was limited in variety, short of vitamin C in winter, perhaps, but it was well cooked, and the portions were heaping.

---

[3] Walton H. Hamilton has conclusively demonstrated that the legal doctrine of *caveat emptor* is only about 200 years old. Before 1700 or so in England, the seller of shoddy goods was subject to severe legal and social penalties. As the face-to-face conditions of scarcity passed, and specialization increased, the personal contact was lost.

Thrown thus on their own resources, the Sheltons, and Americans generally at the time, prized a sturdy individualism. Even if not elevated into a philosophy, it was lived day by day. The neighbors, the community, counted, but not the outside world. Government, with its wars, taxes and laws, was remote and frequently obnoxious.[4] A man should be free to do what he willed with his own. He had carved it from the wilderness, and made it with his own hands. Private property was a "natural right," but it was *use* property, not the paper property of today.

Significant in this connection was the will of the first Daniel. He was a merchant and trader and so a capitalist of his time. Yet only £1,000 of his £9,000 estate was in paper form, "money out in bonds, principal and interest." The other £8,000 was solid stuff, hogs and horses, the sloop "Indeavor," land and houses. Today the ratio for Connecticut capitalists will be reversed—eight units in leaseholds, mortgages, stocks and bonds; perhaps one unit in tangible property. In 1760, credit in the modern sense had not dawned, interest was still close to the obliquity of usury, trade was largely in the form of barter, silver coins were useful when melted down as dower spoons.

Finally, it is difficult to trace the lines of the class struggle in this Connecticut picture. Technically, Daniel exploited Mandy and her black husband, but actually they were part of the family. He paid them no wages and appropriated their surplus, but they never felt it. White children and black rolled on the kitchen floor together, went to the same district school, hunted, fished and played games of ball. Side by side

[4] The town of Cornwall, Connecticut, obstinately refused to enter the Union after the Revolution.

they worked in the fields, and at household chores.
Presently slaves were to be freed in Connecticut with
no recriminations. Presently factories were to spring
up along Connecticut's rivers, and new class lines to
form. But the class struggle, as such, was blurred in
the generic American picture. The cleancut distinction
of lord and peasant, universal for so many ages in
Europe, was found only in the great plantations of the
south. This fact goes far to explain the difficulties of
the socialists and communists in propagating their
philosophies. Americans may be wage slaves today,
but they will not believe it.

In such a setting we see the constitution, states rights,
checks and balances, a weak government control of
economic affairs, the natural right of property, the
sanctity of contracts, the assumption of a stable price
level, the dictum of hard work as the road to success,
oblivion to the class struggle, thrift, rugged individualism—all fitting easily, naturally and inevitably. Scarcity
phenomena all, they deftly locked with the American
Economy of Scarcity in the eighteenth century.

Out from editorial sanctum, gubernatorial mansion,
directors' room, bank, stock exchange, manufacturer's
office, lecture platform, pulpit, academic grove, Park
Avenue penthouse, suburban home—still comes a
reverberating chorus, chanting the chants of scarcity.
We have been too extravagant; we have lived beyond
our means; we have reaped where others have sown.
We must tighten our belts; we must save; we must
economize; we must live within our means. Government is a wasteful meddler; its budget must be cut;
the schools are full of fol-de-rols; the meddling must
cease. Depressions come because hard work has been
forgotten; we must go back to work. Inflation is in-

fringement of sacred property rights. Nothing is gained by tinkering with the currency; hard money is as necessary as hard work.

All this made sense to Daniel Shelton. He believed it; lived it. It makes no sense today. Presently the western world will split between the Scarcity men and the Abundance men; between those who act in one culture and think in another, and those who think as they act. Whenever and wherever a citizen asks: "And where is the money to come from?" he is instantly identified as a Scarcity man. The question is irrelevant in an Economy of Abundance. It is not money which makes the mare go; it is oats.

CHAPTER V

GALILEO'S CANNONBALLS

In 1638 Galileo Galilei published a monograph in which he took *the* philosopher to task. *The* philosopher was, of course, Aristotle, whose shadow lay across European thinking for a thousand years. Members of this school, said Galileo Galilei in effect, sit comfortably in armchairs and use their reason concerning events temporal and spiritual. This may be a satisfactory method for handling spiritual events, but it is a poor one for temporal events; especially physical events in time and space.

Aristotle and his followers had decided that a body ten times as heavy as another would fall ten times as fast. It stood to reason; it made common sense; it was logically justified; there was no more to be said. So, from 500 B.C. to 1638 A.D., bodies fell at a speed proportionate to their weights, in the opinion of all educated men. Galileo Galilei substituted the Leaning Tower of Pisa for the armchair of the Schoolmen. He climbed the spiral stairs loaded with assorted sizes of cannonballs and bullets. He dropped the missiles, one by one, and noted carefully their fall:

Aristotle says that an iron ball of one hundred pounds falling from a height of one hundred cubits reaches the ground before a one-pound ball has fallen a single cubit. I say that they arrive at the same time. You found, on making the experiment, that the larger outstrips the smaller by two finger-breadths, that is, when the larger has reached the ground, the

66

other is short of it by two finger-breadths; now you would not hide behind those two fingers the ninety-nine cubits of Aristotle, nor would you mention my small error and at the same time pass over in silence his very large one.

The two finger-breadths registered, of course, the slightly greater resistance exerted against the lighter body. In a vacuum, the two would arrive at the same instant, together with a leaf or a feather dropped from an equal height.[1]

The scientific method

Those cannonballs shattered the armchair school of physics forever, introduced the scientific method into western civilization, and laid the foundation for the Economy of Abundance. The method, observe, is of more importance than the specific invention, machine or process arising from its application. If every machine were destroyed, but certain books and certain equations preserved, the whole physical apparatus could be reconstructed from the still living laws and methodology of science. Even the layman has been inoculated with the sequence of physical cause and effect. When his motor car refuses to run, he does not summon the nearest medicine man to chant prayers while sprinkling a handful of wild turkey dung and hemlock twigs over the radiator; he summons the trouble-shooter from the nearest garage.

A pretty illustration of the transition period is found in the case of one Whiston, a mathematical divine. He predicted a comet on Wednesday, October 14, in the year 1712, at 5:05 A.M., and the end of the world the following Friday morning. The comet arrived on

[1] Roger Bacon had earlier challenged Aristotle on the same grounds, but not with cannonballs.

the minute. The populace was overwhelmed with the reverend gentleman's prescience. On Friday morning it gathered at the water front, en masse, commending its soul to God in anticipation of prediction number two.

The scientific method is incompatible with magic, pure reason, or common sense—unless the latter has weathered the cannonball test. Common sense tells us, for instance, that if we want to dam two lakes, one ten miles long, and one a mile long, with dams of equal height, the former ought to be ten times as strong. So dams were built in the past. It sounds reasonable, checks with common sense. As a matter of scientific fact, the ten-mile lake, or a hundred-mile lake, requires no stronger dam than the one-mile lake, or a fifty-yard lake. The height of the water at the dam face is the only relevant datum.

Hyman Levy has summarized the great generalizations of science, from which most of our physical apparatus could be reconstructed.[2]

Newton's law of motion
Newton's law of gravitation
Faraday's and Maxwell's laws of electromagnetic action
The laws governing the conservation of matter and energy—
    the first and second laws of thermodynamics
The atomic theory
The theory of evolution
The Mendelian theory
The electronic constitution of the atom
The theory of relativity and its generalization concerning the
    nature of time and space

We must not forget that biology has its place as well as physics. Agriculture has been developed more

---

[2] *The Universe of Science.*

by plant breeding, pest control, and the like, than by tractors and combines. Biology, in that it provides control over living matter, may be the outstanding science of the future, with the new drugs, new disease controls, new foodstuffs, new varieties of animals and plants, and new knowledge of the laws of inheritance, of mutations and glandular control. Already it is actually making us different in our natures and our behavior, according to Julian Huxley.

"We mix measured quantities of common salt and sulphuric acid," to quote Mr. Levy again, "raise the mixture to a definite temperature, and can state with great precision how much hydrochloric acid will be evolved after the lapse of so many minutes. On this form of prediction the whole of industrial science and technology, and the whole of engineering rests. Modern civilization would fall to pieces if it were false. The safety of communities rests on its truth."

Carpenters still build houses by rule of thumb. They guess, on a common sense notion of stresses and strains, that timbers of such and such a size, reinforced by cross pieces and struts, will hold up the roof. The margin of safety is normally huge, and the roof stays up. No such primitive thinking is permissible when an Empire State Building, a Boulder Dam, or a George Washington Bridge is to be constructed. Stresses and strains become an exact science, worked out by higher mathematics. Literally acres of blue prints are necessary before a shovelful of earth is turned. The railroad trains which bear us and our goods, the elevators which hoist us to our daily work, the water systems which preserve us, the motor cars which titivate us, are, at bottom, bundles of abstract equations, as far beyond the carpenter's methods as his are beyond the beaver's. These devices could never have been produced in a million years of trial and error. Imagine driving a tunnel from two sides of a mountain range ten miles wide, and meeting within a fraction of an inch, under trial and error. Imagine it under Aristotelian methods. Such jobs only science can do.

The scientific method has progressively invaded nearly every department of life. Starting with physics (including astronomy), it soon took the magic out of alchemy and made it chemistry; spread to geology, biology, entomology; then into archæology, anthropology, psychology, and now flirts with the hem of economics. As it proliferates, it unifies. Biology is yoked to physics, making bio-physics; Einstein finds matter and energy no longer two distinct phenomena, but one; the ionic theory unites physics with chemistry. The tidy compartments break down, and science emerges as one comprehensive, all-pervading totality. Technology, which is applied science, shows the same drive towards unity. We no longer have a steel industry as such; we have an industrial complex which includes ore, limestone, coal, coke, gas production, electric power *and* steel. This complex can be thought of, and operated, only as an interlocking unit. "Every discovery," says Robert A. Brady, "in electric metallurgy brings these industries into closer and more intimate contact." [3]

The scientific method demands:

That complete results of any experiment be immediately published

That the fullest criticism be invited

That proof or disproof never lie in argument, but only in repeating the experiment under identical conditions

[3] *The Rationalization Movement in German Industry.*

That there be no "patenting" of ideas
That workmanship take precedence over financial return

The method is disinterested; impersonal, and non-moral.

Once the scientific worker has started living the life of intellectual honesty, perhaps in no other spirit than as the condition of success in a field which has aroused his interest, he finds growing within him the realization that he is in possession of something much more than merely a tool by which he may get right answers. The ideal of intellectual honesty comes to make a strong emotional appeal; he finds something fine in the selflessness involved in rigorously carrying through a train of thought careless of the personal implication; he feels a traitor to something deep within him if he refuses to follow out logical implications because he sees that they are going to be unpleasant; and he exults that he belongs to a race which is capable of such emotions. Intellectual honesty appears to such a worker as the last flowering of the genius of humanity.[4]

Science requires a discipline as stern as that of the religious saint or the conquistador, and mentally far more honest. "The world little knows," exclaimed Faraday, "how many thoughts and theories which have passed through the mind of a scientific investigator have been crushed in silence and secrecy by his own severe criticism and adverse examination; that in the most successful instances, not a tenth of the suggestions, the hopes, the wishes, the preliminary conclusions have been realized." Read *Arrowsmith,* by Sinclair Lewis. Or regard Charles P. Steinmetz, who refused to take a salary, asking the General Electric Company only that it pay his frugal living expenses and provide the equipment for his experiments. He died leaving a $300 insurance policy, an outworn automobile, and a few keepsakes. Yet he made possible the high power transmission of electricity, and with it the power age.

[4] P. W. Bridgman in *Harper's Magazine,* December, 1933.

Animals accept nature and make the best of it. So did man up to 50,000 years ago or so. Then he became an earth changer, the "geomorphologic agent." [5] He began to improve on nature, and turned to an active rather than a passive rôle. Animals have techniques— some of them very beautiful—but they are in the genes, and so unalterable save by slow evolution. Man began to develop techniques independent of the life of the species. They were all rule of thumb techniques, found by trial and error, until Galileo dropped his cannonballs. They were passed on from father to son, from master to apprentice, from priest to novice. An Indian boy was taught to shoot an arrow to one side of the fish he saw in the water, but the teacher knew nothing of the bending of light rays—he only knew he could not hit the fish if he shot straight at him. "They knew the sequence of events," says Zimmerman, "but not the causal relationships." As a result, arts could be lost. Many have been lost forever— certain ways of making pottery, certain dyes, certain metal working. When science emerged from trial and error to set up its laws, nothing could be irretrievably lost again.

Between 300 B.C. and 1400 A.D., J. B. S. Haldane is prepared to list only four major inventions: the general use of iron, paved roads, voting and religious intolerance. To these he says coinage and long distance water supply might be added. Modern industry began with the invention of printing in 1450, which had two important results. It was the first example of mechanical mass production—thousands of copies from one inked plate; it cheapened books, spread literacy, and so laid an essential foundation for the growth of

[5] E. W. Zimmerman: *World Resources and Industries.*

science, and for the operation of a machine technology.

The modern worker must be thoroughly literate, able to read and follow printed instructions exactly. Without the printing press, the industrial revolution is inconceivable.

Invention

This is no place to record the history of invention, but a few generalizations covering the invention process are in order. In the stone age it required thousands of years to bring about a new method of chipping flint. Gradually the frequency increased. One invention engenders others, like fruit flies in a jar. "Their growth," says William F. Ogburn, "appears to be somewhat like compound interest: the bigger the principal, the larger the interest." [6] Accumulation was at first very slow, with cases, as we have seen, of actual loss. At the time of the Greeks, the accumulation was considerable, but still so elementary that, for all their intellectual powers, the Greeks could never have invented an airplane. Inventions stand on the shoulders of preceding inventions. It is impossible to invent an airplane without having already in the storehouse a scientific study of wind resistances, an internal combustion engine—which in turn requires advanced electrical inventions; a light, strong metal like aluminum; rubber, a method for drilling oil wells, a gasoline refining process, gauges for tolerances down to one ten-thousandth of an inch—and so on. Leonardo was equally helpless; he had nothing to stand on, and could only do his bit for the future by working out the laws of flying bodies, particularly those of birds.

[6] *Recent Social Trends.*

The history of invention may be roughly divided into four major periods:

(1) Hunting and nomadic culture, from the dawn of man to the first cities of Mesopotamia. A span of upwards of 100,000 years.

(2) Agricultural civilization, from 5000 B.C. to the emergence of the scientific method around 1500 A.D.

(3) The commercial age to Watt's steam engine in 1775 A.D. The groundwork of mechanical science was laid.

(4) The industrial revolution—1775 to date.

The second period of some 6,500 years added more to the stock of knowledge than the first period of 100,000 years. The last period of 160 years added infinitely more than all three preceding periods combined. Invention is a geometric process.

Let us observe a typical invention curve. Here is a tiller on a sailing ship, a simple lever attached to the rudder. It is crude, laborious, exposed to the weather. The next step is to put the tiller between decks aft. This provides a little shelter for the steersman. Next, a primitive wheel is substituted for the lever, which makes steering somewhat easier. Then the wheel is moved forward to a comfortable pilot house. One can see better. Ropes run aft to the rudder. Cables take the place of ropes, and the pilot house becomes a conning tower. Then comes the steering engine to do the manual work of swinging the rudder. Today we have the "metal mike," an automatic gyroscopic compass which holds any course to which it is set.[7]

Not long after Galileo, when the accelerating process had really gotten under way, we begin to note

[7] Ralph E. Flanders: *Taming Our Machines*.

the apparently strange phenomenon of "simultaneous inventions." A man in Germany, a man in France and a man in the United States all announce a new engine, or a new chemical compound, within a few months of one another, unaware of the others' work. This is not so strange as it sounds. All three stood on the same shoulders; at that particular time there was an obvious technical gap to be filled. The whole process is a fabric woven thread by thread, and intolerant of holes. In a sense "the industrial revolution is nothing but one eternal struggle to close technological gaps." In the early textile mills the spinning process would get ahead of the weaving process, whereupon invention concentrated on weaving machinery until it was ahead of spinning; then back it would flow to spinning. By 1857, 800 separate inventions were to be noted in spinning alone. A tidy example of gap filling is provided by the invention of synthetic lacquer paint. The mass production of motor cars had reached a point where thousands of units could be turned out in a day. Under traditional painting methods, however, these cars would require a fabulous acreage of roofed storage space to stand under while the paint dried. If mass production was to be a success, an almost instantaneous method of painting and drying had to be found. It was promptly found.

The physical nature of the country in relation to population has a powerful effect on the invention curve. The United States, with its great distances and low man-land ratio in the development period, tended to specialize on transportation and *labor-saving* devices. Europe, with plenty of men, but more limited natural resources, specialized on *material-saving* devices. Today the two techniques are consolidating.

Inventions are not confined, of course, to the mechanical field; witness the loganberry, the spineless cactus, durum wheat and vitamin concentrates. They are not even confined to the broad field of science. Ogburn lists many important and amusing inventions in other fields—the chain store, basketball, Esperanto, the city manager form of government; the tourist camp —which depended on the invention of the automobile; the trade union—which depended on the invention of the factory. Inventions have strange repercussions. The tin can was in part responsible for woman's suffrage. It helped destroy cottage industries, and gave the housewife more time to look at the world outside. The invention of the mechanical stoker helped the position of the Negro. How? It increased the amount of coal going into the boiler of a locomotive, which permitted more powerful locomotives, which increased the length of trains, which made the distance a passenger carried his baggage greater, which gave more work to Negro porters.[8]

The number of patents granted is not a complete index of invention, but it indicates the curve. Since 1880 the trend, in the United States, has been as follows:

Decade ending 1890—208,000 patents granted
    "   "   1900—221,000   "   "
    "   "   1910—314,000   "   "
    "   "   1920—384,000   "   "
    "   "   1930—421,000   "   "

In the year 1617, the British Patent Office issued exactly five patents. In 1919, the California Walnut Growers' Association offered $10,000 for a machine which would stamp its name on walnuts. Only one ad-

[8] *Recent Social Trends.*

vertisement appeared. Twelve thousand replies were received; including 1100 working drawings and 120 models, one of which was selected. In 1915, the story got abroad that the Distillers' Association was posting a million dollars for a non-refillable bottle. The story was false, but 1,700 United States patents were taken out on the strength of it.[9]

Energy

Reach out your hand for the nearest man-made object—the arm of your chair, a curtain, a shoe, a pane of glass, a radiator, a magazine. The chances are a thousand to one that the object was fabricated and transported to you, in whole or in part, by inanimate energy. A hundred years ago, the odds would have been reversed; the object would have been the result of animate energy, fabricated by manpower, transported by animal power. Technical advance, says Sir Frederick Soddy, is not so much a mastery of materials—of stone, bronze, iron, copper, aluminum—as a "successive mastery over the sources of energy in nature." Given that mastery, we can take our stores of raw materials, heat them, pound them, shape them and deliver them, in any required form. They are the clay, and energy is the potter's wheel. There is plenty of clay, and there always has been. But Galileo's cannonballs have led mankind at last to the secret of the wheel. It will fashion whatever we ask, its only demand—aye, its imperative—that the laws of its spinning be respected. Otherwise, it may burst.

We must rid ourselves of the notion that the machine is the important consideration—unless "machine" is

[9] Harry D. Norton: *Industry and Invention.*

used as a generic term including energy. Man has always been clever with tools. The fundamental thing is the *energizing* of the machine. The use of energy to produce goods and services is not a larger and defter tool—but a wholly new process, as we shall see. Its appearance makes a revolutionary breach in the continuity of working methods, and in the very nature of the effort by which man turns raw resources into consumers' goods.[10]

To tear nitrogen from the air requires a huge amount of electrical energy. When Haber invented and perfected the process in Germany, he fixed not only nitrogen, but the date of the World War. Germany, cut off from the old supply, especially the Chilean nitrate beds, could not have fought three months without it.

The major energy sources in the United States today may be summarized as follows:

From coal: 17,000 trillion B.T.U. per year. Burned in power stations, converted into electrical energy for light, heat and power. Private and municipal power plants. Steam locomotives. Central steam heating in cities. House heating and cooking. Heat processes in industry, such as steel making. Steamships.

From oil: 6,500 trillion B.T.U. Gasoline burned in automobiles, tractors, airplanes, motor boats. Fuel oil in diesel engines, small power plants, house heating, railways, ships. Kerosene as heat and light.

From natural gas: 1,700 trillion B.T.U. Domestic and industrial light and heat. Small power plants.

From water power: 1,900 trillion B.T.U. Central hydroelectric stations with same uses as, and often

[10] See Fred Henderson: *The Economic Consequences of Power Production.*

interconnected with, coal central stations. A little direct mechanical work.

From windmills: 300 trillion B.T.U. Used mainly for pumping water. A little light and power.

From firewood: 1,600 trillion B.T.U. Mainly for heat. A small amount of power.

From draft animals: 750 trillion B.T.U. For agricultural work and some transportation.

From manpower: 400 trillion B.T.U. For odds and ends. Important still, but declining.

Energy as king requires a cabinet. The chancellor is iron, and all the ministers are hard metals. From 1806 to 1913, coal increased thirty-nine-fold, pig iron thirty-eight-fold. Coal and iron marched together; steam power and steel are inseparable. As electricity displaces the steam engine, copper, aluminum, alloys, rise to the top. Where these metals and raw energy are found in the earth together, there appears an industrial civilization. England was such a place, then western Europe, then the eastern section of the United States. The North Atlantic is thus the mother of high energy cultures; no similar juxtapositions of such magnitude have yet been found.[11] We Nordics may be an enterprising people, but above all we have been a fortunate people. Coal and iron outcropped together on our lands.

[11] Russia may unearth them as her geologic survey develops.

CHAPTER VI

THE MACHINE AGE AND THE POWER AGE

WALTER N. POLAKOV draws a useful distinction between two major phases in the upsweep of energy. The first phase, from Watt—or earlier if you like—to 1900 or so, he calls the *machine age*. At the turn of the century we entered the *power age,* and a new industrial rhythm altogether, although no great momentum was gained until the War.[1] The Economy of Abundance made its appearance late in the machine age, but did not come to full stature until the power age was well developed.[2] In the former period, the *mechanism* was the important consideration; in the latter, *energy* becomes more significant than the machine.

Nature, unlike bankers, does not permit the procuring of something for nothing. The laws of thermodynamics see to that. The golden rule of primitive mechanics says: "What is gained in power is spent in time." Thus the lever, wheel, pulley, wedge, while they magnify the muscular power of men, demand a payment, and the payment is time. To heave on the ropes of a pulley may take ten times as long as to push directly, but a ten times bigger stone can be moved. Such methods are like a magnifying glass which in-

---

[1] I follow Polakov closely throughout the following section. See his book, *The Power Age*. Also Fred Henderson, *op. cit.* Unidentified quotations are from Polakov.
[2] See definitions at close of Chapter I.

tensifies detail. One cannot simultaneously look at an amœba and see the countryside. Tools did not decrease human toil, but they provided a larger output of commodities by converting time into force. There was a decided change in the rate of doing work from the invention of the first tool down to Watt. But it was a long, slow change, measurable in centuries.

The labor problem of the pre-machine period was that of spending more time to magnify muscular power. So the pyramids were built, so all great engineering feats of the Economy of Scarcity. Zimmerman provides us with a dramatic comparison between the Great Pyramid and the Empire State Building, structures of about the same mass. To build the first required ten times as much manpower, for forty times as long a period—a ratio, expressed in man-days, of 400 to one. One man-day, aided by energy and modern techniques, can produce 400 times as much as in the era of Pharaoh.

With the introduction of machinery in England in the eighteenth century, time was conserved by intensifying labor, until the strain on the laborers, who furnished the energy, approached the limit of human endurance.[3] This productive level was sharply raised by Watt's invention of the steam engine. The machine age tempo was enormously accelerated; output per man reached heights undreamed of, but *the intensity of the laborer's work was not appreciably lightened.* Steam was added to his muscles, but he still had to use his muscles—often to keep up with the steam—and there was no relaxation in his toil. In the midst of this

[3] The block printing of calico increased productivity 200-fold, but the bigger machines overtaxed the operator's strength. Mule spinning made a man walk eight miles in a twelve-hour day. The improved spinner in 1832 required a twenty-mile walk per day.

period, John Stuart Mill propounded his famous question of whether all the labor-saving devices invented to date had lightened the work of any human being. By and large they had not. A handicraftsman could often work sixteen hours a day; the machine age worker, under more intense strain, broke down after ten or twelve hours. The outstanding characteristics of the period have been listed by Mr. Polakov as follows:

> Human labor was intensified (the robot appeared).
> Workers congregated in great masses.
> Women and children were increasingly exploited.
> Monotony was omnipresent, due to fast, repetitive operations.
> The steam engine accelerated the output.
> Continuity of production was demanded.
> The craftsman was increasingly displaced.

By 1886, so far had the acceleration gone that the Commissioner of Labor Statistics in the United States was able to report that the four million persons then in the manufacturing industries were producing as much as twenty-one million could have done under pre-machine conditions.

The machine age did not necessarily mean more labor efficiency; though, as we have seen, it certainly meant more intensity. "As long as the efficiency of a workman and the intensity of his work remained the same, the output was proportionate to the working time." To increase output, the boss had to drive his helots. He did. He invented the piece rate system of wages to drive them faster. The trade union, socialism, the hated capitalist, the ideology of the proletariat, the class struggle, were the inevitable result. They sprang from the ruthless intensity of work in the machine age. Furthermore, in this period energy consumption was still relatively low, population was growing fast, and output in relation to population meager. High standards of living, except for the few, were out of the question.

The power age appeared in embryo with the first central station generating electricity. Thomas Edison set up the station in Pearl Street, New York City, in the '80's. "The advantages of electricity arise from the fact that this strange manifestation of energy is virtually energy itself—not energy locked up in a material condition and subject to the laws and limitations of matter, but energy, the capacity to do work, freed from substantial form." [4] With the invention of alternating current by Steinmetz, transmission of electricity over appreciable distances became possible. The practicable limit today is about 300 miles. It is not so much the magnitude of this new power which is important, as its fluidity; it adds a new dimension to the industrial arts. Here, after thousands of years, the golden rule of mechanics has been reversed, and "what is spent in power is gained in time."

It is no longer necessary, as in the machine age, to pay for every foot-pound gained with longer hours of labor; not necessary to intensify human work as the price of greater output. "Indeed this is a revolution far deeper than the forerunner ushered in by Arkwright and Watt."

The steam engine, symbol of the machine age, is limited by its harness of belts and cogs, demanding a circumscribed location and floor plan. With electricity and the electric motor drive, these limitations fall away. Power is available where wanted and only when

[4] Gilbert and Pogue: *America's Power Resources.*

wanted; a copper wire and a switch are the requisites. The advance of the power age was marked by the following inventions, in order of their appearance:

1. Electric lighting.

2. Electric motors for cranes.

3. The displacement of the steam engine, and the substitution of one big motor on the main factory shaft. Belts remained.

4. Power generating equipment concentrated in the power house. Fuel economy initiated.

5. The big motor displaced by individual motor drives—one for each machine in many cases. Belts disappeared. Free servicing of machines by cranes; rearrangement of machines by groups; conveyor systems. Human machine tenders began to lose their jobs.

6. Finally, the fusion of transmission, machine tool, loading mechanism, control devices, quality regulation and self-recording, into *one unit* of productive equipment. The whole factory becomes one giant machine. In some cases no human hand touches the product from raw material to packaged output.

A generation ago, a factory was a place where materials were being assembled, where jobs were fairly specialized, where there were many machines, but where *none were able to work to capacity,* because of the failure to synchronize exactly the finishing steps. Hand work still had its place. Men took material from one machine, did what was necessary, and passed it along to another machine. "In such a system," says R. G. Tugwell, "it is obvious the speed of the whole can be only that of its slowest unit—the men who worked by hand. . . . It is the destiny of the machine to be linked with its fellows so that, by careful planning of material deliveries, and by synchronization of speeds and rhythms, the process is completely serialized." [5] In brief, it becomes automatic.

The substitution of electricity for steam permits for the first time a continuous flow of material from raw to finished product, attended by machines arranged in sequence, connected by conveyors, and the rhythm of the whole process geared to automatic controls. The floor plan layout is revolutionized; "the production process becomes, as it were, the function of the electric motor."

Not only does electricity take over, by virtue of its flexibility, an increasing amount of physical labor, thus reducing the intensity of work, but it goes farther: it takes over an increasing amount of mental work. The first remote control system was installed by Mr. Polakov in a power house in 1911. Attention no longer needed to be directed to the physical apparatus, but rather to a series of dials and pointers on a panel. These signals, electrically motivated, reported exactly and instantly how the physical apparatus was performing. After 1919, such devices became standard practice for controlling speed of operations, safety limits, feeding, measuring, quality, precision. They were applied not only in factories, but in power houses, railroad switch yards, mining operations, refineries, ocean liners.

If you have an oil burning furnace in your home, you have an excellent example of the process. When you set the thermostat at 70°, for instance, electricity takes over both your physical and your mental labor. Another homely example is the increasing automaticity

[5] *The Industrial Discipline.*

of your motor car. Presently all you will need to do is to steer—until some inventor puts a battery of photoelectric cells to work providing an automatic steering device. Then all you will need to do at sixty miles an hour is to turn on the radio and look at the billboards. The General Electric Company is now equipped to introduce remote control devices into any sort of process—even as the Fuller Brush man has an implement for every crevice.

"With the power age, the tendency toward specialized men and universal machines is changing toward special, single purpose machines and all-around universalized mechanics." Machine and man change places; the former becomes more specialized, the latter less. While the machine may be highly specialized, however, the whole process becomes more flexible. It is only one in a series of machines. By shifting the controls, a wider variety of end products can be thrown off than was ever the case in the machine age.

Perhaps one of the most startling revelations of the incipient power age was that made by H. L. Gantt and his school of industrial engineers during the War and shortly thereafter.[6] The War marked a turning point in the technological process, and did more to encourage automatic production than any other factor. Time meant victory or defeat. Labor shortages, due to conscription of manpower for the military establishment, enormously speeded up labor-saving devices. Factories revised their management methods and extended their capacities. All mining operations were greatly expanded. Farms were mechanized. Automatic factories appeared in this period; the management engineer became a public figure. It was an era of in-

[6] *Organizing for Work.*

dustrial stocktaking and rapid technical advance, under the twin spurs of patriotism and abnormal profits.

In the machine age, the problem of management was to make labor efficient—with stopwatches, piece work, threats, discipline, orders, and the verbal lash of the gang boss. But Gantt pointed out, and presently Mr. Hoover's Committee on Waste in Industry was agreeing with him, that what really mattered was the arrangement of the plant, the serialization of its machines, the readiness of raw material like water behind a faucet, and the continuous, uninterrupted flow of operations. This was not labor's responsibility; it was that of management—and the committee proceeded to lay from 50 to 80 percent of all industrial waste squarely on management's shoulders. The moral issue need not concern us at the moment; thus was dramatized the fact that labor did not count in the old sense, and that effort expended in driving labor was far less important than effort expended in planning continuous flow.[7]

The stoppage of electric power today would bring 80 percent of all industry in Germany instantly to a halt, and disorganize 80 percent of all agricultural establishments and 75 percent of all homes.[8] The domination of the power age in the United States may be not quite so complete, but at least 75 percent of factory machines are now driven by electric motor. My records show one or more instances of power age techniques in the following industries. Even where a whole factory may not be subject to automatic pro-

[7] Polakov cites instances where it is possible to double output without a dollar of capital investment, simply by rearranging the flow.

[8] Robert A. Brady: *The Rationalization Movement in German Industry.*

duction, it is often shot through with automatic and semi-automatic processes. The poison, having entered, will spread.

Metal refining
Blast furnaces
Steel sheets and plates
Power generating (not a man in some power plants)
Lumber mills
Coking; gas production
Petroleum refining
Matches
Printing—teletypesetter and color processes
Canning
Cigaret making
Flour milling
Bread making
Sugar refining
Paper boxes
Heavy chemicals
Machine tools
Pulp and paper
Motor car frames
Brick and tile
Cement
Leather
Linoleum
Aluminum
Electric light bulbs
Glass

Nails, screws, bolts, nuts, needles, pins, etc.
Rayon
Cotton spinning; cotton sheeting
Shoes
Postal service—many automatic devices
Dial telephones
Automatic restaurants, selling devices, garages
Bookkeeping and statistical devices
The talkies
Automatic steering for ships and airplanes
Automatic switch yards, and freight car dumpers
Betting machines (displacing bookies at race courses)
Automatic firing, heating and temperature control
Traffic control devices
Dispatching towboats on the Mississippi
Automatic transmission of telegrams

Many more could be added to this list if space allowed. The power age is not an engineers' theory; it is taking active charge of process after process, not only in manufacturing, but in mining, transportation, communication, merchandising, clerical work and even recreation.

Certain effects

So the machine age—before which most critics of technology are still cowering—began to give way to "a discipline of mind, complying with the laws of nature." A new kind of worker was demanded; educated, capable of sustained attention, correct perception, quick reaction—a man to understand the process and to assist in its inspection and control. Incidentally his numbers, or his hours, must shrink enormously as compared with the same output in the machine age. The trade union class line begins to dim before this universalized mechanic; white collar and flannel collar become almost indistinguishable.

As the power age gains, the effort of the worker ceases to be an index of productivity. Output becomes increasingly independent of the labor input. Piece rates give way to day rates, a phenomenon noticeable in the whole mass production sector. Ford is almost exclusively on day rates. Alford and Hannum supply some illuminating figures in this connection.[9] They studied best and worst performances, measured in thousands of man-hours, in various industries. Eighty-six blast furnaces show a variation of one to nine; that is, output per man-hour rose from an index of one in the worst furnace to nine in the best. Three hundred and five lumber mills varied from one to thirteen. Three hundred and six petroleum refining plants varied from one to 224. Thus the volume of output stands in no relation to the time worked. The efficient concerns, using advanced techniques, had broken away from considerations of labor efficiency altogether. "If

[9] Applications of KMH Method of Analyzing Manufacturing Operations. Paper before American Society of Mechanical Engineers, December 5, 1932.

a man in one plant produces 200 times the output he might in another plant, the productivity of labor is no longer a factor of time, but of something else. He cannot increase or reduce his productivity at will; the rate of production is predetermined by other factors; it is inherent in the design, and is either carried out, or the production program fails completely." In a modern plant the worker either does his work efficiently or he does not do it at all. Extra effort will not squeeze an extra drop of output. The electrically motivated design of the plant sets the output in accordance with physical, not human laws, and it goes or stops as a unit. The worker can stop it, yes, by technological sabotage; management can keep it operating at this or that percentage of capacity by setting the controls and insuring the flow of raw materials, but sweating labor has no place in this picture.

Returning to Alford and Hannum, they show the value of product per 1000 man hours varying as follows:

Blast furnaces	$2,499 to $ 24,087
Machine tools	918 to 10,673
Petroleum refining	4,563 to 192,908

This gives an overall range of value of output per man hour from ninety-two cents to $192.91. *A man in the best refinery creates 210 times as much dollar value as a man in the worst machine tool shop.* Meanwhile, wage rates varied from twenty cents an hour to $1.09, a spread of only one to 5.5. There is thus no relation between output and wage payments. The power age demands fundamental revision of the existing wage system. The distinction between "direct" and "indirect" labor is passing; all labor in modern plants and processes is becoming indirect.

As labor declines in importance, equipment grows. Idleness in whole or in part becomes fantastically expensive. The function of the structure is such that it cannot operate efficiently except at a full load. This explains two recent phenomena, and drives home a most important conclusion.

Small machine age plants tend to weather industrial depressions better than large power age units. With their costs still chiefly dependent on payrolls, they can fire workers, and cut costs. The large units have no such escape. There the mighty investment stands, eating its head off in depreciation, interest, insurance, taxes and overhead generally. Such costs cannot be fired.

Secondly, we see plainly the reason for the enormous increase in the high pressure selling methods of the mass production industries in recent years. Without great volume, costs per unit become extravagantly high. Volume is fought for by any method, however socially and ethically deplorable.

Finally, it is clear that the Economy of Abundance, based as it is on power technology, specifically electrical power, will function only on one condition—that its industrial units be operated at capacity or thereabouts; that they be given enough to do. Failing this condition, the superb plants, the beautiful technical balance, become so much loss and waste; monuments to be moved to the junk heap. A recent writer in *Advertising and Selling,* under the title, "Is Mass Production Doomed?" raises the bewildering question whether it would not be better to go back to the machine age of little steam plants. The question, I fancy, is academic. The curve of invention cannot be pushed back without a cataclysm. Rivers do not run uphill.

CHAPTER VII

PATTERN AND CURVE

"On the ridges of the coal," says Spengler, "and at the focal points of the lines of communication radiating therefrom, is collected a human mass of monstrous size, bred by machine-technics, working for it and living on it. To the other peoples—whether in the form of colonies or of nominally independent states—is assigned the rôle of providing the raw material and receiving the products." [1]

This was indeed the machine age pattern, and it still holds true to a large degree. Slowly now, soon faster, the power age will mold it to another pattern, assuming that Spengler's gloomy prophecies of general collapse are not fulfilled. Already the human mass on the ridges of the coal tends to grow no greater, as the curve of population throughout western civilization reaches a plateau. Already the mass stirs and moves a few steps from Megalopolis, as electric power demands decentralization. Already the "other peoples" build their own machines, fling their own power lines and make their own mass produced goods.

Modern industry, whether in its remaining machine age phases, or its newer power age development, is one great interlocking process; more and more it takes on the characteristics of a single gigantic mechanism, where every part must be oiled and in good repair, if

[1] *Man and Technics.*

the whole is to function. When the whole *is* functioning, the output of goods and services is great beyond all scarcity age imaginings. When it is not, the stabilities of scarcity look like a hearth fire in midwinter.

Every significant change made in the evolution of the power industry [in Germany] tends to compel fitting, cutting and shaping of plans to fit in with some such basic pattern. . . . Once the step is taken it can rarely be recalled. The logic of technical and economic forces compels ever larger units, more comprehensive geographic systems, more closely woven and meticulously detailed webs. With every shift in these directions, industrial interdependence becomes greater, the necessity for cooperation more insistent, the number and importance of interested groups greater, and the nature of the decisions of the policy-forming control more socially significant. In no other industry are the interdependencies among scientific, technical, political and social forces so coercive and binding; in no other sector is the antithesis between planning and competitive capitalism so clear-cut and decisive. Scarcely a step has been made by even the more capitalistically controlled power units in Germany during the last decade without involving a partial or complete abandonment of one or more of the favorite laissez-faire tenets. And the end is not yet.[2]

Such is the pattern of the industry which furnishes basic energy to one great industrialized nation. Increasingly it becomes the pattern for other nations and for other industries. Already in Germany it has leaped beyond national boundaries to draw alien populations, alien productive processes, into a technological web. A plan is now on foot to yoke all of continental Europe into one high power transmission grid.[3] On the continent of North America, the grid is already laid down.

[2] Robert A. Brady: *The Rationalization Movement in German Industry.*
[3] The Oliven Plan, cited by Brady.

In order that Mr. Ford may provide you with an automobile, no less than forty-eight other industries must be in smooth working order. A strike in a body plant once brought his whole assembly line to a halt. It is not, observe, a question of getting along with forty-five industries or forty-seven; the entire forty-eight must function if Ford is to produce a single car. Modern industry is like a watch. There are, let us say, 200 parts within the watch case. If, in assembling them, one part is omitted, the watch will not run. A sundial has no moving parts. But it will not tell time after sundown, or in cloudy weather. The sundial represents Scarcity; the watch, Abundance. Observe both the gain in accuracy and in output (time telling), and the cost of that gain—complex specialization.

If we are to give up sundials and take to watches—and that is the choice we have made—the parts must be in place, with standardization of measurements, tools, materials, controls. Standard physical measurements are of the essence of the régime, and have run far beyond the financial necessity of standardization, because the process, if not the business man, demands them.

Services must also be standardized. Timetables, steamship sailings, telephone numbers, postal deliveries, telegram codes, radio wave lengths, traffic signals, all must be reduced to exact, measurable terms. "Men are required to adapt their needs and their motions to the exigencies of the process whereby this civilized method of intercourse is carried into effect . . . one's plans and projects must be conceived and worked out in terms of those standard units which the system imposes." [4]

[4] Veblen: *The Theory of Business Enterprise.*

The scarcity pattern is that of a series of largely self-sufficing communities, expending most of their effort in growing food, linked together, over rutted and muddy roads or navigable waterways, with a thin line of commerce in a few essentials and luxuries. The abundance pattern is a group of communities and industries, supplying only a tiny fraction of their local wants. (Muncie, Indiana, for instance, consumes less than one percent of the total products manufactured in the town.) They exchange the overwhelming percentage of what they produce with other communities, not only at home, but abroad—an irreducible minimum even under the severest nationalism; they are linked together with steel rails, cement highways, airways, pipe lines, waterways, a vast network of power and communication lines, and now with the waves of the ether.

PERCENT OF GAINFULLY EMPLOYED—1920–1926 [5]

	In agriculture	All other
England	7%	93%
Belgium	19	81
Australia	23	77
Holland	24	76
United States	26	74
New Zealand	27	73
Germany	30	70
Denmark	35	65
Canada	35	65
Czecho-Slovakia	40	60
Sweden	41	59
France	41	59
Italy	56	44
India	72	28
Poland	76	24
Russia	87	13

This table supplies a rough and ready index of industrialization, with England at the top and Russia at

[5] G. D. H. Cole: *A Guide through World Chaos.*

the bottom. The United States has larger and more advanced industries than England, but its rich lands supply a relatively greater agricultural population. Russia, in the decade since these figures were prepared, has sharply stepped up her industrial ratio; but she still has a long climb before she reaches the levels of the west.

As the abundance pattern develops, engineers have indicated two profoundly important points which every industry must sooner or later reach.[6] The first is the point where the *rate* of growth begins to taper off. New industries tend to expand at a compound interest rate, sometimes for many years. Ultimately, of course, the growth curve must begin to ease, because compound interest rates of development become fantastic. If, for instance, the growth rate for steel obtaining in the '60's in America had been maintained to 1930, it would have demanded, by that year, a production greater than the whole earth. There *must* come a time when the rate of growth declines, although the total tonnage may continue to increase.

The second important point which every modern industry must reach is that of maximum employment. Eventually, despite a mounting demand for the output, the replacement of animate by inanimate energy proceeds so rapidly that no more workers are needed —or ever will be needed—on an eight-hour day basis. Flour mills seem to have reached that point in 1914, railroads in 1920, automobiles in 1923. Just as the physical growth curve peak must ultimately control finance, the employment peak must control hours of labor, wage levels, the extent and severity of unem-

---

[6] See Bassett Jones: *Debt and Production.* Also Howard Scott and others: *Introduction to Technocracy.*

ployment. Both threaten the economic security of worker and investor.

The two points are susceptible to definite statistical computation, but have been completely disregarded by the majority of economists, and, of course, by all bankers and business men. Industrial workers have not made the computation, but millions of them are keenly aware of the results, measured in unemployment. Investors, particularly in securities of railroads—an industry whose growth curve began to flatten after the turn of the century—are also uncomfortably aware of the phenomenon.

Inventions to order

"A really new thing has come into the world," says Walter Lippmann. "That thing is the invention of invention. Men have not merely invented the modern machine . . . they have invented a method of inventing. Mechanical progress has ceased to be casual and accidental, and become systematic and cumulative. We know, as no other people ever knew before, that we shall make more and more perfect machines." Before the War, the inventor was often a lonely crank, working with clumsy equipment in his own cellar. Today, the major inventions are issuing more or less on schedule, from great industrial research laboratories. Some 1500 such laboratories have been established in America since the War. The finest building of the A. O. Smith Corporation in Milwaukee is its research laboratory, built to house 1,000 engineers and scientists. The famous Bell Laboratories of the American Telephone and Telegraph Company have had as many as 4,500 on the staff, and their annual budget is about $13,000,000. Among innovations which have come out of organized research in recent years have been aniline dyes, the radio, television, the cracking process for gasoline, nitrogen fixation, the extraction of radium, and a practicable airplane. When a concern is too small to support a laboratory of its own, it is increasingly common for it to participate in a coöperative research organization, run by a trade association.

Some years ago public utility engineers foresaw that the jumble of power lines on poles in city streets would have to end. The lines would be forced underground. No existing cable could stand the voltages which would be required when that time came. The engineers called the cable producers together and invited them to join in a program of joint research. The invitation was accepted, and when, years later, the saturation point of overhead lines was reached, the cable design was proved and ready for underground transmission.

Some of the research problems involve pure science as well as applied. When the A. O. Smith Corporation decided to manufacture huge pressure vessels, it found that the laws of such vessels had never been developed. The type in use had been bolted together by trial and error. The bolts were large and many, and the hope was general that the vessels would not explode. Sometimes, alas, they did—at a few thousand pounds to the square inch—with distressing results. The Smith engineers substituted Galileo for Aristotle. They made a series of pressure vessels in a variety of shapes and sealed them by a variety of methods. Then they took them to a large, open field and put them under hydraulic pressure until they burst. Instruments were clicking throughout the experiments. The *laws* of pressure vessels were thus determined, and duly recorded in papers for the scientific journals. With the laws worked out, the company proceeded to manufacture the largest, strongest, lightest vessels ever known. 34313

The construction of Boulder Dam, perhaps the greatest engineering feat ever undertaken by man, presented among others two pretty research problems. A vertical wall of water 700 feet high will push against the dam face. How shall the face best withstand such colossal pressure? After months of calculation it was determined that the strongest dam would be one composed of hundreds of concrete columns, thirty-five feet square, rising to a height of 720 feet, and locked together in such a way that the thrust of the water against the horseshoe circumference would press the columns more closely together. Again, it was calculated that it would take 200 years for the concrete in the interior of the dam to return to normal temperature. The chemical action of "setting" produces temperatures of 130 degrees or so, whose duration varies directly in proportion to the mass. The mass in this case is seven million tons. For 200 years, the dam would have been subject to cracking as it cooled. To forestall this danger, a network of pipes will be woven into the columns as they rise. First, river water will be pumped through them at 80°, then refrigerated water at 34°. Thus will the internal concrete be artificially cooled. Finally, the 750 miles of pipe will be pumped full of a special concrete mixture. The finished dam will not only be water tight, but temperature tight—locked against its own shrinkage.[7]

When you try to visualize the Economy of Abun-

[7] New York *Times* Magazine, July 23, 1933.

dance in one specific symbol, think of Boulder Dam —energy container, colossal material mass, superlative scientific research, elegant mathematical equation.

Dams and pressure vessels must obey physical laws. Men in contact with such apparatus, controlling or servicing it or being served by it, must obey them. The penalty of disobedience is frequently death—as when you disregard the laws of momentum in seeking to stop a two-ton motor car, travelling at sixty miles an hour, in the fifty feet between yourself and a stone wall. To decelerate such a mass, at such a speed, needs several hundred feet, depending on the friction of the road surface and the condition of the tires.

By an educational process marked with many dreadful accidents, we are learning to adapt our bodies and our nervous systems to these mandates. We know— most of us—what the signs "Third Rail" and "Walk on the Green Light" mean. A debonair disregard of either is equivalent to joining a suicide club. An illiterate person, or one with eyesight too defective to read signs, is safer in an African jungle than in a modern city or industrial establishment. The physical sciences can no more be argued with than a bolt of lightning.

The technological process in its very infancy destroyed one vast culture pattern. Feudalism fell before gunpowder, the compass and the printing press. The first made the knight in armor obsolete, the second made world trade possible, the third made learning no longer a priestly monopoly. The reading of the bible by laymen was promptly declared a crime; but, like prohibition in America, the law only accelerated the offense. Now, in triumphant adolescence, it is not inconceivable that the technical arts will repeat the destructive process. It is true that science cleared the ground for capitalism, the free market and the entrepreneur; coöperated with the system for many decades. But when finance capital comes increasingly to outrage physical law, as now seems to be the case, the technical arts may wreck capitalism as they once wrecked feudalism. The parallel may not be perfect, but it is worth consideration.

THE FUTURE CURVE OF INVENTION

The growth curves of physical production may—nay, will—reach a maximum and decline, but it is difficult to see an end to the invention process. There may come a halt for a decade, or many decades, as H. G. Wells has prophesied.[8] We noted earlier, however, that invention, unlike money, feeds on itself indefinitely. A collapsing financial system may slow it down, but it will go on again. It may change its course, inventing more simple, rather than more complicated ways of doing things; it may turn from production to distribution; it may flow out of mechanics into biology; it may flow out of both into social, political and financial inventions for a time; it may concern itself more with leisure than with work. . . . The scientific method will go on.

Let us examine briefly certain of the indicated inventions of the not too distant future, with some of their probable results. Observe that I do not hold that such things will come tomorrow; certain forces—especially the principle of vendibility—still obstruct the road. To begin with, what is the outlook for the energy supply?

[8] *The Shape of Things to Come.*

We have observed that one cannot secure something for nothing in nature, which is the reason why all perpetual motion machines went down the trap door with the promulgation and proof of the first law of thermodynamics. Man can get something for nothing by letting nature work for him, but the inanimate energy spent in the process is gone forever. The total of coal and oil in the crust of the earth constantly declines. With waterpower, wind power or tide power, the spending takes place, but at a point beyond all practicable calculation. Water, wind and tide are dependent on the current energy of the sun, and even Mr. Spengler is not looking for the sun to cease functioning in the historical future. With waterpower furnished by an eternal diastole and systole of sunshine, evaporation, rain and run-off, man comes as close to securing something for nothing as the planet allows. The sun pays the bill, but the terms of credit are long.

There is not enough potential waterpower, however, to satisfy even the world's present consumption of energy. In the United States, with every stream harnessed, the ratio would not rise above 18 percent of present demand. Oil will probably be gone in a generation or two; coal as a *cheap* source of energy may be good for several centuries. Long before it goes entirely, mines will be so deep, or so inaccessible, that the cost per kilowatt will be prohibitive. What shall we do then? J. B. S. Haldane summarizes the substitutes known to date: [9]

1. Employ all potential waterpower.
2. Harness the tides in certain favored bays.
3. Bring invention to bear on windmills. A rotor

[9] *Living Age,* July, 1933.

power plant is now being constructed in New Jersey. The Russians are conducting some interesting experiments in this field.

4. Use sun engines to heat water and make steam. They may have a limited use in desert countries like Egypt.

5. Devise an engine which uses cold and warm seawater at different levels. An experiment was recently tried off the coast of Cuba. It was not successful in practical terms. The theory is thermodynamically sound.

6. Exploit atomic energy. A remote and dangerous source. A drop of water contains the equivalent of 200 H.P. for a year. A lump of sugar would raze London. Today it takes more energy to bombard an atom than there is energy released. The net balance is far in the red. No method has been found to make atomic explosions set off other explosions, like a chain of rockets.

7. Make use of the "sunlight cell." A photoelectric cell, exposed to sunlight, releases a feeble amount of energy derived directly from the sun. One has been geared to operate a small motor. The roof of a house thirty by thirty feet receives heat energy equivalent to 200 H.P. as long as the sun shines upon it. No cell can yet collect a tithe of this total. If one could be devised to collect a substantial fraction, the energy supply of the future might be solved. The research men are at work.

8. Make alcohol a substitute for petroleum. It is only about one-tenth as powerful per gallon, but it will run engines. Alcohol can be made from living plants, as coal is made from dead ones. Vast, mechanized plantations in the tropics might grow the required

vegetation. Chlorophyll, the agent which makes plants green, converted the energy locked up in coal production in the geologic past, and probably the energy in oil deposits as well. Perhaps we can learn how to get more energy from alcohol by finding a good catalytic agent.

This list gives us a reasonably cheerful series of alternatives, even omitting sun-steam engines and lumps of sugar to blow up London. Inventors, I am now convinced, will continue to assure the energy supply in one form or another. Tesla promises a complete solution within the next year or two; but we may as well adopt a stern scientific attitude, and wait until we see it in practical operation. Personally, I feel drawn to the "sunlight cell." Perhaps I could install one in my lower orchard, and so be able to tell the Connecticut Light and Power Company a thing or two. . . . But the sun does not shine every day, especially in winter, when I need power most. . . . Yes, it is going to be difficult to escape the transmission net work, and the central power station. The sunlight cell, if and when it is developed, may provide central station power from Florida, Arizona, and other areas with high sunshine exposure. Beam transmission without wires may by that time convey it.

Whatever the future power source, invention will eat steadily away at the inefficiencies of conversion. Mercury as a substitute for water in steam engines may have a future. In power transmission, we note a mounting variety of new insulators, lightning-proof lines, new arrestors and grounding equipment, higher voltages, frequencies and load control instruments, remote control of substations, new relays, reclosing high speed breakers, and other devices too technical to mention here.

In your radio set are several tubes. Their function is to catch the waves which come over the air, and step them up to audibility. Each tube is akin to a photo-electric cell, except that it is sensitive to radio waves rather than to light. Sensitive cells of this character promise to substitute physical law for human fallibility throughout the industrial front in the years before us. They are small, weak, glass-blown trifles to look at, ranging in size from a peanut to a pumpkin; but their reverberations will be mighty. There is no recent invention which I follow with more attention. The function of inanimate energy hitherto has been chiefly to substitute mechanical for muscular work. The photoelectric cell substitutes inanimate energy for the human mind. It cannot do constructive think-ing, but it can cover those mental fields which count, measure, weigh, record, inspect—all the lower brain centers where alert attention and quick response to a given stimulus are required. It can do such work better than any brain.

Recently I watched a photoelectric cell inspecting tin cans. Its job was to see that each can was properly labelled. The cans were coming down a conveyor belt so rapidly that it was difficult to see them one by one. A beam of light played on each can as it passed a given point. If the label was in place, it absorbed the light. If there was no label the beam was reflected into the eye of the watchful cell. Instantly the cell transformed the light impulse, and set a mechanism in motion which knocked the can off the moving line. It happened so fast that one could follow the course only with the aid of a diagram.

Already the uses of the cell are manifold. They include: [10]

Timing motorists over a measured mile.

Controlling crowds in elevators.

Turning on school and factory lights when a storm darkens the sky.

Controlling the amount of smoke from a stack.

Opening doors for quick lunch waitresses, coal mine trucks; garage doors for motorists; railroad station doors.

Counting automobiles passing through the Holland Tunnel in New York, measuring the heights of trucks entering the tunnel, detecting air pollution within the tunnel.

Lighting airports for approaching planes, and signal lights for approaching ships in a harbor.

Trapping burglars. When the beam of invisible ultra-violet light in front of a safe is intercepted, an alarm promptly wails, a flashlight flares, a camera snaps a photograph of the interloper; a tear-gas bomb is detonated, leaving the burglar, if he is so unfortunate as to come without a gas mask, helpless until the police arrive.

Matching the colors of cigars for the top row of a fancy box.

Determining the amount of hæmoglobin in the blood stream.

Detecting breaks in continuous process manufacturing, such as papermaking, and instantly stopping the mechanism before damage is done.

Inspecting gasoline after cracking. Fuel darker than standard contains too much carbon. The photo-

[10] See article of Robert E. Martin in *Popular Science Monthly*, August, 1933.

electric cell detects the slightest variation in color more accurately than the human eye, and turns in an alarm.

Fire protection. A cell sounds sirens if the light flowing into it is dimmed by smoke.

Umpiring sports. Every time a player steps over the foul line in a bowling alley in Schenectady (the home of the General Electric Company), a red light flashes. The decision is infallible. (How about a cell for foot faults in tournament tennis, or for "ins" and "outs" on the boundary lines?)

Shearing hot steel rods at exactly the right length as they come from the rolls.

Locating rust spots, holes, and thin places in sheet metal.

Shunting mailbags to the proper destination on conveyor belts.

Sorting and filing cards in all kinds of office work.

The Massachusetts Institute of Technology predicts the use of cells for automatic steering and stabilizing of ships and aircraft, for the operation of recording instruments, and for gun control.

By 1942, according to O. H. Caldwell, President of the New York Electrical Society, we shall have full automatic newspapers with the photoelectric cell in charge. The reporter will hand in his news story, the copy desk will edit it and turn over the typescript. The machine will do the rest. No compositors, printers. feeders, will be required.

A new order of visual acuity and motor reaction is now possible. The old process, through the human eye, with nervous transmission at about thirty-three feet per second, was relatively clumsy. The photoelectric cell sends its stimulus at the rate of 186,000

miles per second, and can be started by impulses anywhere in the wave-length scale from radio waves
through light to x-rays.

So much for energy and its control. What does
the invention curve promise in the field of food supply?
Two things: an immense increase in yields per acre,
and, almost any day now, a synthetic food which can
be made in factories, like shoes or sewing machines.
The possible progress in the first is shown by the following table, prepared by O. H. Willcox:

YIELDS PER ACRE

	Present Average	Best Present Performance	Theoretical Maximum
Wheat (bushels)	15	117	172
Corn	27	225	225
Potatoes	100	1070	1330
Cotton (bales)	0.5	3.3	4.6
Sugar beets (tons)	?	35	53

We shall never achieve this perfection of yield in
practical farming; but it is safe to say that we shall
continually approach it, so long as crops of this character are required.

"When—not if—we can separate the cellulose-
splitting enzymes from those which break up the sugar
further, we shall be in a position to convert woodpulp
or hay quantitatively into human food." [11] Many animals possess the enzymes in their stomachs. There
is no reason why we cannot isolate them and produce
them in our laboratories. Harder problems have been
solved. When this particular problem is conquered,
mankind need never worry about the basic food
supply again; but one shudders to think of the plight

[11] J. B. S. Haldane: *Science and Human Life.*

of traditional agriculture if the prevailing financial system is still operating.

Nor will traditional agriculture be happy as a developing science of photosynthesis is applied to plants. Waldemar Kaempffert envisions beets and cabbages growing *visibly*—inches in a day; "wheat maturing in a month, vegetables ready to be marketed in two weeks —such are the probabilities with cheap energy and a finer knowledge of genetics and photosynthesis. It is clear that the government must step in and dictate what shall be planted and how large the harvest may be." Only too clear.

We speculated on the future of housing in Chapter III. The pre-fabricated house, made in the factory and bolted together on location in a few hours' time, is undoubtably coming. If you attended the housing exhibit at the Century of Progress Exposition in Chicago, you know how the first designs look. They will be steadily improved. Fabrication will enormously promote mobility in shelter; use-value, as Buckminster Fuller points out, will take precedence over land value. "The idea of boundaries, of a walled city fixed to an unchanging locale, is an anachronism in an industrial society possessing an elastic system of transportation and communication. . . . No longer is humanity space-confined." We look on the skyscraper as a thoroughly modern and scientific construction job. It has, indeed, broken away from traditional building to a marked degree, but the distance it has yet to go is indicated by the fact that the best skyscraper weighs five times as much per useful cubic foot as an ocean liner. Yet the liner is subject to the more powerful strains. I should not be surprised if skyscrapers, historically considered, proved to be a passing fad—like Tom Thumb golf on a grander scale. If we do continue to covet their particular kind of grandiose architectural inefficiency, they will come to weigh no more than ocean liners on end, plus whatever additional weight the vertical rather than the horizontal position demands. (A job for a research laboratory—or possibly only a mathematician's desk.)

Fifteen years ago, a good automobile cost $5,000. Today you can buy a better car for $500. Why? Because traditions were scrapped, and science given a freer hand. (Yet Buckminster Fuller also points out that a Ford is still compounded of 300 pounds of transportation and 2000 pounds of tradition.) Fifteen years ago, a good suburban house cost $10,000. It costs almost as much today. There is no reason why that which has befallen motor cars may not happen to houses. The scientists are ready, though the bankers, tangled in mortgages and real estate values, are diffident. To all appearances, they are frightened to death.

As housing becomes more mobile, and the power network spreads, the great city—a machine age and not a power age product—will rapidly lose population, and again whiten the bankers' hairs as real estate values collapse. The pull of invention, as we have seen, is toward decentralization, smaller industrial plants in rural acres. Alford and Hannum find that small plants are as adaptable to continuous-flow, automatic production as large ones, and frequently more efficient.[12] Farmers and industrial workers will live in the same towns, the former attending their mechanized

[12] The KMH Analysis of Industrial Production. N. Y. Chapter, Society of Industrial Engineers, December 13, 1933.

agricultural units, the latter their automatic, or semi-automatic factories.

No entirely new forms of transportation seem to be on the immediate horizon, but both railroad train and motor car will presently be stream-lined—with *scientific* stream lines, not the present gesture in salesmanship—and much lighter, more comfortable internally, and far handsomer to look at. The fool-proof airplane may arrive any day, but no one appears to be expecting it tomorrow. Meanwhile, Haldane suggests an interesting trilogy in transportation:

Improvements in the art of navigation made the British Empire.

The railroad made the United States.

The airplane is destined to make the World State.

Why the last? Because the airplane leaps all boundaries, respects no national lines, shrinks the planet to a fraction of its scarcity age size, and threatens, by a three dimensional attack and a remote control of bombers, to make war too dangerous for any nation not incurably mad to undertake.

Aluminum is the most abundant of the metals in the earth's crust. For every pound of copper there are 4,000 pounds of aluminum. We shall pass from the present chrome-alloy era, which supplanted the iron era, into an aluminum era. Aluminum can be produced efficiently only in the electrolytic furnace, and is thus a pure child of the power age. It will be employed for the new stream-lined motor cars and railroad trains, for the new fabricated houses, for factories, office buildings, transmission lines, airplanes, tank cars, pipe lines, fences, "tin" cans, and numberless other products. Professor C. G. Fink, head of the division of electrochemistry at Columbia University, predicts that the 1928 output of the metal will be doubled by 1942. With its alloys, like duralumin, it should see us through the calculable future after tin, copper, zinc, lead, and even iron are gone. Nor will iron go in the calculable future—though copper may.

In nature, electrons and protons form atoms, which in turn form about ninety basic elements, which in turn form well over a million different molecular structures, which in turn form everything material on earth—and probably in the heavens.[13] The next problem for mass production to solve is a procedure roughly parallel to nature's fabrication methods. Hitherto mass production has sought to standardize everything, including the end product. This makes for limited varieties. To change from model T to model A, Henry Ford had to spend $100,000,000. Mass production in a mature power age will be guilty of no such blunders. Parts, like the atom or the elements, will be standardized, but flexible machines will be able, by shifting the "servo-mechanisms," to throw out a wide variety of end products, no longer dulling the consumer with rigidly standardized goods. Factories thus equipped could make a model T or a model A or a Lincoln, or perhaps even an airplane—and make them in a variety of sizes, colors, and body constructions. Buying a car from such a factory will not necessarily entail junking it when improvements are invented. The improvements can be bolted home into the old car. This will be possible when the units (elements) are really standardized. The annual model and its ap-

---

[13] T. N. Whitehead: Planning Standardized Components to Secure Variety in Production. *Harvard Business Review,* April, 1932.

palling wastes of labor, materials, advertising and
peace of mind need worry us no more.[14]

The radio, like the airplane, diminishes space in
terms of time. Sir Arthur Salter envisions international conferences to which the delegates need not
go in person. Yet they will sit about a table, watch
each other, and talk to one another. A television
screen will show every movement of their fellow
members. The radio will furnish speeches, questions,
answers, arguments, all complete. Automatic recording instruments will reduce to writing every word.
Let us hope that the delegates will have more perti-
nent matters to talk about than has lately been the case.

Radio is already a key political weapon. In the
future, no candidate can hope to be elected without
it, no revolutionary overturn can have the ghost of a
chance of success unless it controls the air. British
workers went down to humiliating defeat in their
General Strike, primarily because the government kept
its hands on the broadcasting stations. The Nazis now
bombard Austria with air-waves and are sniped at
themselves from Russia. I suspect radio is a more
devastating weapon than a full military offensive.
The press (an old invention) has hitherto been the
dominant factor in molding public opinion. Before
long, an interesting political struggle may come, in
which one party controls the press and the other
the broadcasting apparatus. My money is on the
party of the second part.

William F. Ogburn, in *Recent Social Trends,* specu-

---

[14] The present status of standardization is well illustrated by the
German passenger locomotive, type IcI–H2, as described by Brady.
There are 5,424 parts, of which 1,451 are standard for any kind of
machine—bolts, nuts, etc.; 2,842 are standard for all types of locomotives; 1,131 are still non-standard.

lates on the social changes which must surround tech.
nical advance. With a geometric increase in invention,
the society of the future must be one of accelerating
change. Morality and law require stability to function well. They will accordingly function badly in the
future. The fixity and detail of right and wrong will
give way to social expediency. With industrial decentralization is coming larger and larger political
organization which may end in the World State.
Democracy will not work so well in these great
organizations, and will receive some serious setbacks.
Use property will increase, but commercial and industrial property, now largely represented by stocks and
bonds, will become increasingly socialized.

Lest, however, we should be carried away with the
dance of the learned professors, it will be well to take
a shot of Spengler, neat:

This machine-technics will end with Faustian civilization
and one day will lie in fragments, forgotten—our railways and
steamships as dead as the Roman roads and the Chinese wall;
our great cities and skyscrapers in ruins like old Memphis and
Babylon. The history of this technics is fast drawing to its
inevitable close. It will be eaten up from within, like the grand
forms of any and every culture.[15]

This is a conceivable description, but I presume to
doubt its historical analogy. All civilizations hitherto
have lived by virtue of man and animal power plus a
little wind. All have been fashioned in the Economy
of Scarcity. High energy cultures live by different
and far greater forces, and obey different laws. It is
rash in the extreme to predict either Utopia or cataclysm. We simply do not know.

[15] *Man and Technics.*

CHAPTER VIII

THE WEB

THE story of modern specialization has never, to my knowledge, been told. To tell it fully would tax the entire staff of the Bureau of the Census for some years, and fill many library shelves. In the salt-box house of 1760, Daniel Shelton brought in a pumpkin from the garden, and Mandy cooked it. Two people were concerned in the direct production of the resulting pie. To them, we might in fairness add whatever local labor assisted in planting the pumpkin, cultivating it, and fabricating the tools wherewith it was planted, cultivated or cooked. If the total reached twenty persons, I should be surprised. Such was specialization in the age of scarcity. When it came to imported molasses or London broadcloth, of course the number of contributors jumped—but not beyond reasonable computation. Articles imported from beyond the limits of the town of Stratford, you remember, were few.

You are today reading a book of which I am the author. You presume that one man has produced this book. You are wrong—as a moment's reflection will show. You are probably wrong by some millions of persons. I can never count the people who have coöperated with me in furnishing you this book, but I can indicate, in a rough and ready way, who some of them are.

First, as to its content. The index cards from which

I work show that I have read nearly a thousand documents preparatory to writing: articles, monographs, speeches, clippings, other books. Some, like *Recent Social Trends,* are the joint work of a large number of scholars. Some, like the Census reports, are the joint work of hundreds of investigators. At least 5,000 persons—some of them living, some dead —have contributed data and ideas. Without their coöperation the book, as it stands, could not have been written. Again, to write it, I had once to learn to read, write, calculate and handle ideas. The staffs of three primary schools, a high school and two colleges labored in the past to supply me with the technique of my trade. (They are not responsible for the output.) Certainly 300 persons have had a finger directly in my formal education.

I write with a yellow pencil on yellow sheets of legal size paper. The pencil contains wood, graphite, rubber, and a metal alloy which resembles brass, but probably is not. The wood may mean lumbermen in Oregon; the lead, miners in Colorado; the rubber, coolies in Sumatra; the alloy, mines in Mexico, Cornwall, Utah, heaven knows where. The pencil itself means factory workers in Ohio, let us say. The paper connotes pulp mill operatives in Canada, chemical workers in Delaware, and paper mill workers in Massachusetts. When the manuscript is finally corrected, it goes to a typist in New York. The instrument she employs is a complicated, mass-produced machine, coming from a huge factory in Pennsylvania. The metals and materials in it originate in many different countries. As in the case of the Ford car, a group of collateral industries must rigorously coöperate to keep typewriters sliding off the factory belt.

I approach my publisher, as usual, with a certain diffidence. On the assumption, which may be egotistical, that his staff labors industriously on this book, the roll call is long and varied. Here are executives to draw the contract, expert "readers" to pass on the manuscript, copyright clerks in Washington, indexers, proof readers with their unkind remarks in the margin, advertisers, mail order clerks, field salesmen, packers, shippers, bookkeepers, messenger boys, and those remarkable mystics who figure royalties. It is part of the publishing business, moreover, to enlist the support, so far as ethics permit, of newspapers, magazines, reviewers and radio announcers. The book comes to you—unless you patronize a public library— probably from a bookstore. This involves jobbers, more bookkeepers, retail clerks, and their attendant equipment.

The book is bound in cloth. This means Negroes in Georgia cotton fields, gin operators, balers, stevedores, textile mill workers in North Carolina, bleachery employees, glue from the Chicago packers, dyers, bindery workers in New Jersey. The symbols that you read are put there by compositors, feeders, pressmen, equipped with a complicated and farflung assortment of mechanisms. This means ore workers in Minnesota, blast furnace and rolling mill operators in Indiana, machine shop workers in Rhode Island— to consider but a few of the processes involved. The ink that makes the impression legible is dependent upon the linseed oil, varnish and soap industries, and requires a blue pigment such as indigo, possibly from Bengal.

Over all these more or less direct coöperators in producing the book you are reading, there plays a

network of overhead services which the latest in calculating machines could not unravel. The services
include, in practically every process, energy for power,
heat and light; telephone and telegraph, the mails,
radio communication; the railroads, express service,
trucks, steamships, taxicabs, airplanes, elevators, warehouses; engineers, insurance, legal talent, and the
omnipresent operations of the banking system. Finally, the author and all his helpers, direct and indirect,
must be fed as they produce this book—which opens
up a vista of farmers and food distributors from all
over the world.

I sit at my desk and describe from memory in a
general way the people and the processes that co-
operate with me. With the aid of the Britannica and
the secretaries of certain helpful trade associations,
I could make a strictly relevant list which, I believe, would fill a hundred pages. And what is true
of books is true of nearly every article you use or
consume in your day by day life.

You cannot put through one telephone call without
bringing into play thirteen separate minerals:

Copper—for wires.
Soft iron—for magnets.
Gold, silver and platinum—for switchboard lamps and con-
tact springs.
Lead and asphalt—for cables and terminals.
Antimony—for solder.
Nickel—for springs.
Zinc—for galvanizing.
Coal—for granular carbon in the transmitter.
Aluminum—for diaphragms.
Mica—for insulation.

A midwinter meal in a New York hotel may include
iceberg lettuce from the Imperial Valley in Califor-

nia—3,000 miles; fresh strawberries from Brownsville, Texas—2,500 miles; fresh peaches from South Africa —12,000 miles. The refrigeration process—which is a sort of steam engine upside down, and subject to the same laws of thermodynamics—has enormously increased the area of specialization. In Scarcity, a farmer can market only as far from home as his perishables remain fresh. With refrigeration he can market halfway around the world, and does. The difficulty is that he could count on the market furnished by his neighbors in the old days, but not on the farflung, impersonal markets of today. Iceberg lettuce may go out of style; a war, a revolution, a tariff wall, may shut off a foreign market; an enterprising middleman may insert himself between the farmer and the consumer skillfully to shunt off all profit in the transaction. Or, most common of all, other farmers from other sections and other countries may take to refrigeration too, and presently, the market is saturated. Iceberg lettuce piles up on New Jersey dumps.

Here is the automobile industry, the largest American industry according to value of finished product. It is the greatest single purchaser of gasoline, rubber, alloy steel, malleable iron, mohair, upholstery leather, lubricating oil, plate glass, nickel and lead. It commands 14 percent of the national lumber output, 15 percent of the copper output, seven percent of the zinc, and consumed in 1932, 165 million pounds of cotton fabric for tires. It thrusts a gigantic tenacle around industry after industry; they are dependent on the automobile, and the automobile is dependent upon them.

You buy the finished car and drive away. Suppose, however, that all automobile mechanics and garage men were suddenly removed. Presently the streets would be lined with broken-down cars that you and I were forced, sooner or later, to abandon after a few helpless raisings and lowerings of the hood. In a year, or less, hardly a car would be running.

Specialization comes close to being a mathematical function of the transportation and communication devices available at any time or place. Where man is the chief carrier, as in some Mexican villages today, specialization is slight. Horses and mules increase it; roads suitable for teams increase it more; the rail-road and the steamship step it up enormously; the airplane, the telephone, the radio, are making specialization world-wide.

In the office of the Bell Telephone Company in Detroit sat Mr. Bertil Clason, nervously consulting his watch, on the morning of his wedding day.[1] Beside him sat Judge John D. Watts to perform the ceremony. And where was the bride? She was in Stockholm, 5,000 miles away. The pair were married by telephone and the charge was $47.50 at standard trans-Atlantic rates.

It is still inaccurate to say that every person alive in the world depends upon every other person alive, but such is the direction of the process. Certain great areas, like the United States, Russia, the British Empire, might be made largely self-sufficient by a deliberate program, and the planned invention of substitute materials. They are not self-sufficient today. Every nation in Western Europe would go instantly to ruin if limited strictly to its own resources. In a few wild, remote and primitive regions, communities still carry on completely sufficient unto themselves, but such

[1] December, 1933.

examples are almost museum exhibits. Even hill village Mexicans get their cotton cloth from Manchester and their firearms from Connecticut.

Specialization, furthermore, if we are to be strictly accurate, is not, under power age conditions, a matter so much of persons as of *processes*. In the depression, we released some 15,000,000 workers from gainful occupations, but the processes of manufacturing and distribution continued to operate, so far as there was demand for the product. A certain minimum of personnel is required, *in each process,* or the industrial fabric breaks—but I am not utterly dependent on you, nor you on me. Either of us can be eliminated with, begging your pardon, no great harm done. But some of your kind of people, and some of my kind of people, must continue to keep our particular process in operation, always assuming it is a necessary process. Both of us are utterly dependent on one great mechanism compounded of interlocking processes. It largely feeds, clothes, shelters, educates and protects us—so far as we receive these facilities at all.

Trading in 1760 was either in the form of barter or in transactions but one remove from barter. Producer and consumer were close together. Specialization makes barter and near barter almost impossible. Consider this book which you are reading. You are, let us say, a California grape grower; I know one such who reads my books. Shall you then give a bunch to me, and one or two single grapes to all my thousands of coöperators? And how shall we get the grapes from your hands if I live in Connecticut and my men all about the Seven Seas? There must be some common medium into which grapes, books and everything else can be turned, if you are to read and

I am to eat. As specialization grows the money nexus grows, until the only way that one may secure the tangibles of life is to present a piece of money for them. Presently one takes the tangibles for granted, and concentrates on the pieces of money. Presently one tends to lose all sight of which comes first.

The acute interdependence of the modern world is the direct result of the curve of invention. The facts that I have recited are not new. But the prevailing attitude toward them is more a naïve bemusement with the idea of Chinese furnishing us with silken step-ins and of Caledonians helping us make telephones, than a realistic appreciation of what specialization actually means to our continued existence on this planet. Men still talk of sturdy self-reliance without realizing that such behavior, in fact, disappeared fifty years ago. The awful truth is that we are strapped together in one gigantic collectivist machine lubricated with an abstraction called money. Half the misery and confusion in the world today is the result of an inability to appreciate the straps which hold us; we think we are free agents when we are only parts of one collective total. These are strong words. I wish that I might make them stronger.

Richard Artisan, a good mechanic, weary of punching a timeclock, and with a few thousand dollars in the savings bank, decides to go into business for himself. Such is the common phrase: *business for himself*. Now, Daniel Shelton could go into business for himself in very truth. Richard Artisan has no such choice. He proposes, shall we say, to set up a garage. He can no more build and equip it himself than he can fly to Saturn. He must draw on the services of carpenters, masons, electricians, power company employees, telephone operatives, oil drillers, railroad workers, cement pourers, gasoline refiners, pipe line employees, truck drivers, tiremakers, toolmakers, machine builders, paper manufacturers, insurance agents, government inspectors and bankers—to construct the simplest establishment. He cannot build and operate a garage without their help or permission—and I have named only a few of the necessary coöperators. In the event that he successfully secures his equipment group—and he will, if his credit holds out—there then arises the even more important question of coöperation from his customers.

As the first garage in a small town with 300 automobiles locally licensed, it is conceivable that there is a chance for survival if Richard does his work well. So shoemakers, or millers, set up shop in 1760, with full knowledge of a local market. Poor Richard today will have no such security of markets. If he makes a success of it, another weary timeclock puncher will borrow from his uncle in the wholesale grocery business, and presently there will be a new garage a few blocks down Main Street—and the town cannot support two garages.

If Richard, as is more usual, first takes a chance on setting up a garage at any corner, anywhere, be he the best mechanic in the world, with the finest manners, he is dependent on forces completely beyond his control, such as:

(*a*) The population density.
(*b*) The competitive density.
(*c*) The traffic density.
(*d*) The prosperity of the local community—which may collapse when one factory closes up or moves away.

(*e*) The prosperity of the whole country, as measured by the business cycle.

(*f*) The quality standards of automobile manufacturers; if they increase, the necessity for repairs will decrease. I should guess that 1934 cars do not require half as much garaging as 1924 cars.

(*g*) The finish applied to cars—and the effect on the necessity of washing and polishing. A change in finish styles may ruin Richard's steady income from scouring cars.

Richard in business *for himself!* . . . He is rather sticking his neck out, as the saying goes, with the excellent chance that the collective process will decapitate him, suddenly or lingeringly. Nor is the United States Steel Corporation in a much better fix, when all is said and done—not when a business cycle can slow it down to 12 percent of capacity, and force it to lose tens of millions of dollars for three years on end.

You and I and Richard and the Steel Corporation and everybody else who counts politically must presently realize, with great singlemindedness, the web in which all our economic operations are circumscribed. Every one of us has felt its meshes; but most of us have not perceived that it is all one web; and that it has been spun principally by inanimate energy. When this realization comes, as it must, there will be no more nonsense about sturdy individualism or "going into business for one's self." Our steadfast aim will be to obtain the maximum of security and freedom *within the network;* even as the aim of the ancient Egyptians was to secure the maximum wellbeing consistent with the behavior of the Nile.

Fortunately, the decentralization of industry promises freedom within a network of energy. Geographic specialization will increase in respect to power sources and control, but can relax appreciably in other departments. At the present time we are over-specialized; beyond what the technical arts demand.

ECONOMIC SECURITY

I suspect that the rallying cry of political pressure groups in the near future will not be the dictatorship of the proletariat, prosperity, the tariff, states' rights, inflation, down with Wall Street, or economy and efficiency—but *security;* economic security. . . . Tangible assurance that the citizen is not presently to join the breadline, beg for charity, be dispossessed, have his goods replevined, see his children too ragged to go to school, observe the savings of a lifetime swallowed up in a few months of financial convulsion. The citizen—certainly in the United States and Great Britain—already knows that there is more than enough to go around. It does not take a gigantic intellectual effort to go one step further and demand economic security for all. That demand will become louder and louder. If I were a politician—which thank heaven I am not—I should consider today none too soon to begin orienting my activities in this direction.

We may take it as one of the few dependable laws of economics that, under capitalism, security varies inversely with the degree of specialization. The farther the individual crawls out on the limb, the easier it is for him to fall off. The fact that the fruit is thicker there is not much solace when one is descending at the rate of sixteen feet per second, duly compounded. Specialization permits a vastly increased output of goods and services per capita. But this observation remains a barren abstraction unless you and I actually receive the output and can *count* on it. Have you any sure reasons for supposing that five years from now an adequate share in that output—and by adequate I mean the essentials of a civilized existence—is coming to you? Or even next year? Certainly I have not. Mr. Wiggin of the Chase National Bank was assured of $100,000 a year for life. Certain Senators asked him a few questions and the annuity vanished. The future is a gamble, as every share of stock, every bond, every annuity, every leasehold, every mortgage, every royalty, is now a gamble. In the nineteenth century, with specialization markedly less than it is today, the gamble was less. The investor in British consols, or United States bonds, had considerable assurance. He has none now. Even if he receives his interest in pounds or in dollars, what are the possibilities of inflation destroying, in whole or in part, the buying power of those pounds or dollars? They are excellent. And one cannot eat dollars.

One hundred healthy and prudent men, twenty-five years of age, were examined some forty years ago by the Ætna Life Insurance Company. The following shows their condition just before the depression, when they were 65 years old:

 1 was rich.
 4 were well-to-do.
 5 were still earning a living.
54 were dependent on relatives or charity.
36 were dead.

The dead were secure, and possibly ten of the living. Fifty-four had not found security.

In Sunnyside Gardens, Long Island, live 500 families in one of the finest model housing developments in the country. The group includes writers, artists, architects, businessmen, skilled craftsmen, professional people. I have friends in this community. It represents a cross-section of the intelligent and progressive middle class. After three years of depression, the group found itself in the following situation:

Income from wages, salaries, and business had been reduced 50 percent.

Income from investments had been reduced to negligibility.

40 percent of all families had one or more members unemployed.

50 percent of all life insurance policies had been cancelled, while loans on policies still outstanding had reduced equity by 50 percent.

Bank deposits of the group had been depleted 76 percent.

All assets, as of 1928, had been depleted 78 percent.

50 percent of the group could no longer retain their homes without help; 25 percent more soon would be in the same condition.

Unpaid doctor bills and dentist bills had increased 150 percent.

Other bills, sixty days in arrears, had increased 92 percent.

Personal borrowings had multiplied 578 percent.

Other liabilities had increased 177 percent.

"Garbage eating was reported at Cicero and 31st street, at 35th and La Salle streets, at the loading platform at South Water street, at the I. C. C. Railroad at 25th street, at Fulton and Randolph Markets, at 40th and Ashland, and at the large dump at Summit. These nine places by no means exhaust the list. . . . Around the truck which was unloading garbage and other refuse were about thirty-five men, women and children. As soon as the truck pulled away from the pile, all of them started digging with sticks, some with their hands, grabbing bits of food and vegetables. . . ." [2]

[2] Report of Special Committee on Garbage Dumps. University of Chicago, 1932.

Early in 1933, seven Negroes were killed, seven wounded and one flogged. All were locomotive firemen in the employ of the Illinois Central Railroad, operating in Mississippi. They were ambushed while at work, killed, wounded and flogged by white men, *for their jobs*. White firemen had been replaced in the interest of economy. To such lengths does economic insecurity drive us.

The majority of American workers, says *Recent Social Trends,* are chronically threatened either with total loss of income through unemployment, or with unpredictable fluctuations in the buying power of their incomes due to changes in the price level. In the last fifteen years there have been three huge changes in the price level, and four cycles of unemployment. Technological unemployment increases, as it must with an expanding invention curve; seasonal unemployment is growing, due to the increasing violence of style changes; cyclical unemployment is more devastating with each major depression. Regional shifts in industry, though not increasing total unemployment, make for great local hardships, as when the men's clothing industry in Illinois drops from 33,000 workers in 1919 to 24,000 in 1927; when Massachusetts shoe workers decline from 80,000 in 1919 to 57,000 in 1925. Although the proportion of older people in the total population is steadily gaining, the older workers, even those over forty, are finding it harder to keep their jobs.

College graduates stand today before a world which has no use for them. Said one of them recently: "Look at me, I have been going to school all my life and I have always been told the same thing. 'Get an education. The world has need for you and you must

be prepared. Stick to your books, learn your pro-
fession, and we will do the rest.' . . . I am not bitter.
I believe that ultimately something can be done about
it, but I do feel that I have been let down. I was
urged to prepare myself for a busy world and I find
that I have only prepared myself for a vacuum instead." [3]

From 1929 to 1932, wage rates dropped 19 percent, volume of employment 43 percent, so that the
total purchasing power of wage earners was only
46 percent of what it was in 1929. Twenty-seven
billions in wages was lost in the years 1930 and
1931 while dividends and interest declined but slightly.
The receivers thereof, however, could do little but
hoard and freeze their money. There were no opportunities for profitable investment.

American farmers received sixteen billion dollars
for their crops in 1919, twelve billions in 1929 and a
little more than five billions in 1932. Only 26 percent of farms were tenant operated in 1880. In 1930
the ratio had grown to 42 percent. Do these figures
mean that American farmers are becoming slack and
inefficient? Not at all. Their efficiency is, if anything, helping to destroy them. The figures mean
that farmers, like college boys, workers, investors,
Sunnyside home owners, clerks, professional people,
business men and even bankers, are caught in the web
of specialization from which traditional financial methods offer no escape.

In October, 1930, the Emergency Employment
Committee created a staff of field assistants at $15
a week. Among those engaged—and glad to get the
job—were:

[3] Reported by Joseph Wood Krutch.

5 architects	19 doctors
5 statisticians	22 commercial artists
6 social workers	23 teachers
8 journalists	26 engineers
19 accountants	35 actors
	58 musicians

The market value of all stocks on the New York Exchange on September 1, 1929, was 89.6 billions; on July 1, 1932, 15.6 billions—a shrinkage of 83 percent, though there were some 30 percent more shares listed on the latter date. These pieces of paper are known, somewhat ironically, as "securities."

"In the nineteenth century" (or in 1930, for that matter), says Edward Bellamy, in *Looking Backward,* "when it rained, the people of Boston put up 300,000 umbrellas over as many heads; in the twentieth century" (meaning 1987) "they ran automatic covers over all the Boston sidewalks, and put up one umbrella over all the heads." We have been trying to roof off economic insecurity by the single umbrella method. It will not work.

Complete security will always be unattainable, because we live in a dynamic, not a static, universe— and a jolly good thing it is, too. That is no reason, however, why we must brook the appalling margin of economic insecurity which now obtains. There is no nourishment for the spirit, no "bright face of danger" here; only a picking over of garbage dumps, and a premium on cowardice, greed, crime, and mental breakdown. Six hundred thousand cases of "unemployment shock," a neurosis akin to shell shock, have been reported from England among the ranks of those long on the dole. Since the depression of 1930 in America, deranged and despairing fathers, mad with the strain of insecurity, have butchered their whole families, bloodily with axes. No former civilization has suffered so; the Economy of Scarcity, for all its hardships, never pushed insecurity to such bitter lengths. Slaves at least were fed. No. The condition grows fantastic, explainable in terms of vendibility, but excusable on no grounds. Here is a forty-fold increase in energy ready and willing to end it forever: ready, by the very laws of its technical performance, to produce and distribute material security for all. The laws demand specialization, but in return the demonstrable flow of goods, as we saw in Chapter III, can banish quite finally those mental and material ills which so torture and degrade us now. You see the point. A little longer, and all western mankind will see the point. Then comes the whirlwind. And God help those who stand in its path.

Up to the year 1930, the individual has sought his own security within the financial rules. "He endeavors so to do," says Sir Frederick Soddy, "by accumulating so much property in the heyday of his youth, that he and his heirs may live on the interest on it in perpetuity afterwards. Economic history is the conflict of this human aspiration with the laws of physics, which make such a *perpetuum mobile* [*i.e.,* perpetual compound interest] impossible, and reduce the problem merely to a method by which one individual may get another individual, or the community, into his debt and *prevent repayment,* so that the individual or community must share the produce of their efforts with the creditor." [4]

For 150 years, this method provided security for some—perhaps for five out of 100, to take the Ætna Insurance Company's sample. In 1930, or thereabouts,

[4] *Wealth, Virtual Wealth and Debt.*

the creditors themselves began to tremble. Today, with inflation looming, their chances are little better than a garage mechanic's or a postman's; worse, perhaps, than a farmer's. It is either reasonable security for all or security for none.

CHAPTER IX

THE FORMULA OF CAPITALISM

CAPITALISM operates to a definite rhythm, and upon a definite formula. The rhythm is a curve of development which substantially takes the form of a three to five percent compound interest graph—varying at different times and in different countries. This can be proved by charting the total outstanding debt, or capital claims, over a long period.[1] In 1880 the rate was around four and one half percent; by 1928 it had grown to eight percent in the United States.

For the world as a whole, Robert R. Doane presents the following estimates:[2]

Total world debt (in millions)

1500 A.D.	$ 400
1600	1,000
1700	1,500
1800	8,000
1900	400,000
1929	700,000

In the seventeenth century total debt increased 47 percent; in the eighteenth century 466 percent; in the nineteenth century 52,000 percent. Such estimates are of course open to a considerable margin of error, but the trend is unmistakable.

For the United States, Mr. Doane has calculated

[1] Bassett Jones has done this in *Debt and Production.*
[2] *The New Outlook,* July, 1933.

total interest-bearing debt in his *Measurement of American Wealth:*

Billions of dollars

1860	4.1	1920	116.6
1870	6.2	1925	141.9
1880	9.3	1929	175.6
1890	16.8	1930	163.8
1904	36.8	1931	151.6
1910	41.3	1932	136.3
1915	61.7		

Here we have one of the sublimest curves in all financial geometry. When the compounding process is at last checked in 1929, the decline, while marked, is not so dizzy as in the case of national income, wages, profits and other indices. The debt burden was as great in 1932 as it was in 1924 (135.5 billions in 1924).

Suppose we take a concrete case. Witness the rise of the United States Steel Corporation: [3]

		Capital
1858	Partnership of Andrew Kloman & Bros. $	5,000
1859	Kloman and Phipps	6,600
1864	Carnegie, Phipps & Co.	50,000
1865	Union Iron Mills	250,000
1881	Carnegie Brothers & Co.	5,000,000
1892	Carnegie Steel Co.	25,000,000
1901	U. S. Steel Corporation	1,402,000,000

Invention, as we have seen, grows at a compound interest rate. Physical production through the nineteenth century—indeed up to the second decade of the twentieth, according to Mr. Jones—grew at a compound interest rate. Markets, especially foreign markets, grew at a compound interest rate. The American population so grew until recently, though the rate was lower than for production. Capitalism inevitably adopted this rhythm. Banking, investment principles,

[3] Harold Rugg: *The Great Technology.*

insurance, accounting practice, were all geared to expansion at a compound interest rate.

Presently dealers in these matters, specifically capitalists who had reposed so long in the comforting embrace of invention, physical production and expanding markets for the system as a whole, came to lose all sight of physical realities and to look upon pounds sterling or dollars as growing by themselves according to a special law of metallic parturition. You planted a golden seed in the savings bank or in the insurance policy, and in eleven and three-quarters years, behold! there were two seeds. In a British bank, if not always an American, this was as sure as the next solar eclipse. All those who had seeds to plant did so—the obligation soon became a moral one—and the seeds promptly were transplanted to the capital goods sector of industry, calling labor and invention and raw materials to make locomotives, steamships, power houses, factories, warehouses, and department stores. "Let your dollars work for you," was the solemn admonition. One pictured round, nimble dollars, like so many Brownies, swarming out from banks and stockings to build the imposing plant of modern civilization.

It was a practical formula for many years. Invention encouraged more capital and capital encouraged more invention. As money took precedence in people's minds over physical realities, extraordinary things began to occur. A recent investigation of street railways in Springfield, Ohio, brought out the fact that the company was still insisting on its right to earn dividends on mules that had died in the horse-car days of the 1870's.[4]

[4] Cited by Herbert V. Nelson, of the National Association of Real Estate Boards.

And what should happen when the plant was built?
This impious idea no capitalist has ever been able to
tolerate. It is as abhorrent as the notion that human
wants are not capable of indefinite expansion. He sees
his Brownies swarming to the end of time. When
Mr. Carl Snyder's statistical studies in physical production showed a tendency to abate their growth rate,
he closed his eyes in horror, crying with Euclid: Which
is absurd! There is no end to capitalism but more
capitalism—more dollars saved to invest in bigger
plants to make larger profits from greater markets.

Presumably we build up capital, equipment, the means of
more extensive life by foregoing the full expenditure of our
present resources at any given minute moment. But since we
also propose to continue indefinitely to accumulate, the question
ultimately arises: For what are we accumulating? At what
moment in our economic history do we propose to cash in and
enjoy the triumph of our thrift? But the answer is, never.
There is no such moment. The motive of accumulation is not
society's enjoyment. It is just perpetual accumulation.[5]

Moody's Manual recently listed $1,200,000,000 of
American bonds, dated to mature after 2000 A.D.—
a guarantee that this sum will be paid to heirs
not yet born. Capitalism, says G. D. H. Cole, "is
always urged on by its own successive discoveries, to
production on larger and larger scale; to an unend-
ing expansion of markets as the necessary condition
of productive stability." Squarely in the path of
the enterprising Brownies, now rise two ugly scientific
facts:

*The law of physics do not permit a growth in physi-
cal production at a compound interest rate, beyond
certain rigid time limits.*

[5] C. E. Ayres in *Economic Behavior*, Vol. II.

The laws of biology do not permit an indefinite extension either of population or of human wants.

Somewhere around the year 1910 these facts began to make themselves felt in the United States; at first gently, then with increasing insistence. By 1930, both were roaring their imperatives. England began to feel the effect about 1900, according to Lord Eustace Percy.

The total of capital claims—including long and short term debts, plus common and preferred stock on which dividends are expected—was, in 1929 in the United States, close to 300 billions of dollars.[6] While the growth *rate* (not the total volume) of physical production has declined since 1910, capital claims have increased their growth rate, until the two curves now bear an impossible relation one to the other. If it be objected that common and preferred stocks have no place in the computation, the answer is that, unless dividends are paid, the investment presently becomes invalid. In the last analysis, physical production controls the claims of capital.[7]

---

[6] *Capital claims in* 1929. (Robert R. Doane: *The Measurement of American Wealth.*)

Government debts—U. S. and local	$31,201,000,000
Agricultural debts	14,066,000,000
Commercial and industrial debts	78,319,000,000
Financial security loans	18,396,000,000
Individual debt	33,659,000,000
Total interest-bearing debt	$175,641,000,000
Stocks of domestic corporations	109,858,000,000
Total capital claims	$285,499,000,000

[7] According to the calculations of Bassett Jones in his *Horses and Apples,* we have no dependable index of total physical production. A long series of individual commodities, however, all show declining growth rates from 1900 on. When physical production is referred to in this book, consider it in the sense of the cumulative effect of the series—pig iron, coal, oil, wheat, etc.—rather than as one statistical total. The latter has been computed by distinguished economists, but Mr. Jones has good reason to believe that it is not soundly based.

At this point the puzzled reader may well cry a halt. If the Economy of Abundance is the ruling phase of our civilization, and is linked to a geometrically expanding curve of invention, why cannot markets likewise expand, and so keep capitalism afloat indefinitely? Why, with so many people in America underhoused, underfed, under-clothed, under-provided with comforts, is there not ample room for expansion? And when America is provided for, consider the poverty-stricken hordes of Asia, Africa, Mexico, South America? Even if luxury wants do reach a saturation point, there seems to be a huge vacuum of plain or garden wants yet to be filled. When all consumers have everything they reasonably need, the world over, then, and not until then, is it time to sound a warning to capitalism.

The puzzled reader is suffering from a common point of view. He confuses serviceability with vendibility. The function of capitalism is *not* to supply people with things which they want. Goods are supplied, yes, but only if enough money is forthcoming in exchange for them to cover all costs of production including interest, plus a margin of profit. Markets are not made by human need. The ten million [8] unemployed in this country today would gladly take a volume of goods which would make factory wheels hum. The factory wheels are silent because the unemployed have no money. A market in the capitalistic sense is not a place where people want things; it is a place where people who have money are able to buy things.

Now, if there were some way to equip all citizens wanting things with cash, the financial system, from

[8] January, 1934.

one point of view, could go forward with a rush. But the equipping of people directly with plenty of money is the one thing that capitalists, particularly bankers, cannot tolerate. Equipping people with money, *outside the rules of the game,* is inflation, naked and unashamed. It is more feared—see almost any American editorial in 1933—than loss of markets.

Consumers have bargaining power in the market if they have something vendible to exchange, of which the two chief items are labor and raw materials. Both have been seriously deflated. An abundance economy has enormously reduced the value of labor by supplanting it with inanimate energy. The production of raw materials has been extended and cheapened by technology, leading to what is called "overproduction" by capitalists. Sometimes they call it "under-consumption," without realizing that this is a serviceability phrase, and has no place in their economics. Overproduction destroys the bargaining power of raw material men—especially farmers. As all necessary drafts of labor and raw materials can in the power age be supplied by fewer and fewer individuals, those squeezed out have no place in the market at all, and no way to secure adequate money to buy the goods they need. There is thus little hope, under capitalism, in the poverty-stricken ranks of either domestic labor, or Chinese coolies. They have nothing vendible to offer, hence capitalism can have no use for them.

The rules of the game

Let us observe with some care how people are equipped with money under the rules of the game.

Rule 1. Private bankers control the supply. Government money in the form of gold and currency is comparatively unimportant in the capitalistic world— except that gold sets an outside limit to the volume of bankers' money. Government money is normally about a tenth of the bankers' check money.

Rule 2. An expanding, highly specialized economic system must have more and more money and credit to move its goods. This requires a supply beyond what the capitalist has on hand. The banker enters the picture, and proceeds to manufacture *new money*— veritably out of the thin air of profitable expectation.[9]

Rule 3. This is how he does it: You come to the banker with a commercial proposition—to build an apartment house, let us say. You convince him that it promises to be profitable; population is growing, land values are growing. You give him your note— the debt—and he gives you the right to draw checks for the face of the note—the money. (Of course he deducts his discount.) Here is a new debt, new money, presently a new apartment house—all based on the hope of yourself and the banker that expansion is the order of the day, and that the apartment house will presently have a name under every door bell.

Instead of a note you may give your issue of stocks and bonds to an investment banker who gets the money for you from the public, after deducting *his* discount. The public buys the stocks and bonds in some cases by depositing them with a commercial banker and getting him to create the necessary pur-

[9] Money and credit are used synonymously in this simplified discussion. Strictly speaking, the banker creates, or inflates, *credit,* which can be turned into current purchasing power.

chase price on a note. The net effect is the same—the banker creates the money.[10]

According to Guy Greer, checks are used for 90 percent of the dollar value of all transactions in the United States. Of this check money, the banks create 90 percent through loans. "Thus the banks are charged not only with safeguarding the principal circulating media of the country, but with actually creating the greater part of it." [11] Private bankers cry to high heaven when the government proposes to create some money of its own against, let us say, public works. Why is this more reprehensible than creating money against a shoddily built apartment house which may never be rented; or against Mr. Insull's whirligig of paper pyramids?

Rule 4. The money the banks create is later paid out to labor. Check book in hand, you proceed to build the apartment house. To the contractors you give checks. The contractors pay out the checks to their workers and clerks and dealers, keeping a profit for themselves. When they pay for materials, the material men, after deducting a profit, pay the balance to their workers in the form of wages and salaries. Thus the new check money gets into general circulation.

Rule 5. The wages and salaries are spent for consumers' goods, but always in the aggregate a part is saved for reinvestment in savings banks, insurance, stocks and bonds.

---

[10] It is not too much to say with Sir Frederick Soddy that, under capitalism, all wealth is debt. As wealth grows, debt grows, interest charges grow. Here is where the inevitable compounding factor comes in. Money does not normally appear in the hands of the consumer until *after* it has passed through the debt mill. Robert R. Doane concurs with Sir Frederick when he says: "Debts have come to form, or more accurately to represent, wealth itself."

[11] *Harpers Magazine,* October, 1933.

The interest or profits collected by bankers, contractors, material men, and yourself as capitalist, are distributed—a small part for consumers' goods, a large part for reinvestment.

The total spent by everybody for consumers' goods fixes the amount produced, and the prices thereof. This is the pull of *demand,* and determines roughly the supply. The total saved for reinvestment must try to find, of course, some factory, some steel company, some chainstore, some new invention; *something profitable to invest in.*

Rule 6. The total amount of consumers' goods cannot be bought at profitable prices by the salaries and wages of those who make and distribute consumers' goods.[12] To their contribution must be added the wages and salaries of those workers who make capital goods—steel workers, building trades workers, machine building workers, and the rest. To the fund must also be added the purchases by capitalists of consumers' goods out of their profits, interest, rents and royalties. The latter expenditure, contrary to popular belief, is very small as compared to the purchases of consumers' goods by the masses. The bulk of "unearned income" is not spent but reinvested. *This is the fatal defect in the capitalistic formula.* If capitalists *spent* all their income for consumers' goods and reinvested nothing, the system would be unjust, but stable. But it would not be capitalism. People who spend all and save little or nothing are, by definition, not capitalists.

Let us make this clear with figures:

---

[12] Wages and salaries normally constitute about 60 percent of total national income; profits, dividends, interest, rents, royalties, the other 40 percent, according to Doane.

DISTRIBUTION BY INCOME GROUPS, 1929 [13]

Income group	Spent for goods and services	Savings
	(in millions of dollars)	
Over 1 million dollars	$ 87	$ 1,045
$50,000 to 1 million dollars	2,494	2,695
Total for very rich	$ 2,581	$ 3,740
$5,000 to $50,000	12,145	3,236
$2,000 to $5,000	21,209	3,276
Under $2,000	53,139	2,291
Institutions	1,799	
Total	$90,873	$12,543

Thus the ultra rich spend only nine percent as much as they save, the very rich as a class save a billion more than they spend, while the total of their purchases—yachts, diamonds, penthouses and all—is less than three percent of all consumers' goods bought by the nation. Observe also how those with incomes of under $5,000 saved far more in the aggregate than the very rich, and not a great deal less than all those with incomes of over $5,000. Savings by individuals in this year amounted to twelve and a half billions, but on top of that were corporation and business savings not distributed to individuals. The grand total of all savings amounted to twenty-one billions.

Rule 7. The capital goods sector is the point where reinvestment takes place. *It is the flywheel of the whole capitalist process.* Unless this wheel is actively turning, consumers are not supplied with adequate money; markets languish.

Thus people get money, and markets are made only through a roundabout method. They will not get enough money, and there will be no profitable markets,

[13] Robert R. Doane and Vergil Jordan in the *Business Week.* Pamphlet reprinting the issues from April 27 to September 7, 1932.

unless ever-expanding profits are reinvested in an ever-expanding capital goods sector.[14]

You see why this must be. Each year the capital goods sector provides *more* factories and machines for the manufacturing of consumers' goods. Customers will have money to buy the new goods only if the capital goods sector is busy making *more* factories for next year, and supplying its workers with *more* wages and salaries. Round and round the spiral must go. To put it another way: As a result of the increasing application of science to industry, consumers are unable to purchase more than a *continually decreasing* fraction of industrial output. In order to maintain existing levels of consumption, an increasing quantity of capital goods must also be constructed—leading ultimately to overproduction and excess capacity.

M. J. Bonn in *The Crisis of Capitalism in America* illuminates the psychology of capitalists during the New Era (1922–1929). "America behaved in much the same way as did German industry when it borrowed so heavily. Both saw only one-half of a period of time: the half during which, with the aid of credits, one creates new plants and furnishes work, pays wages, reaps profits and gives a new impetus to production. Meanwhile they completely forgot the *second half*

[14] Broadly speaking, the capital goods sector comprehends:

1. Labor applied to the construction of plants and facilities for making and furnishing consumers' goods. Rayon mills, department stores.

2. Labor applied to the construction of plants and facilities for making other capital goods. Locomotive works, machine tool factories.

3. Materials for the above. Steel, concrete.

4. Overhead services for the above. Executives, lawyers.

5. Commercial housing.

The line between capital goods and consumers' goods is not always distinct. A dwelling house is a capital good when a capitalist builds it and rents it to you. If you build it yourself, free of debt, it is a consumers' good. If there is a mortgage on it, it partakes of both.

of the period, during which the new factories ought to be producing, but owing to restricted market potentialities, are unable to do so to the full extent."

Rule 8. Nothing is ever undertaken by capitalists without the reasonable expectation of profit.[15] If the capital goods sector has developed its plants and processes to a point where no further profitable opportunities are offered, savings will not flow into it, new factories, new filling stations and new skyscrapers will not be built. The savings freeze in hoardings, capital goods workers are deprived of their jobs; their wages and salaries cease, they can no longer buy consumers' goods. The price of consumers' goods falls as total demand shrinks; business men in this sector reduce their inventories, cut down their payrolls and so decrease purchasing power further. Presently the whole capitalist machine is in reverse—as we have observed it from 1929 to date.

Rule 9. Any depression is surmountable where opportunities for profitable investment, *on a sufficient scale,* lurk in the background, ultimately to call men and women back to work in the capital goods sector, and so, through their salaries and wages, to revive the consumers' goods sector. All depressions prior to the present have been surmountable because expansion was ready and waiting.

Rule 10. Capitalism officially ends when the fly-wheel—the production of capital goods—ceases permanently to turn over at its accustomed compound interest rate.

A system might be devised which got rid of this clumsy method of issuing purchasing power, crab-wise,

---

[15] Profit meaning interest, rent and royalties as well.

through the capital goods sector; a system which dealt directly with consumers by giving them enough money to buy back the goods they helped to make. This might be a good system, but it would not be capitalism, for it would mean distributing almost all the national income in the form of wages and salaries, and little or nothing in the form of interest, profits, rents and royalties. All income would be "earned" income, and the total prices of consumers' goods and services sold would, over any period, equal total wages and salaries distributed. Savings might be permitted, but not for reinvestment, and above all not for interest-bearing debt. For such capital goods as were needed, the State, or other controlling authority, would have to levy a tax and build them out of current income. Private bankers would have no place in such a system.

As a matter of fact, we have this system in embryo, functioning coincidentally with capitalism. Government distributes money directly to government employees, who render many vital services—and some not so vital. Foundations, charities, endowed institutions, do the same. This procedure often bypasses the capital goods sector, the bankers and the debt mill. The extent of this extra-capitalism has never been computed to my knowledge, but we know that it is growing. Mr. Doane shows an increase of "non-productive wealth," including government buildings, churches, endowed universities, country clubs, public parks, etc., from 19 percent of all wealth in 1914, to 28 percent in 1929. That it is a foreign body in the corpus of capitalism is evidenced by the repeated protests of business men against taxation, and against the diversion of funds from the channels of "legitimate" investment.

If the above ten rules give a true account of the processes of capitalism, broadly interpreted, the question above all others in the immediate future is the fate of the capital goods sector. If the sector can be revived, capitalism can continue so long as expansion continues. If it cannot be revived, private capitalism is self-liquidated.

How can the capital goods sector be revived, and the formula set in motion again? Lawrence Dennis has pointed out one way: a Grade A war.[16] . . . Munitions, battleships, airplanes, submarines, barbed wire, chemicals, Big Berthas, steel, cement, rolling stock, copper, aluminum, lumber, wool, cotton, rubber, zinc, drugs—profitable investment everywhere, wages and salaries for all. The proposal is open to two difficulties, however. Would any of us be left alive after the next first class, mechanized war, to enjoy the benefits of a revived capitalism? Again, would not the load of debt, inevitably created by the expanding process, prove even more disastrous in the long run than the debts of the late War? War is a shot in the arm of capitalism, followed by extreme lassitude in the patient.

Another obvious method is to scale down all debts by inflation, devaluation of the dollar, or otherwise, and start over again. This sets the compounding process back on its haunches, reduces the volume of money seeking profitable investment, and requires a smaller capital goods sector to keep the formula in balance. (The volume of consumers' goods must also shrink, of course.) Germany and Italy have already put creditors through this wringer. It has served to keep the community afloat, but produced fascism from an infuriated middle class, stripped of savings. France

[16] *Is Capitalism Doomed?*

officially dropped the franc from twenty cents gold
to four cents, without producing fascism—as yet.
Capitalism cannot be said to be flourishing in any of
these nations. Furthermore, the method, like war,
only postpones the day of reckoning.

In earlier depressions, debts were reduced by bank-
ruptcies and repudiations spotted over the economic
front. As Bassett Jones has shown, these were sufficient
to bring the debt curve into alignment with physical
production, allowing both to move forward with the
next wave of expansion. Far more serious surgery is
needed today. There are six specific reasons for a
halt in the tempo of expansion. Some of them I have
already mentioned, but categorically they are:

1. Population in western civilization is approaching
its peak, soon to decline. This chilly fact, so contrary
to the lush growths of the last 150 years, cannot fail
to affect land values and business markets adversely.

2. Nations hitherto considered backward have built
their own factories and energy systems—with the
help of the output of our capital goods sector. They
do not provide the markets they used to provide. Nor
does the drive of the whole world towards economic
nationalism help. A minimum of imports is the slogan
of the movement. We must remember, as Karl Marx
long ago pointed out, that capitalism soon exhausts,
under its peculiar formula, the profitable possibilities
of the domestic market, and turns to foreign expansion
and imperialism, to keep its flywheel turning over.
Foreign markets are now shutting up like so many
accordions. The London Economic Conference of
1933 was a last despairing wheeze. Some foreign trade
must go on for the exchange of vitally needed materials. The point is that so far as we can look into

the calculable future the rhythm of expansion seems quite finally broken.[17]

The United States is particularly handicapped in respect to foreign trade. The War turned her into a creditor nation. If foreign loans are to be serviced, she must import more goods than she exports to balance her earlier advances.

3. The American industrial and agricultural plant, as we have seen, is built to a point where it can care for about twice the active demand for consumers' goods. It does not accordingly offer—as a whole—a field for profitable investment. Here and there are opportunities, of course, but are they sufficient, in the aggregate, to employ ten million workers? They are not. And that personnel is approximately what the formula now demands. Let us drive this home with more of Mr. Doane's figures:

BILLIONS OF DOLLARS

Year	Gross savings	Total capital outlays	Additions to plant	Corporate net profits
1909	4.5	5.0	4.2	2.9
1912	6.3	6.3	5.4	3.5
1915	7.5	6.7	5.8	4.3
1918	11.4	14.9	12.0	6.6
1920	16.4	19.4	12.4	5.9
1922	15.4	15.0	12.2	4.8
1924	17.9	16.0	13.0	5.4
1926	19.0	18.8	14.2	7.5
1928	21.6	21.0	15.3	8.8
1929	24.8	19.2	15.3	10.8
1930	13.7	9.9	8.2	1.4
1931	6.7	2.1	5.9	—1.7
1932	7.1	—3.3	3.3	—6.6

Gross savings include corporation as well as individual savings. Capital outlays include additions to work-

[17] See especially G. D. H. Cole: *A Guide through World Chaos.*

ing capital and foreign loans, as well as additions to plant. The great reduction in working capital in 1932 throws the whole total into a minus quantity. The figure which most concerns us is "additions to plant," for this is the heart of the capital goods sector. It includes industrial machinery and equipment, farm equipment, commercial equipment and new construction. In 1928 and 1929, the outlay was more than fifteen billions. At an average wage of $1,500 a year, this turnover would require the services of ten million workers. As $1,500 is above the national average, the figure is conservative. Observe the pitiful collapse of the sector after 1929. The year 1933 will be little better than 1932 for capital goods.

The last column is significant in furnishing an index of the possibility of servicing the claims of capitalists in the form of bonds and capital stock. If total corporate profits continue in the red, the claims obviously cannot be serviced. To maintain the debt structure at its 1928 and 1929 level, profits must run from nine to eleven billions a year. In 1932, profits were sixteen billions short of meeting that demand. 1933 will show but little improvement. "More than 60 percent of all debt," says Doane, "is dependent entirely upon future income . . . Any violent fluctuation in the total income immediately jeopardizes a substantial portion of the total debt structure."

Revivalists point out that many industries need to be reconditioned and brought up to date. They do. But such a program means either increasing their debts, increasing the service charges on those debts, and so increasing the demand for profitable investment, or a widespread repudiation of debt, the elimination of the least efficient concerns, with consequent unemployment and loss of purchasing power. When expansion, *for other reasons,* is moving briskly forward, modernizing also goes forward at the cost of the inefficient, and cheerfully heedless of the additional debt. As a prime method, it cannot of itself provide a fraction of the volume of expansion needed. Indeed it might only make matters worse in the long run by further stimulating technological unemployment. Reconditioning means speeding the power age.

4. The American continent has substantially completed its experiment in transportation. The frontier has long since closed. The stimulation and excitement of conquering a raw new territory are over. Many refinements are in order, but the original expansion drive has exhausted its growth rate.

5. There are no great new industries on the horizon to stir the capital goods sector as canals, railroads, power developments, automobiles, stimulated it in the past. There is, of course, the gigantic task of rehousing twenty million families. But this is a job which private capital seems singularly loath to undertake. Rehousing, on this scale, is a serviceability job or none at all.

6. Technological unemployment is steadily whittling away at purchasing power in both sectors, regardless of booms or depressions.

David C. Coyle in *The Irrepressible Conflict* points out another very important consideration. The power age promises to produce an equivalent output with a declining outlay for capital goods. He says: "An automatic factory, with all its expensive instruments, may be more productive than an old-fashioned plant of equal cost and much larger size . . . If a million dollars invested in new plant can force the abandonment of more than a million dollars worth of existing plant, the time may come when the total capital investment of the country will diminish as industry grows, instead of increasing as it did all through the machine age. . . . Apparently the power age is going to have comparatively little use for either labor or capital."

The situation is something like the case of a growing boy. The boy is market expansion, the parents, capitalism. For years father and mother have been adjusting their pocketbook to larger shoes, longer trousers, bigger hats, heavier meals. Some day the boy will grow up, and reach a replacement rate in his requirements. Such is the law of biology. Human parents know this. Capitalism does not know it, but expects the boy to grow forever. . . . Gentlemen, the market has come to the end of its adolescent growth. The boy has reached maturity.

A last factor deserves mention. Specialization has produced economic insecurity. Insecurity seriously depresses purchasing power, by causing people to save rather than freely spend such income as they possess. Haunted by fear of unemployment, old age, destitution, they feel they must put something by. This increases the demand of funds seeking profitable investment, and diminishes the active demand for consumers' goods. If avenues for profitable investment are closed, the funds are sterilized in banks or mattresses. Thus a large fraction of the "money in circulation" is not circulating. This is the factor which neutralizes "buy now" campaigns. For psychological reasons the plain citizen dare not buy beyond his cardinal wants. Only when insecurity abates will he or she go to market. The principle operates most forcibly in depressions, but is not absent in so-called normal times.

The capitalistic formula has run out. The boy has grown up. The growth curves of the nineteenth century will never rejoice this country again. Capitalism might be revived by war, by ruthless inflation, or by a series of great new industries. So revived, however, it can be a matter of only a few years before the demands of the capital goods sector overtake the new expansion, and another, and final, crisis is reached. I profoundly doubt if further expansion is to be granted, but I do not deny that, theoretically, there may be a quiver or two in the formula. Capitalism remains a tough and persistent tangle of economic habits. It has been officially buried before, only to burst belligerently from its coffin. What we can safely say is that never in the past has the corpus of capitalism had such a copper-riveted coffin.

Observe that in describing the formula and its collapse I have not mentioned the aberrations of particular capitalists. Such cases have filled the newspapers in recent years to the shock and delight of the populace. Many believe that if only the bad capitalists —the Mitchells, the Wiggins, the Insulls, the Kreugers—and their practices could be eliminated; if only all bankers protected their depositors, all investment houses their investors, all stock exchanges their lambs, all corporate directors their stockholders, capitalism would not have fallen on evil days. I do not hesitate to affirm that had every banker, every investment house, every stock exchange, every director, been pure as the driven snow,[18] the formula would have

---

[8] "Clean as a hound's tooth" is Thomas Lamont's phrase.

collapsed just the same. Indeed, it might have collapsed earlier. Debts and the capital goods sector might have compounded even more majestically, undiminished by the losses of reckless manipulators. Individuals are unimportant in this analysis. The epilogue we have sought to write is for a system.

CHAPTER X

MARCH TO ZERO

THROUGHOUT the early stages of the Economy of Scarcity, and later, as barter gave way to pecuniary exchange and vendibility gained, demand was normally in advance of supply. Prices on the market, accordingly, were well above the cost of production. This was a condition which eminently satisfied the early business man. Whatever the commodity he dealt in, his gain was at a maximum when the commodity was scarce.

In due time, vested interests clustered about these price levels; relative scarcity was duly capitalized. Bonds, mortgages, leaseholds, shares of stock, in the hands of capitalists, *rentiers,* banks, trust estates, insurance companies, and the inevitable widows and orphans, set, like concrete, in a rigid mass about a given price level and flow of profit. Recipients of the bounty did not desire any industrial change or development which would increase the supply of their commodity to the point of reducing prices. They had a vested interest in scarcity.

Into the tidy price walls came crashing science and energy, particularly in the form of mass production, driving down the direct costs of goods and services, and so undermining prices.[1] Consider one specific

[1] The fact that all prices move up and down in secular swings is not important here. The important thing is the particular price

case: the American railroads. Something over twenty billions of dollars has been invested in the system, every dollar expecting its three or five or ten cents of free income a year. Railroad investors were quite content to let transportation progress halt at this happy peak. Progress would not halt. It produced the internal combustion engine, the motor car, the truck, the long distance pipe line for gas and oil, the high voltage transmission of power to replace in part the haulage of coal—and so undercut the stability of the whole railroad investment. Carriers are now dropping like rotten apples from a tree into the courts of insolvency and into the treasury of the Reconstruction Finance Corporation. Their owners tried to maintain prices— and did maintain high rates—through the agency of the Interstate Commerce Commission, but the commodity could not be kept dear, because of technological advance. The posted rates availed them nothing in the long run. The twenty billions is earning only a despicable return today.

SCARCE MONEY

The commodity the banker handles is money. The scarcer the commodity the higher the price, that is, the interest rate. He protects his business and his profit by keeping this commodity relatively dear. Thus he clings to a position taken by money-lenders centuries ago, when all cash was metallic; when gold and silver were genuinely rare metals and highly prized. For all his downtown urbanity, the banker is still at heart a goldsmith, with a side line in usury.

which yields a reasonable margin of profit at any given time. A "reasonable" profit, as Veblen points out, is always the highest obtainable profit.

What keeps the industrial plant on part time, even in periods of prosperity? Lack of mass purchasing power. Why were mass incomes so low even in 1929? Manufacturers and farmers were eager to produce more goods; labor was eager to assist; railroads and trucks were eager to carry; merchants were eager to distribute. The engineers' system was straining to go; the leash was the bankers' system. The banker is a private middleman who has thrust his way into the economic system and set up a toll bridge. One cannot deny that the bridge has had its uses. Nor can one deny that it is the tendency of all private bridge keepers to charge what the traffic will bear.

As the technical arts fostered the production of goods, money and credit had to expand also, or the goods could not be moved. The banker met that situation by creating check money, which could expand with production.[2] But a nice balance had to be maintained; money and credit must be "sound"; that is, scarce in relation to demand. The bankers' money followed the engineers' factories but always somewhat behind them. This is proved by the fact that purchasing power has never been level with plant capacity, save in isolated cases. Furthermore, for every dollar of check money created, a dollar debt, bearing interest, was also established. The sound money men solemnly warn the nation against the perils of government inflation, perversely ignoring the fact that from 1922 to 1929 in the United States, they themselves inflated credit and debt to the tune of fifty billions of dollars, until the rotten paper mass was punctured in one devastating

[2] Guy Mallon in his *Bankers vs. Consumers* shows how the American constitution contemplated the issue of money as a strict government function, and how the private banker proceeded, in due time, to usurp the function.

explosion. They had not financed mass purchasing power, except as a side issue. The object of this gigantic credit inflation was a flow of free income to themselves.

One of the prime agents for keeping money relatively scarce was the gold standard. It set an outside limit to the money bankers could manufacture. A gold standard is in effect a guarantee by the government to bankers that mass purchasing power will not become too plentiful. When a government leaves the standard —as did England in 1931, and the United States in 1933—bankers are naturally seized with panic. Nothing remains but habit and political promises to stop inflation. The government has withdrawn its guarantee, and can, if it chooses, print money and deliver the same to citizens without the bankers' permission; ignoring the usual channels of debt, the capital goods sector, and compound interest. Worse, when money is thus made abundant, the existing debt fabric is threatened. The creditor loses his scarcity position; the bankers' toll bridge faces the competition of free bridges.

This touchstone reduces the gigantic controversy now prevalent in industrial nations over inflation, sound money and the gold standard, to one orderly pattern. Broadly speaking, it is a conflict between private bankers and creditors who want to keep their commodity scarce, and the pressure of an abundance economy which demands that purchasing power also become abundant. Governments waver back and forth between tenderness for bankers, and attention to political clamor from the mass of their citizens, roaring for the wherewithal to obtain the necessities of life.

SCARCE GOODS

The producer of tangible goods and services also seeks to maintain prices at profitable levels, which means insuring a relative scarcity in goods. Henry Ford was one of the first of his class to renounce this business-like philosophy and try deliberately to make goods abundant by cutting prices *below* what the traffic would bear.[3] His was not a bargain sale or a "loss leader" policy, but a universal, permanent procedure for all his output. A few have followed in his footsteps, but not many. The scarcity pattern is still the prevailing one.

But technology with its pressure on costs moves relentlessly onward. Many price walls have been breached by the impact; many more are swaying. Such is the tragedy of the producer under capitalism. Remember, he does not deal primarily in goods but in money values—vendibility.

High scarcity values once obtained for the following. Where are they now?

Matches	Tinware
Pins	Icecream
Clips	Electric light
Safety razors	Watches
Printed matter	Bottles
Pens and pencils	Cans
Rubber bands and string	Imitation jewelry
Paper	Underclothing
Towels	Cartridges
Buttons	Coathangers
Nails and screws	Hairpins

I was tempted to include used cars in the above list, but they are a special case. New cars, due to the an-

[3] The Ingersoll dollar watch antedated Ford.

nual model selling method, normally have a value well above cost, but after they have been purchased and driven one mile, that vendible value falls a third, sometimes a half. Presto! into the sea of abundance leap two to five million cars a year; their scarcity value gone. Although technically they are better machines after a few thousand miles of operation, they may presently be had from $5 up. Sometimes they are given away. In due time they are thrown away—to litter the roadsides of a nation. American secondhand motor cars are the sublimest exhibit of collapsed scarcity values in all economic history. And of course the final effect is to drive new cars also towards the brink of the precipice.

Robert R. Doane gives us a hint of the pressure of technology toward lower prices in the following figures:

	Expenditure in billions of dollars 1929	Average annual rate of growth
Industries with diminishing costs	80.8	6.7%
Industries with stationary costs	11.5	4.7%
Industries with increasing costs	20.7	3.9%

Thus industries whose costs are diminishing are far in the lead, both in magnitude of business done and in growth rate.

In any five-and-ten-cent store you will find scores of articles which used to cost dollars; articles that our ancestors prized and carefully saved. We fling them carelessly about, valuing them little more than air or water. Indeed, as Consumers' Research has pointed out, you will find articles (hardware is a case) in the five-and-ten which still do cost dollars—or at least far more—in other stores, with no better quality. Thus the scarcity position of an identical article may have disappeared at one place on the industrial front, while at another, strenuous efforts are made to preserve it.

At some point in the history of each commodity listed above, capital was forced to readjust itself to a sickening drop in costs and prices; and those concerns which held to older methods were driven out of business. Few men will be driven out of business without a struggle. As technology threatened greater aggregations of capital, the struggle to survive took the form of deliberately fostering scarcity by bringing the whole industry under one effective control; in short, by creating a monopoly, *de facto* if not *de jure*. As Veblen says:

> Ever since the mechanical industries first came into the dominant place in the industrial system, the defects of this business-like management of industry have continually been encroaching on its qualities. . . . Having begun as an industrial community which centered about an open market, it has matured into a community of vested interests whose vested right it is to keep up prices by a short supply in a closed market.[4]

What is cost?

Economists and accountants have been debating this question for years, without coming to any agreement. They never will, because under vendibility, cost is anything which helps to maintain prices. It is subject to no exact appraisal, but varies from plant to plant. From the point of view of serviceability, however, cost can be accurately defined:

The cost of production is the energy consumed in making the article or rendering the service. This includes both inanimate and animate energy—food and maintenance for workers. The real cost of goods

[4] *The Theory of Business Enterprise.*

made in any period is the amount of goods—both consumers' and capital goods and both reducible to terms of energy—used up in the period.[5] If the amount of goods on hand at the end is greater than at the beginning, the cost of the new wealth has been less than the output and a net gain in wealth has been registered. For 150 years, cost, so defined, has been below output in western civilization, resulting in a colossal accumulation of "wealth." The trouble is that much of the wealth is without serviceability—excess plant capacity and other forms of waste. Production has always exceeded consumption—think steadily in terms of *tonnage*—even during the War. Never has the United States "lived on its capital" or been extravagant and prodigal in the sense of consuming more than it produced. Never. During the New Era, new capital goods accumulated prodigiously, export tonnage exceeded import. Only when we twist our minds back to vendibility can a case for "extravagance" be made out. For debt, operating by the formula of capitalism, ran clear off the chart in the New Era.

H. L. Gantt was enough of a serviceability engineer to paralyze business men with a revolutionary cost system. "The indirect expense," he said, "chargeable to the output of a factory should bear the same ratio to the indirect expense necessary to run the factory at normal capacity, as the output in question bears to the normal output." [6] All other cost systems neglect this principle, thus covering up the true waste of plant idleness. Suppose when the factory is running at capacity, the overhead cost—interest, insurance, depreciation, repairs, office expense, etc.—is twenty

[5] Following Soddy, Henderson and Hattersley.
[6] *Organizing for Work.*

cents per unit of output. When the factory goes on
half time, this cost jumps to forty cents, on all traditional cost sheets. No, said Gantt, overhead should
remain at twenty cents, and the balance be charged
direct to the profit and loss account, not loaded upon
the output. He was, of course, correct from the
serviceability point of view. The article does not
cost any more in energy when the plant operates on
part time. The cost is the same, but waste has now
appeared. The business man serenely adds the waste
to the true cost, and keeps prices at a level which
covers both, plus, if possible, a profit. This is sound
vendibility cost accounting. I learned to practise it
myself, and I ought to know.

Thus, great as may be technical economies and
improvements, they can be blanketed by the collection
of too high a price. It takes a long time, accordingly,
for technology to emerge from the wrappings of
vendibility—which is prone to pad its costs as out-
rageously as any travelling salesman. Here we find a
classic example of the war between the engineer and
the business man. When the engineer wins, prices
must come down to the vicinity of true cost, to the
great benefit of the consumer. If most business men had
been as bold as Henry Ford, they would have shattered
the capitalist formula at an earlier date. The Ford
principle—though he does not know it—is one of the
most vicious attacks on capitalism ever made. It is
directly counter to a shrewd, business-like scarcity in
goods; it threatens untold vested interests in high,
relative prices.

When expansion of the capital goods sector over-
reaches itself in excess plant capacity, values based on
scarcity obviously become precarious. At any time,

some outlander may, and frequently does, cut prices to true cost, bringing down the whole level of the industry; driving the least efficient concerns into bankruptcy, skimming the cream of profit from most concerns. Small wonder that trade associations brand the price cutter as a criminal.

In the rubber tire industry we are given an instructive example of what happens to costs and prices when monopoly or other business-like restrictions do not seriously impede the work of the engineer. Costs for tube and tire combined fell from $17.91 in 1921 to $9.63 in 1929, to $7.19 in 1931.[7] The average price to the consumer was $30.50 in 1914, $15.70 in 1929, $12.07 in 1931. The industry had no protecting monopoly; open to the blasts of competition, it was forced to pass on to the consumer its operating efficiencies as they were made. The serviceability of the industry has accordingly been high; its vendibility is one of the poorest on the stock exchange.

Let us consider an hypothetical case which is the reverse of this sad tale of Akron. Suppose a group of enterprising gentlemen could get hold of the atmosphere, create an air-tight monopoly, and meter it out to every family in the nation, like gas, water or electricity. Immediately there would be a huge increase in financial wealth—particularly if the technical process of controlling the supply were very costly. What a balance sheet! What a gorgeous statement of the costs of reproduction for the sweating accountants of public service commissions. What a resounding item for goodwill and patents. What an array of thirty million accounts receivable; what hordes of

[7] *Monthly Labor Review.* U. S. Department of Labor, December, 1932.

bookkeepers, inspectors, officials, vice presidents, field service men and meter readers. Surely, with such responsibilities, the salary of the president should be not less than $150,000 a year; surely he must be allowed a bonus, and the opportunity to sell a little stock—just before the corporate report was made public—on the side. What requirements of legal talent, of goodwill advertising, of appraisers, auditors and legislative lobbyists. What issues of preferred, common, Class A stock, Class B and C, and gold Debenture 5's, maturing in 2034 A.D. What pools on the stock exchange, and what opportunities for an enterprising "control" to double cross the owners of the property.

By reducing air to vendibility, scarcity could be capitalized. Business would be richer—and every man, woman and child in the country would be poorer.

The early enterpriser a century ago was technician, manager and financier, all in one. He had an expanding market to play with. He could use all his output profitably. About the middle of the nineteenth century in England, and somewhat later elsewhere, the "productive capacity of the mechanical industry was visibly overtaking the capacity of the market, so that free competition without afterthought was no longer a sound footing on which to manage production." [8] A policy of combination and restriction of output set in. The date in the United States was about 1880, when corporation finance made its bow. The enterpriser then became afflicted with a split personality. Part of him remained in production, part of him went over into finance, to become the dominating voice. In due time

[8] Veblen: *The Engineers and the Price System.*

the investment banker developed an even louder voice.

Real costs were high a century ago, because a pin, a pad of paper, a match, required a tangible quota of human time and energy. Now, with inanimate energy to cheapen costs, labor ceases to limit volume of output. To operate a given machine by electric power costs, let us say, $1. If the same power were furnished by laborers at $5 a day, the cost would be $230. This dramatic contrast, calculated by C. M. Ripley,[9] shows the intense downward pressure on real cost.

To put costs under pressure threatens a complicated layer of annuities, fixed charges, investments, contracts, mortgages, bonds, salaries, perquisites and other financial arrangements which, like barnacles, have crusted upon the old price and profit margins. Somehow, anyhow, this layer, and what Veblen calls "the flow of free income," must be maintained. If *real* scarcity has disappeared, an *artificial* one must be created. Thus, when petroleum threatened to submerge the nation, Mr. Rockefeller, senior, promptly set up the Standard Oil Company to confine the flow to more seemly price levels.

Devices for artificial scarcity

Monopoly is probably still the favorite method for maintaining a spurious scarcity. It was the first method tried two generations ago, when technological advance was making itself felt in meat packing, aluminum, steel, sugar refining, paper making, ship building, copper, matches, harvesting machinery, and the like. Then we saw, in effect, group after group of our most distinguished captains of industry jumping with both

[9] Of the General Electric Company.

feet on these incipient volcanoes; stamping and pounding them back to scarcity.

Another standard procedure is, of course, destruction of goods. I have before me a picture from a recent bulletin of Consumers' Research,[10] showing an embankment of oranges in California, some ten feet high and a mile long. There appears to be enough Vitamin C here to keep the whole world healthy. The fruit has been dumped to rot in order that price levels may be maintained. Cotton, coffee, wheat, corn, bananas, milk, potatoes, fresh vegetables, also come to mind. The Agricultural Adjustment Administration is now officially experimenting with this technique.

Allied to physical dumping is the figurative method. Goods are dumped in foreign markets at prices sometimes scandalously below the domestic price. This has long been common practice in dealing with "the surplus." Hence the regulation which you may read on the back of your customs declaration, which forbids you to bring into the country any American-made goods you may have bought abroad.

A method popular since the War is the "quick replacement" technique. Following the sale of flimsy goods, or highly styled goods, depreciation or obsolescence takes a rapid toll, and supply does not outrun demand so readily as when quality is better. The so-called "annual model racket" is an organized form of this procedure. The method is inconceivable without the help of advertising—about a billion dollars worth of advertising at last accounts.

"The business man's object," says Veblen, "is to get the largest aggregate gain from his business. It is manifestly for his interest, as far as may be, to shorten

[10] October, 1933.

the process out of which his earnings are drawn, or, in other words, to shorten the period in which he turns his capital." This reduces quick replacement almost to formula. The technique is now evident in:

Women's dresses and cloaks	Sparkplugs
Men's coats and suits	Crank case oils
Hats	Furniture
Collars	Radios
Shoes	Razor blades
Kitchen utensils	Golf clubs and other sporting
Motor cars	goods
Watches	

A time honored source of artificial scarcity is, of course, the protective tariff. How is the domestic manufacturer to keep prices at profitable levels if consumers are permitted to indulge themselves in cheap imported goods? The interloper is summarily, and legally, thrown out, amid a welter of crocodile tears as to the pauper labor of this and that member of the League of Nations.

A fifth method is the loading of distribution costs. Even if the product, f.o.b. factory, can be almost given away—say safety razor blades—by the time it has been loaded with jobbers, wholesalers, speculators, commission men, salesmen, canvassers, mail order campaigns, calendars, illustrated brochures, sales engineers, fancy containers, travelling allowances, crosshauling, captive balloons, retainers to college professors, telegrams, conferences, trips to Washington, cigars, presents to purchasing agents, accountants, long distance telephone calls, radio programs, liquor, lawyers—by this time, I repeat, the razor blade, the radio set, the washing machine, the steel tennis racket, or whatever the article may be, is reasonably secure in its scarcity status.[11] The price to the consumer is three to three hundred times the factory cost. Interestingly enough, this method, unlike monopoly, is not deliberate. A new man in the field might be glad to forego this expense and undersell his competitors. But he finds he cannot break into the market without a spirited promotion campaign. Once in, he has to maintain his position by unremitting ballyhoo.

Incidentally, the doubling or trebling of jobs in the ballyhoo force is less beneficial than it sounds. In the last analysis these jobs rest *on a commodity held to a limited output.* It is output, not jobs, which finally determines standards of living and material well-being. . . . Millions of artificial jobs are created by an artificial restriction of output. It is a shaky formula. Yet on this dubious foundation, the learned faculties erect their case for the inconsequence of technological unemployment. The chorus runs: "There is always plenty of room in the overhead trades for those displaced by technology."

Salesmanship aims at capacity operation, to keep operating costs low and profits high. But so onerous is the burden of salesmanship that low factory costs— provided they are achieved—are promptly offset by high distribution costs, and thus the whole effort tends to cancel out. The irony in the case is unnoted by most business men.

Dr. H. S. Person of the Taylor Society has well summarized the broad situation: "Advancing technol-

---

[11] In July, 1916, wheat averaged exactly $1 a bushel, according to the *Consumers' Guide,* published by the A.A.A. The average price of a pound loaf of bread was 7.0 cents. In November, 1931, wheat averaged 50½ cents a bushel. The average price of a pound loaf was 7.3 cents. The difference was not all profit to bakers. Most of it, we may be sure, was overhead, distribution and ballyhoo.

ogy demands ever lower prices, other things remaining the same, for the commodities produced with ever lower costs. Business finance, on the other hand, demands fixed prices. It succeeds for periods in actively resisting the glacier-like pressure of technology for lower prices, until now and then the latter breaks through and confuses all the fine adjustments and stabilities of finance, and we have such a crisis as that from which we are now trying to extricate ourselves." [12]

The deliberate suppression of new invention is another standard method of achieving scarcity. Inventions themselves are bought up and put away in safe deposit vaults; or still better, inventors are bought from competitors and put away on the home payroll. Like authors in Hollywood, they may find nothing to do but draw their salaries. All large corporations retain a legal staff whose business and pleasure it is to sue for infringement of patent, prepare injunctions, throw every possible barrier known to the law in the way of an unassimilated new invention or process.

A final and somewhat curious method claims our attention. Racketeering, when applied to business, is nothing whatever but a device to insure artificial scarcity. We find in Chicago, for instance, the well established "collusive-agreement racket," whereby the astute business man turns gunmen, corrupt labor leaders and politicians against his competitors, establishes a local monopoly, and maintains his price levels. He but follows the golden rule that the preservation of business is the prime consideration of all good Americans. "Organized crime, like war, is

[12] Address before the Boston Retail Distribution Conference. September, 1933.

the savage but logical extension of the sales system to its ultimate absurdity." [13] Now that repeal of prohibition has taken the supreme scarcity value from alcohol, other forms of crime are expected to increase.

Ultimately technological pressures break through the price barricades. We have noted various material goods which have lost their scarcity status. Utilities are following commodities—Charles P. Steinmetz before he died prophesied that electricity would soon become as common as water. It is significant that the great boom of the New Era, from 1922 to 1929, *produced no appreciable increase in the average price level;* in defiance of the precedent of all previous periods of business prosperity. Monopolies are even harder to maintain in a period of rapid technological change.

"Nothing in the world," says Katherine H. Amend, "will save the Tennessee Valley Authority from a volley of dead cats for producing for common workers a charming town, which has even been located with the desire to provide for every dwelling vistas of the beautiful, misty hills. It is rank heresy to give cheap homes, beauty, comfort and convenience. If that can be done for $2,500, what happens to the market for $10,000 and $15,000 houses?" [14] What indeed? The United States government is building the town of Norris for workers on the new dam, without benefit of real estate speculators, agents, subcontractors or other vested interests. It will build for $2,500 a better house than any individual could build for $7,500, with fireplace, screened porch, electric stove, heaters, refrigerator installed, and all public service connections.

---

[13] Albert M. Newman: *Enough for Everybody.*
[14] The Government Builds Homes. *Nation,* December 6, 1933.

Each house will stand on one-third of an acre of land, allowing plenty of room for home gardens, and will rent for around $20 a month. How long can the scarcity gentlemen in the building industry survive such competition?

Here is a $10,000 machine to stamp out a lighting fixture. Overhead costs on the machine continue day and night. This creates an imperative to use the machine at capacity throughout its life. "The wish of owners to keep the price high, or to stop operations because of a market glutted with high-priced goods, is controlled by the fact that it is cheaper to go on to enlarge the market by reducing prices than to stop, or slow down and keep prices high." [15] In brief, it is sometimes cheaper to go on manufacturing and to sell at a loss, than to close up shop and secure no revenue at all against continuing overhead. As the practice expands, it tends, according to Tugwell, to take the production program out of the hands of the absentee owners. Their wishes, and hopes of dividends, no longer prevail. The technical process prevails.

Monopolies and restrictions have been dramatically in evidence for half a century. Laws passed against them have been disregarded with the same easy conscience as the late prohibition amendment. Many honest citizens still insist that all our troubles arise from having left the benign principles of free competition. If, they assert, the free market had been a reality all these years, prices would have come down naturally with each advance in technology; the consumer would have got more for his money, and secured automatically all the benefits of an abundance

[15] R. G. Tugwell: *The Industrial Discipline.*

economy. It is an attractive picture, but overlooks several collateral effects, both of technology and of the capitalistic formula.

What would have happened to huge mass production investments if a chance invention had the right to scrap them over night—as the electric house furnace now threatens the oilburner investment? Do you really expect, gentlemen, the owners of these agglomerations of capital—so much greater than the tiny competitive shops which Adam Smith discussed—to obliterate themselves without a fight? Human nature does not work that way. Again, is there any reason to suppose that the profits of free competition, accruing to the fortunate, would not ultimately have swamped the capital goods sector in due time, and thus have brought the capitalistic formula into jeopardy just the same?

Of all impractical dreamers, those who would have us go back three or four generations to unadulterated competition are perhaps the most quixotic. To talk today of allowing the good old law of supply and demand to operate freely, is to talk of allowing the good old horse cars on Third Avenue to operate. Big business has ruined the one as electricity has ruined the other.

A last idea intrigues me. Certain large industrialists are hoping to escape from their dilemmas by virtue of President Roosevelt's recovery program, specifically the N.R.A. The various codes now provide in effect for an abatement of the anti-trust laws, and tend to promote price fixing. Here is a means, possibly a strictly legal means, to get clear away from the terrors of competition, make every major industry a monopoly, restrict production to profitable levels, eliminate the small fry, and allow distraught super-executives at last to play golf with some peace of mind. This picture has more to recommend it than the forlorn nostalgia of the free marketers. For one thing, it moves forward, not backward. . . . On to the legalized cartels and rationalization, with government sanction, but with private business still in the saddle.

But if we look carefully again at the formula of capitalism, we see that Mr. Swope [16] and his friends, while they might indeed put the idea into temporary operation, would find it exceedingly difficult to keep their saddles. In seeking to restrict production, they could only diminish the possibilities of expansion, shrink the capital goods sector, diminish total wages, salaries and purchasing power. The debt edifice would have to crash, carrying banks, insurance companies, untold vested interests down to ruin.

Only on one condition could the program be made to work: to wit, an industrial dictatorship which scuttled the constitution, outraged traditional capitalism, abrogated most debts, made itself responsible for an enormous army of unemployed; in short, became the government. One doubts if Mr. Swope has either the qualifications or the ambition for the rôle.

[16] Proposal of Gerard Swope, in the fall of 1933, on behalf of the United States Chamber of Commerce, to take over the National Recovery Administration.

CHAPTER XI

ESSAY ON PROPERTY

In feudal times, property was tangible: land, a house, a castle, gold, jewels, horses, tapestries, tools, slaves. If the accumulation was large, it was protected by armed retainers. The armed retainers were hearty eaters and so diminished the net value of the property. The insurance rate was high. When gunpowder and the printing press overthrew feudalism, the free market and capitalism—an infant capitalism to be sure—gradually substituted law for private retainers. The protection of property was socialized; one community police force replaced the liege lord's mercenaries. Thus protected, property became more fluid and vendible.

Early law regarded property as something with which a man "hath mixed his labor." Knut Hamsun's great novel, *The Growth of the Soil,* provides a perfect illustration. Isak arrives with an axe in the Norwegian wilderness. He clears ground, builds a hut, and plants a crop. Patiently, sturdily, year by year, he adds to his homestead. Ultimately he acquires a few clumsy farm machines, but never any inanimate energy, beyond firewood and kerosene. If ever property rightfully belonged to a human being, it was this farm. Every foot of soil, every stone, every beam, every pound of supply, was mixed with Isak's labor. Daniel Shelton of Stratford was spiritually close to the Norwegian pioneer. All the early settlers of America were his blood brothers.

Why is the western farmer the most belligerent of citizens today? Because depression is depriving him of property with which he has mixed his sweat and toil. "When a man is thrown off his farm," says A. A. Berle, Jr., "it is a fighting, tearing, weeping matter. All the human bonds are working overtime. . . . More than one mortgagee who has tried to foreclose on a farm in recent years has discovered that the transaction was not purely financial. But when a man loses his money in General Electric, although everybody is sorry for him, and the personal consequences may be disastrous, the human bonds do not work. . . ." [1]

As pioneering gives way to civilized communities, and specialization of labor grows, property ceases to be so much a tearing, weeping matter; the proportion of labor mixed with it declines. One's possessions are largely fabricated by others. Witness the book you are reading. It is *your* book, but many thousands of people have helped to produce it, as we saw in Chapter VIII. In so far as the property is personally used, however, the attachment remains close. One may not dynamite bridges for such property, like Iowa farmers, but one will fight for it, after his fashion.

Here on my little Connecticut farm, I note only the woodpile, some slight land improvements and a few built-in bookcases and benches, which are the result of my physical labor. Yet house, furnishings, orchard, garden and personal effects, are *mine*, in a

[1] *Scribner's Magazine,* June, 1933.

deep, emotional way. They become, with the years, a kind of *alter ego*. I would not sell them; their vendibility means little; but I would furiously resist being deprived of them.

Use property attaches to the individual, or to the family, in a cardinal, human way. To socialize such property is truly against human nature, as the Russians have been forced to learn. Collectivization among the peasants can go to certain psychological limits only. The old ironmaster, the early entrepreneur, retained something of this feeling. It was *his* shop, his little factory, his store. He often lived in it. He knew every corner of it. He was *responsible* for it. A broad definition of use property would be that for which one is actively responsible.

Socialists in spreading their propaganda have not always been careful to make the distinction between use property and the commercial property of absentee owners. Their enemies have been quick deliberately to confuse the two. "Ah!" they cry, "socialism means dividing up. Would you, my good Republican farmer, share your house, your pigs and poultry with wastrels from the city?" The good Republican farmer emphatically would not. When the opponent desires to be particularly nasty, he pushes the conception to the point of dividing up the ladies. Of course, no collective program—unless the program makers are quite mad—should lay a finger on use property; rather, it should seek to safeguard and extend it. Money, be it observed, is not use property. It has no use as such. Gold has use to goldsmiths, but little to ordinary citizens. Paper money makes an indifferent material with which to light fires. Stock certificates are very little better.

In cities some aspects of use property are declining. A hospital surgeon, for example, may use professional tools which do not belong to him. He may live with his family in an apartment which he rents furnished, be conveyed to his work in a public cab, perform operations wearing a white uniform which has the name of the hospital embroidered upon it, but which is owned and cared for by a service company. To a degree this depersonalization of property can be extended, but there must remain a minimum of strictly private possessions.

With the conception of use firmly in mind, it is easy to see how property came to be legally regarded as a "natural right." It was long, however, before one had the power to sell that right in all circumstances. Even in parts of Europe today, an heir cannot sell an entailed estate. The interest-bearing function of property was unknown. The notion that wealth must increase at any "ordinary" rate per year would have been regarded as necromancy 300 years ago. The increase of wealth was a purely fortuitous matter.

The chief financial agent in the spread of the free market was the contract. By this legal instrument, property could be transferred expeditiously and widely. Incidentally, it was assumed that the unit of money, which measured most contracts, would remain stable; otherwise long term contracts would have been too hazardous to undertake.

With the rise of technology and a maturer capitalism, property concepts began to grow beyond the simple natural right of use, and of contract for the delivery of tangible goods. Under the pressures of vendibility, the legal mind evolved a sublime property metaphysic, a veritable triumph of pure reason. Property rights were finally to be found in physically indivisible oil pools under the earth [2] and in air waves over the earth; in factories and railroads that owners had never seen—let alone mixed their labor with, or personally used; in the industrial output of generations yet unborn; in goodwill which represented nothing one could kick with his foot but only earning power in excess of average earning power; in the labor of street railroad mules which died fifty years before; in all manner of intangibles and grotesques. Furthermore, as Berle says: "It was never quite clear where the kind of property you could hit with a hammer ended, and the kind of property that you could see only with an imaginative vision began."

The law surrounding corporations has been particularly lush in providing new metaphysical and intangible concepts of property. For one thing, it removed personal responsibility. The stockholder (nominal owner) of a corporation was held not liable for its debts. This was an impressive step forward for vendibility. Good old Adam Smith regarded the joint stock company—as the corporation was first called—with precisely the same horror with which Mr. Hoover regards socialism. It was a hit below the belt of sturdy individualism; ownership without responsibility.

Today, corporations dominate American economic activity.

---

[2] At law, the owner of a piece of land 100 feet square above a petroleum deposit, has title to whatever oil lies thereunder as bounded by imaginary planes extending vertically downward from his land. Whether the section extends to a final point at the exact center of the earth has not, to my knowledge, been determined. Alas, a policeman cannot be sent down the pipe line to keep the oil in place.

TOTAL VOLUME OF EXPENDITURES [3]

	Corporate	Non-corporate
Agriculture	1%	99%
Professional work	20	80
Trade	39	61
Construction	55	45
Mining	64	36
Finance	79	21
Transportation	94	6
Manufacturing	95	5
All activity	60	40

Furthermore, in 1928, six percent of the corporations did 90 percent of all corporate business, and one-half of one percent of them collected 54 percent of all corporate profit.

The corporation was the legal mechanism which above all others furthered absentee ownership. (Absentee ownership of land, of course, was relatively ancient.) It came to provide the main reservoir for profitable investment. Most of the goods in the capital goods sector are owned *in absentia*. "Absentee ownership," says Veblen, "is the ownership of an industrially useful article by any person or persons who are not habitually employed in the industrial use of it." There are many one-man corporations where the owner of the stock runs the enterprise; but such corporations represent only a small fraction of American business.

Under absentee ownership, property, which takes the form of stocks, bonds, notes, mortgages, leaseholds, becomes extremely liquid, readily passing from hand to hand. As the only measure is money, it can be instantly converted into other forms of wealth. The stock market operator "owns" Steel in the morn-

[3] Robert R. Doane: *The Measurement of American Wealth.*

ing, and Coca Cola in the afternoon. Wealth is less and less in a form to be employed directly by the owner. Only through sale in the market can he obtain ultimate use—by exchanging his property for money with which to buy consumers' goods. Ownership is thus tied to the market, particularly the stock market, as never before. Doane says: "The development of the negotiable instrument with its element of high convertibility, permitting a daily flow of capital from one corporate security to another, has given to capital a sensitive volatileness far from any exact correlation as to its actual or original nature." Seventy-five per-cent of all profit-bearing wealth is of this character today. The total in 1929 was appraised—for the moment—at 238 billions of dollars. In the depression of 1893, only 20 percent of income-producing wealth was of this highly convertible and volatile nature. The cardinal importance of the stock market in modern capitalism is thus thrown into bold relief. It is a gambling joint, yes, but it is also the wheel on which the whole vendibility system now turns.

The owner of corporate property has a token—a bond or a share of stock.[4] The token acquires value primarily because of its liquidity. Property in a non-liquid form (the factory itself) is worth one price; in liquid form (securities covering the factory) another price—higher or lower as the case may be. "Tersely, the shareholder has a piece of paper with an open market value, and as holder of this paper may receive from time to time, at the pleasure of the management, periodic distribution. He is forced

---

[4] The professors in their textbooks make impressive distinction between bonds, preferred stocks, common stocks. Actually, as Berle and Means point out, the distinction becomes increasingly academic.

to measure his participation, not in assets, but in a market quotation; and this market quotation 'discounts' or appraises the expectation of distribution. This idea does not accord with the popular or the legal concept of a shareholder. Economically, however, it seems inescapable." [5]

You own a piano. You can play it or not as you please. You can keep anyone else from playing it. It is use property and the arrangement seems fair enough. You also own a factory employing 500 men. You can work it or not as you please, and keep anyone else from working it. Such is the law. The factory, unlike the piano, is not for your use and pleasure. You may know nothing about its technical operation. When you refuse to operate it, not only your income is cut off, but that of 500 others—who probably are more dependent on the factory income than are you. Or it may be the only factory in the country making a certain essential preparation for hospitals. When you shut it down, the hospital patients suffer. Perhaps, again, you own only 51 percent of the stock of the factory corporation. The other stockholders desire to keep the factory running, but you order it closed. You have that legal right. Absentee ownership is thus deeply involved with the public interest; factories are not pianos for owners to play upon.[6]

If you own a factory, not only may you legally keep others from using it, but also if it is held to be worth a million dollars at a given time, you have a theoretic right to the usufruct of a million to perpetuity. On this quaint conceit rests the whole theory of public utility

[5] Berle and Means: *The Modern Corporation and Private Property.*
[6] Following O. F. Boucke: *Laissez Faire and After.*

regulation, according to Donald Richberg.[7] Utilities are allowed six percent or eight percent on a "fair value." Yet there is no such thing as fair value in the capitalist system. "Physical properties have no intrinsic value. All material values are in the nature of illusions. The wealth of yesterday is gone tomorrow. A factory or a railroad that cost ten millions yesterday may hardly be worth the price of destruction today."

When prices were rising, from 1915 onward, the utility gentlemen, with their learned counsel and their agile accountants, were demonstrating beyond peradventure, indeed with tears in their eyes, that the fair value of their gas companies and street railroads meant the cost of reproduction today. As costs were now higher, value would be higher, and the permitted eight percent fatter. When prices fall—as in the depression—the utility experts leave "cost of reproduction," like rats a sinking ship, and swim stoutly back to a valuation based on "original cost." Pity the poor Interstate Commerce Commission. It spent fifteen years and millions of dollars trying to find the "fair value" of the railroads. Along came the falling prices of the depression and reduced the whole computation to waste paper. In the last analysis, the only value of a commercial property is its earning power, duly capitalized. It has no use value as such. It is just an orderly junk heap of cement, steel and lumber unless it is operating. It is junk to absentee owners unless it is operating at a profit. We remember Mr. Doane's calculation which showed 60 percent of all debt dependent entirely upon future income.

Industrial property, then, has got away from labor

[7] Economic Illusions Underlying Law. *University of Chicago Law Review,* May, 1933.

value, away from use value, away from all tangible foundation in many cases, to become a mathematical abstraction. The courts follow, panting, in the wake of corporation lawyers. A flow of dollar income to absentee owners is now about all that gives such property validity. A piano is a piano, but stocks and bonds are bundles of pious hopes. The hopes were realized, by and large, when expansion was holding the capitalist formula together.

Finance capital

We now approach the holy of holies—the operations of finance capital. All that has gone before in the way of property transvaluations is petty change. The absentee owner is very small fry compared with the magnificos of finance capital, where the principle of vendibility reaches its climax, and the concept of property is furthest removed from reality. Corporation lawyers performed the miracle, and they should have their due. In fact, they got it. Veblen in *The Theory of Business Enterprise* anticipated the story thirty years ago; Brandeis in *Other People's Money* carried it forward; Berle and Means superbly documented it from the available records; the Banking and Currency Committee of the United States Senate is now engaged in adding a rich deposit of case material hitherto unpublished.

The principle of finance capital is very simple. There is more money to be made in manipulating the securities which represent tangible property than in manipulating tangible property.

Commercial operations began in primitive times with simple barter, the exchange of goods for goods. Vendibility was hardly discernible. Then came the free market, the contract, absentee ownership, where goods were sold for money and vendibility grew strong. At last appeared finance capital to buy and sell *the presumptive evidence of future earning power.* Vendibility, like the curve of compound interest, soars out into the stratosphere, with Orion as its goal.

"The ultimate conditioning force in the conduct and aims of business," wrote Veblen, "is coming to be the prospective profit-yielding capacity of any given business move, rather than the aggregate holdings, or the recorded output of products." As the conditioning became more pronounced, the business man began to lose his fear of debt, and borrowed more freely. By borrowing he could turn his own capital more rapidly. If he was turning at ten percent and borrowed at five percent, he added five percent to his own capital gain. The banks were glad to issue new money on the prospect, and bank credit began to soar. The technique became very general—and contributed its bit to making bigger and better business cycles.

Above all it blurred the lines between the capital of the owner and the capital he borrowed. Capital began to mean the "capitalized putative earning-capacity expressed in terms of value, and comprised the use of all feasible credit extension." The value fluctuated from day to day, and bore only a remote relation to the underlying physical equipment. Goodwill now becomes the most important item—though it may not appear on the balance sheet at all. It always signifies some variety of monopolistic advantage; something which yields a rate of return over and above the normal, or freely competitive, rate. All enterprising new corporations begin immediately to collect goodwill— in patents, trade-marks, clientele, consolidations, tariffs, brands, advertising campaigns, what not. The word "halitosis" was worth millions in goodwill. "The substantial foundation of the industrial corporation is its immaterial assets," observes Veblen.

In the world of finance capital—which appeared with the turn of the century and reached its apogee in the United States in 1929—the manipulation of immaterial assets is all-important. "Commodities bought and sold on the goods market are the outcome of a process of production, and are useful for a material purpose; those bought and sold on the capital market are the outcome of a process of valuation and are useful for the purpose of pecuniary gain." The capital values which are the stock in trade of the process depend on the *tension of the market,* and on presumptive future earnings.

. . . "Gentlemen, with this merger consummated and destructive competition eliminated all down the line, the yield on Class B common cannot be less than $5 a share. Here are the figures, carefully prepared by Yessir, Yessir and Pleesir, Certified Public Accountants." The gentlemen glance at the figures and put in a long distance call to their brokers. . . .

Fluctuations in the capital market turn upon imagined future events.[8] The capital is subject to constant revaluation and reappraisal—as the ticker moves on the stock market. The distinguished financiers who

[8] The Senate Committee on Banking and Currency brings out a typical case. The International Projector Corporation carried a book value of $2,225,000. When taken over by the General Theatres Equipment Company (connected with the Chase National Bank), it was valued at $28,489,000, a mark up, made overnight, with no change in tangible assets, of more than $26,000,000, or 1000%. When asked the reason for this huge increase, Harley L. Clark, who had engineered it, said that it was "based on prospective earnings." (Reported in the New York *Times,* November 11, 1933.)

manipulate it are only rarely the owners of the property. They constitute what is known in Wall Street as the "control." The group in the United States consists of some 2,000 individuals all told. Of the 200 largest non-banking corporations in the country in 1930, Berle and Means find that real power, as distinguished from legal ownership, lodged as follows:

	Percent of companies
Controlled by management	44%
By legal device	21
By minority of stockholders	23
Total	88%
By owners (majority of stock, etc.)	11
In receivers' hands	1
Total	100%

Thus 88 percent of our greatest non-financial corporations are controlled by gentlemen other than their legal owners, through management agreements, voting trusts, non-par-value stock, minority blocs, and other devices of the legal faculty. Incidentally the 200 corporations account for one-half of all corporate wealth in the country, and showed combined assets of 81 billion dollars in 1930. In only 11 percent of cases did the owners have anything mandatory to say about "their" property. "Ownership of wealth without appreciable control, and control of wealth without appreciable ownership, appear to be the logical outcome of corporate development."

Not the owners, but the control knows whether a corporation is over or under-valued on the stock exchange; "the information of the outsiders does not coincide with the information of insiders." The insiders are privy to the appropriate time to sell short or to sell long. The properties which they manipulate are managed primarily with a view to profitable sale in the capital market, and not with a view to the future prosperity of the company. So there come to be *three* sets of interests involved:

1. The public at large, which is interested in a maximum of serviceability in terms of output.

2. The corporation and its legal owners, who are interested in long term stability and steady dividends.

3. The control, which is interested in maximum disruptions looking to a profitable sale, long or short, of the corporation's securities.

Finance capital thus bisects the heart of capitalism —a point the Marxists have never properly appreciated. The owner—popularly known as the investor— is exploited by the control only to a less degree than worker and consumer are exploited. In case after case cited by Berle and Means, the control achieves its end by deliberately wrecking the company. (If the stock stands at 100, and you have private knowledge that the corporation will presently be insolvent, you sell short at 100 and cover at 35. Boy!) "Profits at the expense of the corporation become practically clear gain to persons in control, and the interests of a profit-seeking control run directly counter to the interests of owners." Witness the wrecking of the Chicago and Alton Railroad, the Pere Marquette, the Rock Island, the New Haven, and the 'Frisco.' [9]

[9] The chief methods whereby the control can damage the company or the owners, or both, are these:
1. Forcing the company into receivership.
2. Shifting profits from parent to a subsidiary company, in which the control has a large personal interest.
3. Diverting profits from one class of stock to another in which the control has personal interest.

As the power of the control grows, the traditional defense of capitalism takes a strange twist. The historic argument has run that when each man pursues a maximum of private profit, the community is best served. There is something to be said for it when competition is freely operating. There is less to be said for it when 200 great corporations, dominated by scarcity concepts, monopolize the community's supply of food, shelter and clothing. Still, if dividends are to be regular, it is to the interest of the owners of these corporations to keep them operating. It may or may not be to the interest of the control to keep them operating. *Private profit for the group of 2,000 men who direct corporate property is frequently best served by wrecking the corporation, and is always best served by a maximum of disruption resulting in shifting valuations on the stock exchange.* It is not to be understood that the control is *always* ruthless in respect to the interests of stockholders and the public. Sometimes it is very polite; but when it is polite it is acting against its own best (profitable) interests.

The connection of these supermen with any individual enterprise is often transient. It can be terminated speedily and silently. At the same time we must remember that the owner can terminate *his* connection speedily on the stock exchange. The investor has no sentimental affection for his patent medicine plant or railroad, and we must beware of

4. Amending the corporate charter—a very important last resort of the control.

5. Inside information, enabling the control to buy low from present stockholders and sell high to future stockholders.

For a very fine full-length portrait of the whole process, see *The Investor Pays,* by Max Lowenthal.

becoming too sentimental concerning his plight. It is a metaphysical game all around; a far, far cry away from the realities of use property.

Finance capital first appeared in railroad securities, and spread rapidly to industrials, utilities, and even to merchandising corporations like chain stores. Through the New Era, mergers and investment trusts claimed the imperial attention. Up to the collapse of the formula of capitalism in 1929, it would be unjust to call the controlling gentlemen speculators. They had a sure thing. Here we find the reason for the unparalleled size of American fortunes. A mere trading in tangible property could never have produced them—only trading in the moonbeams of presumptive future earning power. "Nothing so effective for the accumulation of private wealth is known to the history of human culture."

Our success story has apparently led us away from the main thread of the analysis—the effects of technology and the machine process. It is there, luminous beneath the shuffling papers of high finance. Advancing technology and its threat to scarcity prices, produced monopoly, as we noted in the last chapter. Owners under modern conditions of large scale industry cannot manage their property. The web of specialization has been spun too fine to permit it. To the ten million stockholders, more or less, in this country, their property means chiefly a right to a conventional dividend—and a proxy which they forget to mail.[10] A proxy, furthermore, is not a means whereby an owner controls his property, but a means whereby

[10] 18,000,000 stockholders, including duplications, according to Berle and Means.

control is taken out of his hands. Owners normally know nothing about operating management. They are dispersed and unorganized. There is no human bond between them and their vast, impersonal holdings. Use property they can understand and fight for; the new conceptions of property are too much for them altogether.

In brief, the exercise of free contract, natural rights, traditional usages in respect to property, is incompatible with a high energy civilization. Business discretion must come to settle in other hands than those of the legal owners; hands, alas, even more irresponsible. The investor becomes a pensioner to finance capital. The general body of business men, dealing in goods, is similarly disfranchised. As for the public at large, it is simply raw material for the sublime process. No serviceability is to be detected anywhere in the picture.

The owners are at the mercy of the control. But both are at the mercy of the formula of capitalism. And the formula is at the mercy of the technical arts, as we have seen in Chapter IX. If, for one reason or another, the flow of free income dries up, and the calculations of putative future earning capacity have no reasonable expectations behind them, what becomes of the modern concept of property? Let us see.

Goodwill, as the most ephemeral element on the balance sheet, vanishes first, depriving the control of its chief asset. The promulgation of mergers, the profitable pyramiding of securities through investment trusts, come to an abrupt halt. The distinguished gentlemen are driven to the dreary and uncertain business of organizing pools on a declining stock market. Their great days are over. Some go to Greece, some go to rejoin their Heavenly Father, some go to jail—and some sit tight, waiting for the formula to revive, while manipulating the aforesaid pools.

As for the physical properties themselves—the steel mills, the great machine shops, the railroad lines— they become, *with any permanent collapse in the formula,* valueless to their owners. One cannot camp out in them; one cannot consume a tithe of the output. Under a vendibility system, they have value as a source of money income, but not otherwise. If there is no income, then owners have no further use for them. These great plants with their trained labor and their operating technicians are left, in the end, homeless; swinging in an industrial vacuum. Even if the workers and engineers should seize them, they too would be helpless without a market. The product is too specialized to be consumable by the operating staff, save to a very small degree. Tires might be consumed by tire makers, but hardly tappet valves by valve makers.

No such impasse has come as I write, but it must come unless the formula of capitalism be revived. Corporations cannot go on paying interest charges and dividends out of surplus indefinitely. Already dividends have been cut to a third of the 1929 disbursement.[11] Use property is as important as ever, indeed more important. *Rentiers* with no *rentes* are retreat-

---

[11]Dividends to individuals, reported by Doane:

1920	$3.274 billions
1925	3.848
1928	4.905
1929	5.439
1930	3.100
1931	2.872
1932	1.830

ing to little houses in the country, preparing to dig in for the worst. The root cellar and the garden patch look better to them than a safe deposit box full of mortgages. Vendible property is no longer vendible, over great areas.

The Economy of Abundance promises presently to socialize the bulk of commercial and industrial property. If the owners have no use for it, the community has. Without its regular operation, the community must starve and freeze. It is part of the web of specialization. The corporate owners have never been responsible for either its debts or its regular operation; finance capital even less so. The community will have to become officially responsible if the community is to survive, and I doubt if either workers or technicians will demur. Perhaps even the Supreme Court will not demur. I quote from Vol. 169, page 393 of its records:

> It is a settled principle, growing out of the nature of well-ordered civil society, that every holder of property, however absolute may be his title, holds it under the implied liability that its use may be so regulated that it shall not be injurious to the equal enjoyment of others having an equal right to the enjoyment of their property, nor injurious to the rights of the community.

In the Economy of Scarcity, a responsible owner of tangible property was protected by the law. Must it follow that an irresponsible owner of more or less intangible property, who has surrendered the control of his wealth to expert manipulators, must also be protected to the full? This is the weak link in the corporate structure. Deny the protection to "owners;" deny the right of the "control" to make personal profits by depth-bombing the company—and the whole mechanism must fall automatically into the hands of the community.[12] It has nowhere else to fall.

Finally, it is highly improbable that the technical operation of the physical properties could be managed worse by agents of the community, than by the agents of finance capital. Indeed, it is difficult to conceive of a method more sinister from the standpoint of efficiency than that of managing industrial property with a view single to a profitable turnover of imagined future earnings on the stock market.

[12] The law, as a matter of fact, has not yet caught up to the operations of the "control" gentlemen. They are, according to Berle and Means, in effect outlaws. For all their financial strength, their legal status is exceedingly weak. Nor is their financial status what it was in 1929.

CHAPTER XII

PLANT PLUS

EXCESS capacity in the industrial and agricultural plant is the plain result of technological advance. It seriously jeopardizes, as we have seen, the revival of the capitalistic formula; diminishing as it must the field for profitable investment in the capital goods sector. Why put one's money into woolen factories, for instance, when capacity is thrice normal demand? Again, excess capacity has been a major agent in undermining the property values of absentee owners. Their property becomes too productive in terms of market demand, prices fall, dividends are passed, and the plant turns into a white elephant, costly and useless to its owners. The effect on the "control" is equally distressing. It prevents these gentlemen from calculating those bright visions of future earning power which are at the heart of their trading in intangibles. Overcapacity regards the capitalization of goodwill with a broad, ironic smile.

Like technological unemployment, to which it is akin, excess capacity is a reasonably new phrase, and as in the case of all new things, has been discounted by students of a conservative turn of mind. No one in his senses denies the fact that American plants as a whole do not operate at capacity. The points are made, however, (1) that capacity is a loose term; (2) that many plants are rickety and obsolete and should be scrapped anyway; (3) that human need is far in excess of capacity and so it is ridiculous to talk of the plant's being overbuilt; and finally, (4) that it is a question whether or not plants should be run at capacity; our manufacturing forefathers observed no such standards. With these observations delivered, the student turns back to his charts of competitive prices covering the panic of '73.

The first objection has considerable merit. Excess capacity is difficult to define quantitatively. Only in the power age has it come to have exact meaning. When one of Mr. Polakov's continuous process, electrically controlled mechanisms starts on a productive schedule, the gauges are set to turn out, for example, 10,000 units an hour, neither more nor less. This is the number for which the mechanism is designed; it cannot be speeded up or slowed down without damage.

For older machine age plants, capacity is a matter of shrewd estimate. Most managers with whom I have discussed the question do not hesitate to make that estimate. Whether the plant is to run on single shift, double shift, or twenty-four hour operation, is of course very important. Some processes, like steel making, demand the latter. In brick manufacturing the size of the kilns determines capacity, even though the brick molding machines themselves are capable of a greater output. Most machine age factories have one or more bottle necks of this character.

A frequent method of estimating capacity is the total output on an eight-hour day basis for 300 days in the year, less an allowance for shutdowns due to necessary repairs. Such a method is inapplicable, however, to highly seasonal production, like the canning of fruits and vegetables. For a few weeks such plants may work double shift, only to remain idle for the rest of the year. Excess capacity here should be measured against the canning season only. It should be remembered that many operations which are now highly seasonal—like garment making—technically do not need to be seasonal.

Let us examine a typical report on excess capacity. "It is generally agreed," says the National Cottonseed Products Association, "that the daily average crushing capacity of one press is fifteen tons. There are 2,731 presses or their equivalent in the ten principal cotton producing states.[1] These presses, operating 300 days a year, could crush 12,289,500 tons, which means an equivalent production of about thirty-five million bales of cotton. The three-year annual average crush—1927 to 1929—was only 4,700,253 tons, according to the Bureau of the Census. It is obvious, therefore, that the mills in these states are equipped with sufficient press capacity, on the basis of each press handling fifteen tons daily, to crush the average available crop in 115 days, or 38 percent of 300 days." There are thus almost three times as many presses as are needed on a balanced load basis for three prosperous years averaged. Cotton is a seasonal crop, of course, but cottonseed can be stored, and does not demand immediate crushing.

Whatever the difficulties of appraisal, a working ratio between capacity and actual output can be arrived at in most cases, even as the Cottonseed Association arrived at it. This is all that is required to establish the general fact of excess capacity. Ask any operating manager if, over a reasonable period of

[1] *Facts about a Great Southern Industry.* Pamphlet published May, 1931.

time, he is selling all the goods he can make. In most cases he will tell you, bitterly, that he is not, and that he was not before 1930.

The second objection of the sceptical student is naïve. Granted that many plants are obsolete, if they continue to operate, they constitute an item in the nation's capacity. Granted that from the efficiency point of view, they should be scrapped, what is to be done with the workers who are discharged, and the small investors who lose their investment? "Savings invested in industry," says G. D. H. Cole, "can only realize their purpose if consumers' demand expands fast enough to absorb the goods which the new and old factories together are able to produce." [2] Scrapping old plants may delight engineers, but there is no delight in it for the workers and investors therein, or the mortgage holders thereof.

The third objection, that human needs are in excess of capacity, is but one more example of the confusion between serviceability and vendibility. Of course needs are in excess of or equal to the capacity of most industries. (Though not of all. In some cases, such as filling stations and radio plants, capacity is beyond any conceivable domestic need.) The fact is irrelevant when vendibility is dominant. Excess capacity, under capitalism, is always registered *when the plant can produce more than it can sell during a substantial period of normal business activity*.

The fourth and last objection is a throwback to the days of scarcity. Our ancestors did not worry about the capacity of their fulling mills and blacksmith shops because they were operated by hand labor and were not loaded down with overhead expense. If

---

[2] *A Guide through World Chaos.*

business was slack, the helpers could go back to the farm for a while; the shop was not seriously affected. Plants today are capitalized on the expected low costs of capacity performance. Excess capacity means excessive overhead costs, and an excessively burdensome debt. There is no parallel whatever between conditions in a blacksmith's shop and in the United States Steel Corporation.

The only attempt I know of to appraise the extent of excess capacity in the American plant as a whole, including agriculture as well as industry, is that of Robert R. Doane, covering 1929, a year of abnormally high business activity.[3] The appraisal runs in pounds, as follows:

Total capacity [4]	5,000 billion pounds
Total production	3,800 " "
Total consumption	3,000 " "

Agriculture weighs heavily to reduce this estimate; for the agricultural "plant" does not show capacity greatly in excess of actual production. Crops can readily be stepped up several times by fertilizers, irrigation, tractors; but we do not call unplowed, arable acres "farm excess capacity." Even with this allowance, Mr. Doane shows capacity in 1929 as 32 percent in excess of production, and 67 percent in excess of consumption. Consumption signifies roughly what was sold. The difference between consumption and production shows "overproduction," or material presumably stored to keep prices at reasonable levels. Warehouses bulged with cotton, wheat, corn, steel products, textiles, what not; awaiting more favorable prices. The prices never came.

[3] *New Outlook,* October, 1933.
[4] On a one-shift basis for most lines.

Mr. Doane notes that the poundage actually saved in 1929 was no less than 27 percent of all consumption —about twice the ratio of money savings to national income in that year. The shadow of coming depression is conspicuous in these two ratios. Goods were piling up beyond all possibility of profitable absorption.

Excess capacity, for both industry and agriculture, on the basis of Mr. Doane's estimate, was 67 percent for the year 1929. The market furnished purchasing power to carry off only 60 percent of the total the plant could produce. If he had used a two- or three-shift basis, excess capacity would have been far greater.

The American Engineering Council reports as follows:

> This last boom was the first major one in which industry as a whole did not receive orders in excess of its capacity. Deliveries were not greatly delayed at the peak. It was a "buyer's market." For the first time, there was ample equipment and labor with which to meet the extreme demands of unrestrained business enthusiasm.

The plant represents capital goods. Bassett Jones in *Debt and Production* has been at some pains to chart the growth curves of both consumers' and capital goods in the United States for many years back. He finds that the plant is growing as the square of the time faster than consumers' goods.[5] At these rates, by 1950 each citizen would consume only 1.2 times as much as he did in 1900, while the plant would absorb 5.3 times as much. Increasingly the plant has been eating its own output (consuming bricks, steel, energy, lumber, cement), leaving the con-

[5] Assuming that the indices of physical production heretofore furnished, on the highest authority, are valid. In his *Horses and Apples* Mr. Jones questions their validity.

sumer a steadily decreasing share in total physical production. This is obviously a kind of economic pernicious anemia. Furthermore, it coincides with the formula of capitalism as set forth in Chapter IX. Pressure for profitable investment, combined with limited purchasing power, has pushed the capital goods sector beyond all possibility of profitable use.

"In a rough sense," says Robert Lynd, "plant expansion follows consumer demand; actually, however, guided by guess and plans for capturing the volume market, expansion tends to leap ahead of actual demand; and it outlasts demand. Once built, on the basis of whatever expectations, expanded plant facilities increase overhead and become compelling stimuli to sales pressure on the consumer." [6]

Car lots of iceberg lettuce rose from 2,078 in 1917 to 46,401 in 1928—at which point market garden facilities were far in excess of demand. At which point the lettuce producers raised $250,000 for an advertising campaign. The secretary of the producers' association launched the campaign with these significant words: "Naturally, increasing the consumption of iceberg lettuce is an imperative matter in order to keep ahead of ever-increasing production. Inasmuch as there is no way to curb production, consumption must be increased." . . . Good. The consumer must buy more iceberg lettuce—or hats, or radios or mouthwash. But the consumer has only so much purchasing power, fished painfully out of the capitalistic formula. Captivated by rosy portraits of bathing beauties munching lettuce, he buys more lettuce and, let us say, fewer umbrellas. This throws it squarely up to the umbrella producers and calls for another $250,000 to be handed

[6] *Recent Social Trends.*

over to the advertising agencies, and bathing beauties now parading under cerise umbrellas. So whirls the merry-go-round.

"The success of certain selling appeals has led to great over-optimism in industry," says R. G. Tugwell.[7] "The expanding income of Americans involves a flow into an ever more varied set of goods. But each industry seems to assume an almost unlimited market for its own kind; and commitments of capital—plant, machinery, materials—are made optimistically by each out of its surplus. The result is over-expansion. When the facilities are not used, their expense goes on and is added to the price of goods, and thus makes marketing progressively more difficult." In an upswing, too many producers think of the same thing at the same time.

William Wren Hay, writing in the *Annalist,* presents two admirable case studies, covering radios and rolled strip steel. Let us briefly follow his analysis.[8]

Radios

The all-electric plug-in radio set was marketed on a large scale in 1928 under the stimulus of the presidential campaign, which was the first great political struggle to go "on the air." Capital investment poured headlong into the industry. Some of the pioneers made very large profits, which they promptly reinvested to increase capacity. At the same time, the cost of production was drastically lowered by the technical improvements of one concern, and a complete console set brought within reach of a great many more buyers. *In eighteen months, capacity was increased three-fold,* bringing the total up to fifteen million sets

[7] *The Industrial Discipline.*
[8] July 28, 1933.

by the end of 1929. All that consumers took off the market in that year was four million sets. "A great deal of the capital which had been pumped into this industry never earned any return, and the rest of it, because of excessive competition, was soon limited to such a low rate of return, that when the large market dried up with the depression, all the surviving capital was doomed to be idle and unproductive."

In 1931 I wandered through the deserted aisles of one of those great radio establishments. The technical equipment was superb, but no energy flowed into it; the machines were cold and dead. Radio, we remember, was a magnet for the fluid funds of absentee owners in the New Era, and one of the prize footballs for the operations of high finance.

Strip steel

The growth of the motor car industry brought a large demand for strip steel. Steel of this variety had been made by a few "merchant" mills in a pedestrian way, with steady prices and adequate earnings. As demand grew, the research scientists went to work. In 1928 they produced a continuous rolling process, with electric drives and automatic controls. Costs of production promptly fell 20 percent. Mills with older machinery were forced to install the new process. Presently capacity was far ahead of demand, and "the market price of hot-rolled strip continued to decline under the pressure. Unquestionably the drop in the cost of production of hot-rolled steel strip, in 1928, stimulated a much larger use of this class of steel because it was relatively cheaper than the older shapes. It is equally irrefutable that the enlarged demand brought forth a much larger supply which has since operated to force the market price still lower. As soon as demand fell off, in 1930, many of the economies which it was thought would be gained by the newer production units, were absorbed by fixed charges which made it more advantageous for them to run at a loss than to shut down." In 1929, capacity stood at 3.6 millions of gross tons; production at 2.5 millions. In 1932 production had fallen to 1.2 million tons, while capacity presumably is unchanged.

I say presumably. For the steel industry as a whole, the *Iron Age* reported in 1931 an increase in capacity of 4,075,000 tons *during the depression*. Yet for a time in 1933 production was down to 12 percent of capacity.

Filling stations and films

Glen B. Winship, after an exhaustive survey, finds 156,671 filling stations in the country, while consumers would be adequately served by about 45,000. The superfluous investment he calculates at $1,000,000,000. Filling stations, so gaily run up on each of the four corners of busy intersecting streets, illustrate both an ancient and a comparatively new form of excess capacity. The old form is the plethora of retail stores. The consumer would be better served with a quarter the number. They represent not so much a business phenomenon, however, as a psychological one. Their proprietors—nine out of ten of whom are doomed before they receive their first credit from a wholesaler—set up shop to escape the factory timeclock.

The new form represented by the filling station is excess capacity resulting from chain distribution methods. Rival chain store corporations battle for locations on Main street, hoisting real estate values for

choice positions to fantastic heights. Rival movie
theatre chains do likewise and thus pile the costs of
out-palacing their rivals on top of heavy real estate
costs. They are built "not for the entertainment of
their audiences, but the embarrassment of one another." [9] Meanwhile to shift the industry from silence
to sound cost the movies $500,000,000—$25,000 per
sound-equipped theatre. When the installation was
accomplished, their customers had, of course, no more
money to spend than before.

Sir Frederick Soddy draws a physical analogy.[10]
Here is an empty reservoir. To fill it, water must
flow in faster than it flows out. Ultimately a head of
water accumulates which drives the water out as fast
as it flows in, at which point the level remains constant.
"So with each increase in the flow of wealth by scientific discovery. At first, part of the wealth accumulates
as new capital, but the only possible permanent condition is where the rate of inflow equals that of out-
flow, or the rate of consumption equals that of
production." Mr. Doane's figures show production
27 percent ahead of consumption in 1929. This reservoir, one would have said, was going to burst. It did.

Granting, as one must, the existence of excess
capacity, and consequent loss to property owners, it
may be objected that the condition has always obtained
under capitalism. New inventions, shifting markets,
have been wiping out investors for decades; yet net
progress has been registered. True. The answer to
the objection is that the *rate* of technological change
is now so great, and the *size* of investment in many

undertakings so large, that the weeding-out process, which was tolerable in a condition of small businesses with a relatively light obsolescence rate, is intolerable in the power age. It all comes back to the point at which a given curve of development, expanding at a geometric rate, leaves the plane of reality and zooms off into the ether.

Excess plant capacity is overproduction in capital goods, just as huge wheat and butter carry-overs are overproduction in consumers' goods. It does not become advocates of vendibility to weep for these surpluses. The first held the capitalistic formula together throughout the New Era. By releasing wages and salaries to the men who built the movie theatres, the skyscrapers, the filling stations, the hot rolled steel mills, the radio factories—it provided purchasing power to keep the flywheel turning over. Surplus food stocks were the result of an effort to maintain artificial scarcity in consumers' goods. Both phenomena were inevitable in a system based on vendibility.

Shifting the point of view back to serviceability, both are obviously unmitigated evils. The plant surplus should be used, and the food surplus eaten. Mr. Justice Brandeis, in the case of the New State Ice Company, has supported the serviceability philosophy in an opinion which has become famous. If indeed the community is to fall heir to properties which owners can no longer either manage or derive income from, the law must adjust itself to the economic facts. Justice Brandeis held:

Increasingly doubt is expressed whether it is economically wise, or morally right, that men should be permitted to add to the producing facilities of an industry which is already suffering from over-capacity. . . . Many insist there must be some form of economic control. And some thoughtful men of wide business experience insist that all projects for stabilization and proration must prove futile unless, in some way, the equivalent of the certificate of public convenience and necessity is made a prerequisite to embarking new capital in an industry in which the capacity already exceeds the production schedules.

A working formula to this end has been proposed by David C. Coyle, a distinguished engineer: [11]

(1) If no new machinery were permitted, but only replacement of old machines, obsolescence would be at a minimum, but progress would be slow, and overall efficiency low.

(2) On the other hand, if continuous scrapping and modernizing were permitted, excess capacity would be prevented, but "most of the energies of the people would be devoted to setting up and taking down equipment." Progress would be rapid, with obsolescence at a maximum, and overall efficiency again low.

(3) Somewhere between these extremes lies the maximum overall efficiency. "It will be most nearly approached if the machinery of production is kept so scanty that it will work the maximum number of shifts and wear out as fast as possible before some new invention renders it obsolete. The optimum rate of progress will be where the costs of production, including not only new capital costs but costs of eliminating old plant and finding work for displaced men, add up to a minimum."

Mr. Coyle is careful not to overlook the question of technological unemployment. To its consideration, in some detail, we will now turn. Excess capacity—too many plants—embarrasses property owners. Technological unemployment—too many men—devastates flesh and blood.

[11] *The Irrepressible Conflict: Business vs. Finance.*

CHAPTER XIII

MANPOWER PLUS

I

"CIVILIZATION," says Sir Frederick Soddy, "is pursuing two precisely opposite goals at one and the same time. On Mondays, Wednesdays and Fridays, it invents new methods of abolishing labor, and on Tuesdays, Thursdays and Saturdays, new labors to relieve the consequent unemployment."

Broadly speaking, the Tuesday shift kept up with the Monday shift, from the first steam engine to the laying of the corner stone of the Empire State Building. Nothing less than heroic, however, were its efforts from the World War on. In 1928 and 1929, unemployment began to grow despite prevailing prosperity. Even if the depression had not come, there is reason to believe that the Monday shift would presently have prevailed.

Sir Frederick speaks with a certain poetic license. The technical arts were unquestionably inventing new methods of abolishing labor, but the invention of new methods to absorb the labor displaced was a purely fortuitous matter. Nobody planned anything; the question was ignored. It was assumed that a worthy and diligent citizen could always find a job. Worthy and diligent men without number, throughout the whole course of the industrial revolution, have searched for months, sometimes for years, and found no jobs.

Whereupon they killed themselves, or climbed numbly down a psychological ladder into the ranks of the unemployable. Statistically the new job was there— perhaps a thousand miles away, perhaps at an untried vocation. Cold statistics helped Thomas Tryhard, for example, a Rhode Island mill hand whose factory had moved to North Carolina, not at all.

In 1920, in the United States, employment reached its peak in all the great productive industries—in manufacturing, mining, agriculture, transportation— and thereafter, despite an increase in physical production, began steadily to decline. No more men were wanted in these industries, and if the curves of invention and population follow their indicated course, no more will ever be wanted. The millions displaced drifted into garages, hot dog stands, filling stations, public service, house-to-house canvassing, insurance, taxi driving, bond selling, Wall Street running, marketing Florida swamps by the front foot—a hundred curious and insecure occupations. Presently the operating economies of an advancing power age were to rend this flimsy statistical veil.

It has been customary to make a nice distinction between various kinds of unemployment: to ascribe it to *seasonal* causes—as in the canning of vegetables; to *cyclical* causes—in major and minor depressions; to *technological* causes—as when the dial telephone displaces manual operators; to *financial* causes—as when a corporate merger dispenses with superfluous clerks and executives; to *industrial shifts*—as when much of the Massachusetts shoe industry moves to St. Louis; to *obsolescence*—as when carriage makers disperse before the motor car; to *managerial* causes—as when time study methods double the output per man hour of workers assembling carburetors. These distinctions have their uses, but in the last analysis each comes back to the scientific method; in a broad sense all unemployment today is technological. Mergers are the result of the drive for monopoly to hold prices threatened by lower costs of production; geographical shifts have technical reasons, such as the desire to be nearer sources of raw materials; business cycles are linked with excess capacity, and so on.

Strangely enough, women were among the earliest victims of technological unemployment. Middle class housewives lost their jobs by the million to labor saving devices in the home. Mary Shelton spinning with both hands, a baby on her lap, knew nothing of electric light, central heating, washing machines, tin cans, fireless cookers or gas stoves. I should find myself in an uncomfortable amount of hot water, if I charged that the good suburban mother—well, pretty good—was left with empty hands by these inventions. She went, let us say, on part time. Her hands were freed at least sufficiently to deal a round or two of contract bridge.

Somewhat later, other friends of man began to suffer. In the last fourteen years, according to *Recent Social Trends*, farm machinery, especially the tractor, has condemned ten million horses and mules to technological unemployment. Presumably the farmer, on bringing home the new tractor, turned the faithful animal loose with the admonition that "any worthy mule who really wants a job can find one."

Expansion of markets, of population, of new industries, has concealed the displacement of workers by labor saving devices. To produce the simple requirements of the Shelton family in 1760 for every one in the country today, would not take, I suspect, ten percent of our available manpower—leaving 90 percent unemployed. The modern family, however, has mired itself in very wasteful urban centers, and demands all manner of goods and services which would have seemed wanton luxuries to the Sheltons. So the 90 percent has—until recently—found jobs in servicing waste and providing for wants and luxuries unknown in 1760. To be specific, jobs have been created for:

1. Making new and useful commodities—bathtubs, tractors.

2. Making new and silly commodities—Tom Thumb golf courses.

3. Making quick replacement commodities—razor blades.

4. Ballyhooing commodities—new and old.

5. Constructing new and essential capital goods—factories, power houses.

6. Constructing excess plant capacity.

7. Padding distribution outlays.

8. Servicing Megalopolis.

9. Providing some excellent new services—in research, education, medicine, recreation.

So partly by waste, partly by genuinely increasing living standards (we noted in Chapter I that standards had probably doubled over the scarcity base), partly by covering great geographic distances through specialization, the job market was kept at par. It makes no difference in a vendibility system how wasteful or disagreeable or even vicious the job may be. If it carries a payroll envelope, it is a job, and he who claims the envelope is not unemployed economically, however much he may be spiritually. Should we have survived the depression at all without the purchasing power released by a million bootleggers? Without this vendible traffic, bootleggers would have been unemployed, and much of the money spent for their merchandise hoarded and frozen. They kept the pecuniary ball rolling—which is all that vendibility demands.

So long as expansion is brisk, technological unemployment remains within bounds. Let market expansion slacken, however, and unemployment will come out from behind its draperies, naked for all to see. Its progress then becomes the inverse of the expansion curve, climbing as the latter falls. When expansion halts, furthermore, there is no halt in labor saving devices. Business men seek every possible way to cut costs.

When Howard Scott tells us that there is a rayon factory being constructed in New Jersey to operate without a man on the floor, the news is of scientific interest, but means little as to unemployment as a whole. Perhaps at the same moment there is a brisk demand for Wall Street messengers, or for highway workers, which more than compensates for dismissed rayon employees. When he tells us that scores of factories, in various industries, are introducing continuous process, electrically controlled production, the observation becomes more impressive, but still inconclusive as to total unemployment. He may prove to our complete satisfaction—and I think he and his group have done so—that the Monday shift is making remarkable progress. We remain unconvinced of a *net increase* in unemployment, until the reports from the Tuesday shift are in: How many new jobs elsewhere are being created?

Scott was dreadfully manhandled by the business economists because he concentrated on one side of the equation, apparently disregarding bootleggers, bus boys, billboard pasters, and young gentlemen of forty working their way through college by selling subscriptions to *Good Housekeeping* from door to door. The "service" trades were expanding as fast as productive jobs declined, said the business economists. (They waived the depression, of course, as an abnormality which would soon be over, allowing the service trades to expand as heretofore.)

Perhaps no economic dispute has been productive of more figures, pro and con. Newspapers and magazines bristled with them in the early months of 1933; there was hardly a citizen who did not produce a case: "I remember when they put that new stamping machine into number two shop, there were three men. . . ." The unfortunate part of it is that there are no accurate figures to prove or disprove the net effect. The United States, to its shame, has never maintained a regular census of unemployment which permitted comparisons between different periods to show the trend.

"It is true," says George Soule, "that while industrial productivity has been increasing in the past, a larger and larger proportion of the population has found industrial employment. . . . But it has been a period of change from handicrafts to machinery, from small-scale to large-scale enterprise. People who used to be independent workers have become employed by others—that is the real meaning of the figures showing the growth of employment." [1] This is an important point. When Carolina hill-billies come down into

[1] *New Republic*, December 28, 1932.

new cotton mills, employment figures swell; but what really has happened is an exchange of jobs—from hoeing a corn patch to mending broken threads on a factory loom.

The figures of the technocrats were invulnerable from one point of view. Whatever was happening to net unemployment, the fact of a change in the rate of displacement, due to power age methods, was indisputable. This operated to throw more and more workers into temporary unemployment. "Aside from the possibility that the pace of mechanization may make the permanent displacement of labor a serious problem not encountered in this form in the past, temporary displacement, involving both unemployment and absorption into new industries, is already a problem of increasing gravity." [2]

Here is a group of workers displaced in various industries in the closing years of the New Era. Isadore Lubin, notebook in hand, follows them one by one.[3] Less than one-third found new jobs in the industry to which they were trained; two-thirds had to find places in alien industries. The journey from the old job to the new took a long time for most of them; many men were out of work for more than a year. Unemployment and insecurity may be, from the human point of view, almost as severe in a period of increasing technological change, as in a period of increasing net unemployment. The effect on the worker is disastrous in both cases.

It is easy to prove that employment in the great productive sectors is declining. Here, for instance, are figures from *Recent Social Trends:*

[2] Wolman and Peck in *Recent Social Trends.*
[3] The Brookings Institution Pamphlet Series, Vol. I, No. 3.

UNITED STATES MANUFACTURES

Index numbers

Year	Persons engaged	Volume of production	Output per person
1919	100	100	100
1923	96	122	127
1924	89	114	128
1925	92	128	138
1926	94	131	140
1927	92	129	139
1928	91	136	149
1929	94	145	153

Employment never reaches the 1919 level again, even in such a year of great activity as 1929. Yet production is steadily rising, while output per worker gains 53 percent in ten years. Here are more figures from the same source:

EMPLOYMENT ON STEAM RAILROADS

Year	Number of men	Index
1920	2,013,000	100
1923	1,880,000	93
1925	1,769,000	88
1927	1,761,000	87
1928	1,680,000	83
1929	1,686,000	84
1930	1,511,000	75

Thus in a decade the railroads lose a quarter of all their manpower, but steadily move more traffic.

The number of farmers drops from 6,387,000 in 1920 to 6,012,000 in 1930; coal miners from 759,000 to 646,000; all miners from 1,083,000 to 983,000; lumbermen from 195,000 to 159,000. The 1930 Census of Occupations, from which these figures are taken, did not take unemployment into consideration. The occupations are listed in the Census whether the individual was working at the time or not.

Going as far back as 1910, C. S. Slocombe, of the

Personnel Research Federation, presents some significant findings. Analyzing the Census returns, he calculates that in the twenty years to 1930, employment in the basic industries increased only six percent, population increased 35 percent, and physical production 86 percent. We must remember that a smaller gain in employment than in population means unemployment. What are the boys and girls leaving school and college going to do? The business economists have a habit of forgetting the population factor when they deny an increase in net unemployment.

It is also possible to prove, again from *Recent Social Trends*, that the service trades are *adding* to their numbers:

Number employed (in thousands)	1910	1920	1930
Total wholesale and retail trade	3,447	4,215	6,094
Road transportation	822	955	1,386
Total clerical	777	1,540	2,102
Domestic and personal service	3,805	3,605	5,448
Professions	1,727	2,203	3,110

The trades whose upward curves are marked include:

Teachers
Engineers
Nurses
Draftsmen
Librarians
Authors
Taxi and truck drivers
Elevator men
Janitors
Hairdressers

Restaurant employees
Highway maintenance workers
Policemen
Firemen
Store clerks and retailers
Insurance agents
Realtors
Commercial travellers
Bankers and brokers

Home + grounds architects

It is impossible to determine accurately the net balance between the decline of employment in basic industries and gains in the service trades, up to the year 1929. We must approach the problem from another angle.

Mathematical pincers

Bassett Jones, with a precision almost diabolical, has charted the course of employment as he has charted the course of physical production and capital claims.[4] "We are not interested," he says, "in whether human beings are satisfied or not with the performance of the productive plant, but only as to how it works, and has worked. We want to know the measurable relation between output and the number of workers. . . . Only when we know this can we decide what changes are required, if any, to relate properly the number of workers demanded to operate the plant at any time, and the needs and satisfactions of the workers as human beings." To determine how the plant works, Mr. Jones tabulates and calculates six series of data, drawn from the best available sources:

1. Total number of workers
2. Total physical production
3. Output per worker
4. Hours per worker
5. Total man-hours
6. Man-hours per unit of total production.

Based on a 1900 to 1929 moving mean, the number of workers, the output per worker and total production showed curves which all tended toward maxima to be reached at, or earlier than, 1950. But, in 1921, output per worker suddenly jumped and began to increase at nearly the same rate that production was increasing. This indicated that the *number of workers*

---

[4] *Debt and Production.* See earlier discussion in Chapter IX of this book.

*to support increased production needed only to remain
constant.* "Shortly after 1921, American industry
had to solve the problem of whether to reduce the
number of workers, or hours per worker, in direct
proportion as the growth rate of production declined."

While total production has increased, its growth
rate, like that of population, has been decreasing. Man-
hours are inexorably tied to that growth rate. When
it slackens, working hours must come down, or unemployment must result. There is no escape from
these mathematical pincers. Production as a whole
will probably never increase its growth rate again, due
mainly to the unprecedented expansion of the nineteenth century. It follows that unemployment in the
industrial plant must become a chronic condition,
unless working hours are deliberately reduced.

Mr. Jones does not deny that the service trades can
mitigate the situation to a degree. He says, however:
"Thus it seems that this ever-increasing number of
people outside the plant, but dependent upon it, becomes very similar to a growing mortgage on the plant
and on the total goods it produces." The service
trades, however useful—and most of them are not
useful at all—are parasitic on the physical output of
the plant. It must feed, clothe, shelter and energize
them. They are a kind of debt against it—and there
is a limit to the burdensome possibilities of all debt.

The cusp in Mr. Jones' curves in 1921 is particularly
interesting. That was the time when the power age
techniques began to function, when electrification and
the automatic process proceeded to step up output
per man-hour. We have already summarized Mr.
Polakov's account of this important change in Chapter VI. Taking an arithmetic average of the studies

of Alford and Hannum covering blast furnaces, lumber mills, petroleum refineries and machine shops, Mr. Polakov found that productivity in kilo-man-hours could be theoretically increased forty times by employing the best known technical methods—or that 625,000 workers could produce, in equal time, what 25,000,000 now produce. No such *reductio ad absurdum* will, of course, ever be reached, but the calculation shows the goal toward which industry moves.

"Manufacturing methods," says David C. Coyle, "have improved during the present depression to such a point that many hundreds of thousands of workers who lost their jobs because of the depression have now been permanently displaced. They will never return to their old places in industry. No conceivable expansion of demand can overcome the accelerated rate at which manufacturing is dispensing with human labor."

David Weintraub makes the observation concrete, in perhaps the most acute study of technological unemployment yet undertaken.[5] In manufacturing an output x, 100 men were required in 1920; 68.2 men in 1929; 65.2 men in 1931. Output per man increased 8.6 percent in 1931, a rate far in advance of the average for the New Era. His study indicates that:

1. Output per man tends to increase in depression periods.

2. Given a constantly rising output per man-hour, an increase in physical volume is accompanied by a *less* than proportionate increase in the volume of employment; a decline in physical volume by a *more* than proportionate shrinkage in employment.

3. Physical volume must increase *faster* than the

[5] *American Statistical Association Journal,* December, 1932.

increase in output per man-hour to keep employment from falling.

The last finding fits Mr. Jones' pincers. Mr. Jones observed that even when output per man-hour increased only as physical production increased, unemployment was inevitable. Mr. Weintraub concurs.

I shall not weary the reader with further formulæ and figures. If he could stand it, I am prepared to submerge him with sad examples of technological displacement for nearly every industry, and for many of the service trades as well. Here, for instance, is a method—not a machine but a method—for depositing in a central agency the certificates of stock traded in by Wall Street brokers, which promises to eliminate the services of thousands of messengers, clerks and runners. It was devised in connection with the proposed bank for the New York Stock Exchange.[6]

Enough, I believe, has been said to warrant the following summary:

1. That technological unemployment is a fact.

2. That output per man-hour took a sudden leap after the War, accelerated through the New Era, and continued uninterrupted in the depression. The rate of technological displacement has followed the same general course.

3. That there is reason to suppose that the absorptive power of the service trades has reached its limit, under a vendibility system.

4. That even if the service trades still retain some margin, the *rate* of displacement is so high that the effect on the worker is as pernicious as would be the case with permanent technological unemployment.

[6] Reported in New York *Times,* October 8, 1933.

CHAPTER XIV

MANPOWER PLUS

II

We have noted how the Economy of Abundance is undermining the efforts of bankers and manufacturers to preserve the scarcity values of their commodities. Let us examine the operations of this principle in the market, not for money or goods, but for labor.

Under vendibility, labor is of course a commodity like pig iron or cotton, to be bought and sold. Tender-minded observers have tried to soften this fact by soothing words as to common humanity, the dignity of labor, man is more important than the dollar, and so on. These words have had no effect whatever on manufacturers under the necessity of keeping costs to a minimum. Low wages, they reason, are to be preferred to insolvency, and profits are to be preferred to high wages. The price of labor has normally been the least that men—or women or children—could be coerced into accepting. Sometimes it has even failed to cover the cost of bare subsistence, necessitating the labor of two or more members of the family, to keep the family alive.[1]

[1] Alford and Hannum, as a result of a seven year study covering twelve billion man-hours in American industry, prove conclusively that high productivity has a plus correlation with high wages, and vice versa, but manufacturers as a class never have believed this. It is a scientific truth and contrary to common sense. (Paper before the New York Chapter of the Society of Industrial Engineers, December 13, 1933.)

In these circumstances it is to the advantage of those who have labor to sell to make their commodity also relatively scarce. In the development of a new continent there is more work to be done than manpower available. Wages in frontier communities are accordingly high; wages in the United States as a whole, during the period of its expansion, were high, compared to those in settled foreign communities. If an eastern manufacturer paid starvation wages in the nineteenth century, workers would take to covered wagons and find a better life in the west. Millions did. There was a safety valve for brutal exploitation.

Slavery in the south was fought for because planters were afraid, and rightly, that if slaves became freemen, subject to supply and demand in the labor market, wages would be high. If the black freeman did not like the wage rate in Georgia, he would trek to Kansas.

As the continent began to fill, labor unions inevitably formed. Through collective bargaining, apprenticeship rules, "make work" devices, restrictions, and often downright waste, an artificial scarcity was set up. The labor organizer was motivated by precisely the same principles as motivated banker and manufacturer. He tried to make a monopoly of his commodity. Here, however, an important distinction must be drawn. The labor leader seeks a decent standard of living—which sometimes means life itself—for his group. The banker and the manufacturer have other ends in view.

In certain trades and industries—the railroads, for instance—the union drive for monopoly achieved a measure of success. In most of the old line craft occupations where skill was important, unions secured a foothold, and here and there afforded substantial protection to their members. At no time, however, has trade union membership in American exceeded ten percent of all those gainfully employed. No such success has crowned the efforts of labor to stave off the effects of abundance as has crowned the efforts of business men.

The outlook is for even less success. The future of labor as a commodity is black and ominous. Workers are now confronted with an exceedingly difficult problem; so difficult indeed that I see no possibility of its solution under capitalism.

In the Economy of Scarcity, to make two coaches required twice the labor expended on one. The A. O. Smith Corporation in Milwaukee doubles production of motor car frames with only ten percent more men, by installing an automatic frame mill. Not without significance is the fact that few of the newer mass production industries have been organized.[2] Skill is not required for the majority of jobs; labor is a smaller item of cost than materials in some cases; than overhead in most cases. Where can the labor organizer find a foothold? He cannot find it; his paper organizations collapse—not so much under the onslaughts of the management, as under the technological conditions set. As long as there is a surplus of labor outside the gates, and no special skill required within the gates, the shop cannot be organized except temporarily and precariously.

The only thing that can keep the price of labor from falling headlong in a free market is for total production to grow fast enough to absorb the slack. Production, as we have seen, did so during the nineteenth

[2] Until Mr. Roosevelt threw the power of the government behind collective bargaining in the summer of 1933.

century, and for the first decade of the twentieth
century. The incipient depression of 1914 might have
proved critical for labor had not the War interrupted
its course. When the United States joined the conflict,
approximately one man in four was lifted out of normal
economic activity, and put in uniform or to making
munitions. This reduction in the ranks gave labor, as
Arthur Dahlberg points out, a high scarcity value.[3]
The services of the remaining 75 percent were in
demand. Wages rose; labor's share of the national
income increased; silk shirts were sported by machinists, to the horror of the well-to-do; mass standards
of living advanced. Considerable progress was made
in trade union organization.

Alas, the new freedom was not long maintained.
The army was demobilized and the munitions workers
were released. The three men were now four and
their bargaining power collapsed. You remember the
cartoon of the doughboy in uniform: "He risked his
life for you; give him a job." Presently labor began
to feel the additional pressure of the power age.
In the depression of 1921, unemployment rose to
6,000,000.

Labor has never regained its scarcity position, and
failing another world war or a Black Death, never
will. Unemployment remained serious, as we have
seen, throughout the New Era; insecurity grew in the
midst of prosperity. Wages as a whole did not increase; labor's share in total national income fell.
What kept the worker from excessive unemployment

[3] *Jobs, Machines and Capitalism.*
Dahlberg adduces a pretty parallel from the fourteenth century.
When the Black Death struck Europe in 1348, it wiped out half the
population. Wages promptly rose; nobles were ruined by the prices
they had to pay.

during this period was, you recall, the forced activity of the capital goods sector. He was reasonably busy building skyscrapers—which were destined to remain half occupied; factories and machines—to stand half idle; goods for export—which were never to be paid for; subdivisions—never to be lived in.

But with the collapse of the capital goods sector in 1929, labor became as abundant as oranges in California. The situation is precisely similar to the surplus stocks of wheat, cotton, coffee, copper, which have overhung the market with such disastrous effects on price, except that in the case of labor the decline of purchasing power makes it worse. Wheat can be burned, cotton plowed under; the unemployed are not disposed of so summarily.

In the summer of 1933, President Roosevelt took a step of the utmost importance. In setting up the N.R.A. he declared in effect that labor was not a commodity. In prescribing maximum hours and minimum wages, he removed labor from the free market; took it clear out of the vendibility system. It was none too soon. As I write, the tangible action has not been far-reaching enough to have more than a relatively slight effect on unemployment and payrolls, *but the principle has been laid down*. May heaven have mercy on the soul of American labor if it is ever rescinded.

A NOTE ON SKILL

One of the famous bugaboos associated with advancing technology is that of the so-called robot in industry. The philosophers who still raise the issue are about twenty years behind the times. The robot was a serious problem in the machine age. He was the man who worked to the limit of his strength at dull, repetitive tasks. In the power age, the robot all but disappears. In a full automatic factory no worker, by definition, touches the product, from raw material to finished goods. There are plenty of old plants still in operation, filled with altogether too many robots, but, as technology gains, the robot goes. I calculated in 1929 that the robot jobs in the United States might possibly number five million.[4] Today they are far fewer.

What kind of worker does the power age demand, and what should be his training? Labor becomes a supervision of the transformation of energy—to follow Soddy.[5] The intuitive metabolic process, as he calls it, which is the age-old labor pattern, is replaced by other processes depending on reason. Man ceases to be an energy source, and becomes a director of energy. For this job attention, alertness and an intelligent understanding of the broad principles of the whole process are required. For an hour's attention, a worker can get as much product as used to cost him days of physical labor.

"The human labor factor is constant supervision, watchfulness and readiness to adjust the controls of the power-service as required," says Fred Henderson in describing the work of a man in a telphar cabin feeding coal a ton at a time to giant furnaces.[6] An intelligence and responsibility are required which have nothing in common with what hitherto has been known as craft skill. Production is escaping not only from human energy, but from all limitations of traditional skill. When trained machinists and other skilled

[4] *Men and Machines.*
[5] *Wealth, Virtual Wealth and Debt.*
[6] *The Economic Consequences of Power Production.*

operators in England were conscripted during the War, their places were often filled by girls, clergymen and university dons. To the surprise of all, especially the skilled workers, the makeshift crew learned how to turn out perfectly good munitions with only a few weeks of training. Why? Because it was the *process,* not the worker, which counted. And that was twenty years ago.

The work of the mature power age employee will fall increasingly into a common pattern. His alertness and intelligence can be applied equally well to the production of rayon or to the production of locomotives. Remember he is handling energy, not goods. He can pass readily from one industry to another if he has the necessary qualifications—and if someone else does not beat him to the job.

What will he do specifically? In the higher grades he will design, plan and supervise the layout of the productive process; he will be research worker and operating manager. He will be part scientist, part engineer. In the lower grades he will be inspector, repair man, dial watcher and switch thrower, operating the electrical controls according to performance schedules worked out by the management. Many of the tasks in this category, furthermore, will presently be taken over by the photoelectric cell—whose alterness and dependability are practically infinite.

So we may chant a dirge for the craftsman, who has been trisected:

His physical energy has been given to coal.

His operative skill has been taken over by a machine sequence.

His craft knowledge has been captured by technician and research laboratory.

It is clear that for every 100 men employed in the machine age, ten will suffice in the power age; presently fewer.[7] If it is objected that the men who make the machines must be counted too, engineers answer that this industry too is becoming a standardized process, subject to automatic controls. Some men should be counted, of course, but their numbers will not be great. "Manufacturing is rapidly tending," says David C. Coyle, "to become the specialized province of a very limited number of highly trained and experienced operatives." He also points out that it is ridiculous, in plants of this character, to talk about retaining displaced workers on the payroll, and working the whole staff shorter hours. They would be falling all over each other; there would be nothing for them to do. No. The technological process demands so many men, on duty so many hours. The work will be too responsible to subdivide on a chain-gang basis. The workers displaced must get out and stay out. They must try to find jobs on some other sector of the industrial front.

It is also clear that distinctions between direct and indirect labor will collapse, and that piece rates will have no meaning. Indeed all the old formulæ for wage payments will be meaningless, for labor has become a function of energy transformation, and produces nothing which can be measured against the effort expended. An entirely new basis for compensation will have to be found.

Nor is the factory the only field for transformation. "Technological progress is rendering useless much of the traditional skill of the worker in a growing number

[7] The ratio between employment in the A. O. Smith automatic mill and machine age mill, for equivalent output, is exactly one to ten.

of occupations. . . . The model of factory production is being copied in transportation, trade and clerical work." [8] Already automatic switchyards for railroad traffic are in operation. Statistical, clerical and bookkeeping work is being taken over by electrically controlled mechanisms. Even the ticker on the Stock Exchange has been speeded up.

To drill four holes in a number of metal plates so that they bear a fixed relation to the edges of the plates, requires a highly skilled craftsman to operate the ordinary drilling machine. But if a jig is devised whereby the plates can be secured by set screws, the drill can come down to a thousandth of an inch every time; a semi-skilled, even an unskilled worker can direct it. If the quantity of plates to be drilled is large enough to warrant the expenditure, a machine can be installed which will do the whole job, hour in, hour out, with nobody in attendance. Both skill and thought have been replaced by the mechanism. An immense amount of thought is required, however, in first designing the automatic driller.

The skills now in demand are, specifically:

> Designing machinery
> Toolmaking
> Setting and repairing machines
> Designing the final product
> Laying out the factory or process
> Managing the process
> Working out specifications
> Inventing and improving the process (research work)

The worker, in transforming energy, transforms himself into a major or minor technician. He dares no longer trust to common sense, rule of thumb,

[8] *Recent Social Trends.*

"experience" or tradition. His job is to understand the laws of physics as applicable to his particular process. As the power age gains, the proletariat diminishes. The scientist, technician and engineer seize the controls of production. Only so will the process operate; it has no use for the "instinctive metabolisms" of horny handed toilers. Human labor continues to be cardinal, but it has been transferred from the mass to a small, alert class, possessing a new kind of skill altogether. When that class becomes conscious of its power and importance, we may expect some startling political developments. It can act more swiftly, directly and intelligently than any mass of semi-literate workers has ever acted. Already, due to the interlocking network of specialization in the United States, it could in a few hours' time bring every productive wheel to a full stop.

We must be careful, however, not to give the power age more emphasis than the facts warrant. Its promise is so exciting that the temptation is strong to overgeneralize. Millions of manual laborers are still required in industry, and will be for years to come. Even with automatic processes dominant in manufacturing, transportation, pre-fabricated housing, communication, and over large areas of distribution, there must remain great numbers of jobs as a necessary skirmish line about the automatic or semi-automatic front. Men will be needed to service the mass produced automobiles, oil burners, electric furnaces, ice boxes, and other articles turned out for home consumption. Prefabricated houses will require skilled erection crews. Truck drivers, delivery men, will continue in demand. Highway construction, however mechanized, must have its supporting crew of unskilled or semi-skilled workers, as must nearly all engineering projects.

A process which lends itself to exact specification, regularity and standardization, can be taken over by inanimate energy. And will, failing a general smash. The trend is unmistakable. A process which cannot be standardized, such as building a mountain road, or a Norris Dam, or even a Paris hat, must remain in whole or in part outside the technique.

A surprising number of products on the budget of a comfortable standard of living are readily susceptible to these new methods. Here for instance is a partial list of goods in and about my own house, classified three ways. *First,* goods susceptible to quantity production where individual taste is not important. I take what the factory sends, hoping the design will be functional. Increasingly it is. *Second,* goods susceptible to quantity production where individual taste is important. Automatic factories can handle most goods in this class without much difficulty on the Whitehead principle of flexibility in the end product. *Third,* articles not susceptible to mass production, either technically, or because their very nature demands the craftsman's hand.

Susceptible to Quantity Production

Individual taste not important

Plumbing	Nails, screws, hardware
Furnace	Cement and plaster
Electric pump	Windowframes (steel)
Electric heaters	Glass
Electric stove	Screens
Refrigerator	Bedsprings
Toasters	Mattresses
Kitchen cabinet	Sheets

Kitchen ware
Sewing machine
Typewriter
Filing cabinets
Sunlamp
Electric bulbs, fuses, etc.
Flashlights
Household tools

Razors
Toothbrushes, combs, etc.
Cameras
Phonograph
Garden hose
Roller
Garden machines and tools

Taste important

Piano
Tables and chairs
Dressers and chests
Beds
Lampshades and stands
Table silver
Table crockery and glass
Firescreens
Draperies

Blankets
Towels
Suits
Shoes
Underwear
Baggage containers
Books
Automobile

Not Susceptible to Quantity Production

Pictures
Ornaments
Rugs

Craft glass and pottery
Violin
Women's hats

As I go about my house and garden, I have the greatest difficulty in finding articles, other than the few which are purely ornamental, that are not susceptible to mass production techniques, particularly when a wide choice of colors, shapes and sizes is allowed, under the Whitehead principle. Certain articles even in my short third list—pictures, rugs, a violin, for instance—are there not because factories do not make them, but obviously for reasons of taste. Some people satisfy their esthetic needs with expensive rings, perhaps from a jewelry factory. Many would prefer machine-made modern orientals which cost far more than the Mexican sarape on my study floor.

Obviously all consumers' goods are not subject to complete automaticity. It will be exceedingly hard if not impossible to make all processes of textiles and clothing manufacture automatic. But at point after point in the flow from raw material to installation in the consumer's home, the process can be inserted to advantage. The glass will be so rolled, even if a glazier cuts it to mend a broken window. Meanwhile furnaces, refrigerators, pumps, flashlights, hardware, light bulbs, plumbing and many such things can fall, if they have not already fallen, into the pattern of continuous process, electrically controlled production.

If my house burns down, I shall certainly investigate pre-fabricated models before I build another. One tires of unremitting warfare against mice, wasps, flies, moths; against dampness, cold drafts, rust and dirt. If I find a model to suit me—or, better, if I find one to suit my wife—and we have the means to finance it, the whole house slides out of the craftsman's sector and into that of quantity production.

Already the technician is the arbiter of most goods which go into the average home. Presently he may direct everything, including the structure itself, except a few *objets d'art*—good, bad, or indifferent. He will direct it, but you will choose it from a catalogue of exceedingly wide range.

The robot never knew what his work meant; he was a cog in a productive line which began somewhere in the dark to the left, and ended somewhere in the dark to the right. As Simon Patten has shown, this condition inevitably set up psychological frustrations.[9]

[9] In *Product and Climax*.

One wants to know what one is working so hard at; to see some tangible result of one's labors. A fat pay envelope is little recompense for this very human desire. An actor must have his audience; work, to be rewarding, must lead to the shaping of some visibly completed end. The technician of the power age recaptures what the robot of the machine age lost. Standing before his dials and controls, he can see the whole process; before he can control, he must understand it. He has the satisfaction of steering it, step by step, to the completed goal.

Heavy physical labor is biologically inhuman, in so far as humanity is distinguished from animal life by its skilled hand with the opposed thumb, and its relatively big brain. The craftsman was more human than the ditch digger; he used the hand and thumb. The technician is more human than either; he uses the big brain. Said Oscar Wilde:

> There is nothing necessarily dignified about labor at all, and most of it is absolutely degrading. . . . To sweep a slushy crossing for eight hours on a day when the east wind is blowing is a disgusting occupation. To sweep it with mental, moral or physical dignity seems to me to be impossible. . . . Man is made for something better than disturbing dirt. All work of that kind should be done by a machine.

Wilde was a poet. One of the greatest of engineers echoed him. Steinmetz once remarked that when a job became so inhuman or monotonous that no one could take any interest in it, it should be abolished. . . .

CHAPTER XV

FARMERS PLUS

AGRICULTURE was once a way of life. Now, for the great bulk of its production in America, it is just another business. The Shelton family of Stratford were more than farmers; they were a cultural unit, providing not only most of their own economic goods, but educational, social and spiritual values as well. They farmed for the good life as well as for food. The land was not a capital investment to be put on a businesslike basis; it was a mother.[1]

Throughout the development of the continent, the majority of Americans who have gone on the land have had this attitude. Their farms have fallen under the head of use property. The year 1915, according to Lawrence Dennis, marked the wholesale stampede of farmers into business, and the concentration upon a money crop rather than a life crop. Whereupon

[1] From break of day
Till sunset glow
I toil.
I dig my well
I plow my field
And earn my food
And drink.
What care I
Who rules the land
If I
Am left in peace?

Unknown Chinese poet, 2300 B.C. Translation by Henry H. Hart, University of California Press.

235

they lost their self-sufficiency and were duly locked into the vendibility system, dependent no longer chiefly on their own efforts, but on a market, over which they had no control.[2] Hard times for the life farmer meant more work; never eviction and unemployment. Hard times for the business farmer often mean utter destitution. A recent survey of 166 agricultural counties showed one family in eleven on public relief rolls. The average for all counties, both urban and rural, was one family in ten. The farmer is thus in the same boat with the urban worker.[3]

Farmers have borrowed great sums of money during their matriculation into business. Agriculture became a major channel for the flow of profitable investment. With the credit extended to them, farmers bought land, water, combines, tractors, electric milkers, energy. Output per man-hour began to rise on the farms as it had long been rising in factories. Efficiency led ultimately to overproduction, price collapses, foreclosures. Observe the growth of debt:

	1910		*1931*	
Value of all farm property	$40.9 billions		$43.0 billions	
Mortgage debt	3.6	"	9.5	"
Personal debt	1.0	"	3.6	"
Total debt	4.6	"	13.1	"
Percent of indebtedness	11%		30%	

The bulk of the new debt went into buying land as prices rose during the World War. Up to 1920, farmers made large profits, partly by reason of the demand for their products at home and abroad, even

[2] *Is Capitalism Doomed?*
[3] Agricultural Adjustment Administration. *Consumers' Guide,* Nov. 29, 1933.

more by reason of increments in land values. The
fortunate sold out at the peak, to rejoice the realtors
of Los Angeles. Buying farm land, however, was like
buying investment trust stocks during the New Era.
One thought expansion was going on forever. For
six or seven years American agriculture was an item
in high finance.

	1913	*1919*
Value of farm property	$45 billions	$79 billions
Gross farm income	7 billions	17 billions
Physical production on farms (index number)	100	108

Mortgage debt increased seven billions in the period.
Yet all this stupendous swelling of dollar totals was
accompanied *by only an eight percent increase in
tangible output*. The paper balloon was pricked in
1921. Agriculture as a profitable business has been
prostrate ever since. In 1932, gross farm income was
only a little more than five billion dollars, and the
money value of farm property *less* than in 1913.

The drainage of the locally germinated income has not been
neutralized through a compensating return flow of incoming
payments. This growing adverse balance between the network
of industrial and financial centers, and the ten to twelve thousand small agricultural communities, has resulted in a mounting
indebtedness of almost forty percent of the population to the
external agencies of insurance, finance and government. That
the saturation point was reached by 1924 is clearly evidenced
in the total volume of agricultural debt and the stationary and
declining resources of country banks.[4]

Ten years of business dealings were enough to put
American agriculture hopelessly in debt to city slickers,
and to end all hope of profitable transactions for farming as a whole.

[4] Robert R. Doane: *The Measurement of American Wealth.*

This sad story, which we have taken chiefly from the researches of Mr. Dennis, illustrates the fact that the farmer is not a good business man. (There are many individual exceptions, of course.) Invading late a field in which he did not know his way about, he presently encountered the utmost difficulty in maintaining scarcity values—which, as we have seen, is the essence of good business. For a time, due to the fortuitous circumstances of the War, his paper profits were extraordinary. But in the end he was like the elevator boy who bought radio stock on margin in the spring of 1929.

In the face of oncoming technology, the farmer is more helpless even than the working man—unless, of course, he keeps an anchor to windward by retaining some degree of self-sufficiency. Workers have protected themselves here and there with trade unions, and social legislation. American farmers with their pioneer traditions have no training in coöperation, and do not know how to organize business-like monopolies. (Again, there are a few exceptions, such as the California fruit growers.) By and large their prices have been subject to devastating competition; naked to the winds of the market, and to hailstorms loosed by the packers, the canners, the jobbers, the elevator companies, speculators and middlemen galore. Let us set forth categorically the reasons for this helplessness:

1. The inability to establish monopolies.

2. Counting on food demands of a population which never eventuated. Between birth control and the cessation of immigration, agricultural expectations, based on past experience of population growth, were disappointed.

3. The over-expansion of acreage due to abnormal demand during the War.

4. Mechanization and scientific development of farms, tending to increase output faster than the markets.

5. Mechanization and development of agriculture in other nations—specifically Canada, the Argentine, Australia, North China, Russia and South Africa— which limited the export market for American products. The movement has been in full swing for a decade and more.

6. The growth of economic nationalism abroad, which has encouraged domestic agriculture in each country by bounties, and excluded, by high tariffs, farm products imported from other countries.

7. The growth of economic nationalism in the United States. If we raise tariff walls against the importation of foreign goods, foreigners are forced to buy less of our products. In the last analysis, goods in foreign trade can be paid for only in goods. If we will not accept alien goods, we can ship ours only as Christmas presents. The Santa Claus rôle was overplayed.

8. The limited size of the human stomach. The production of food reaches a saturation point long before the production of clothing, shelter or luxury goods. The working man spends a third of his income for food; the rich man less than one percent.

9. The fact that "a people on wheels eats less than a people on foot." The automobile reduces the need for energy foods. The decline of hard physical labor in industry does likewise, and so does the great extension of central heating by coal and oil. (Makers of red flannel underwear have also suffered.)

10. Changing styles in food. Even when the gross expenditure is maintained, large groups of farmers are seriously hurt from time to time by decreased demand for their particular crop. In recent years Americans have been eating more fruit, fresh vegetables, dairy products, sugar, pork; and less beef, potatoes, wheat, corn meal and other cereals. Remember the carloads of iceberg lettuce, which probably meant fewer carloads of potatoes.

Here are ten good and sufficient reasons why American agriculture has failed as a business proposition. The fact that farmers have been good citizens, have worked hard, have improved their efficiency, have fed the nation well, is beside the point. They have been unable to hold prices to a profitable, or even a survival, level—which is the only point that matters in vendibility. Mr. Dennis bids them retreat posthaste to farming as a way of life; to get out of the vendibility system altogether. His warning comes too late.

These observations throw into bold relief the activities of President Roosevelt's Agricultural Adjustment Administration. The government's program, as we observed in Chapter X, is primarily a heroic attempt to resurrect a lost scarcity status. Plow under your wheat and cotton, slaughter your brood sows, that the curse of abundance may no longer fall upon you. Desperate illness requires desperate remedies. Possibly the emergency justifies the legislation. Note, however, that it is the same old story, so common in the business world; the attempt to maintain price levels by waste. If vendibility is to continue, any relief the farmer receives from the government today will be absorbed tomorrow. Even if acreage is reduced, surpluses will presently be sprouting from greater yields per acre. The agro-biologist has the technique all prepared.[5]

Technology on the farm

The total mechanical power used in agriculture increased from one-half H.P. per worker in 1900, to 5.6 H.P. in 1930, according to *Recent Social Trends*. Inanimate energy stepped up its flow eleven times. For the decade 1922–1931, output per farm worker rose 22 percent over its average in the previous decade. The statistical abstraction known as the average farmer now provides food for eighteen persons—four in his own family, twelve Americans outside his family, two foreigners outside America. In the world at large today, it still takes two farmers to support their families plus one urban family between them—in other words, two-thirds of the whole population is engaged in agriculture. Certain highly industrialized nations, of course, reduce this proportion; for Asia alone the figure would be still higher.[6] Despite this eighteen-fold load upon American farmers, higher than any civilization has ever known, there is not work enough to keep ·them busy. Technological improvements forced a million and more people from the farms between 1920 and 1930, while total production advanced.

Dr. O. E. Baker, of the Department of Agriculture, calculates production per acre has increased 20 percent

[5] From a number of sources, I have heard that the tobacco, cotton, and wheat farmers, after signing an agreement with the government to restrict acreage, are preparing to beat the gun in 1934 by intensive cultivation.

[6] See M. P. Taylor: *Common Sense about Machines and Unemployment.*

since 1900, and production per man 34 percent—
the bulk of the increment since the War.[7] "While
our population in 1950 may be six times as great
as in 1850," says Professor E. A. Stewart, "yet
it is conceivable and probable that the decrease in
farm workers which started to take place in 1910
will continue, and by 1950 no more farm workers will
be required to supply food for a population of
150,000,000 than were required in 1850 for a population of 25,000,000."[8] What is not probable, in view
of 1934 trends, is a population of 150,000,000 by
1950. It will be nearer 140,000,000; which, if Dr.
Stewart is correct, means even fewer farmers than in
1850.

Only about ten percent of American farms are as
yet electrified. As decentralization and giant power
gain, cheap current will come increasingly to agriculture. Already in certain areas where rates are moder-
ate, "a nickel's worth of current will milk ten cows,
separate 1,400 pounds of milk and cream, churn
twenty pounds of butter, sharpen an axe on the grind-
stone six times, pump two days' supply of water for
people and animals, run a sewing machine five hours,
or do two big family washings."[9]

The application of electricity to industry produced
the power age. Its application to farm machinery-
promises equally dramatic results, according to Cooke
and Polakov.[10] The horse, mule and ox were superior

---

[7] Address at University of Minnesota, December 2, 1932.
[8] Before the State Agricultural College, University of Minnesota,
August, 1928.
[9] *Harvest and Highlines,* published by Middle West Utilities
Co., 1930.
[10] Morris L. Cooke and Walter N. Polakov. Report to Power
Authority of State of New York. 1932.

to manpower for plowing, harrowing and carting. But a horse eats whether it is working or not, and requires much care. A gasoline engine does more work than a horse and does not eat when idle. Unfortunately, it depreciates when idle, and if it is to pay its board, it must be kept busy. Electric power brings in an entirely new factor. "Electricity costs nothing unless used and can be drawn from the power line any time in such quantity as the job calls for. When farm machinery is driven electrically—whether it is hoisting or hay drying, pumping or refrigeration, lighting or heating—the farmer is placed in the position of a boss over slaves which need no housing, no clothing, can work twenty-four hours a day and are paid piece rates for actual performance. Electricity makes the farmer largely independent of the hours of the day or night and even of the weather." Pests are beginning to be controlled by electrical devices. Electric hotbeds, the direct stimulation of germination and growth in plants, are being experimented with.

"The Saratov combine plant produced the first Soviet electrical grain harvester in August [1932]. This machine can harvest ten acres an hour, almost four times the speed of an ordinary combine. It reaps and stacks the grain simultaneously. Only two men are required for its operation. It was invented and constructed by a group of young Soviet graduates from the Moscow Agricultural Institute." [11] Electricity may have a future in the actual operation of field machinery. It is too soon, however, to be sure of this.

The United States Department of Agriculture calculated in 1924 that the average cost per horse-power hour for all forms of power used on American

[11] *Economic Review of the Soviet Union,* September, 1932.

farms was about nineteen cents. The most costly form was the horse; he reduced the farmer's budget at the rate of twenty-five cents an H.P. hour. The least costly form was electricity from a large central power station—five cents an H.P. hour at that time. Rates are now lower. When the Tennessee Valley Authority begins supplying power to agriculture, we may see a further substantial reduction.

Let us turn to another branch of technology. The agro-biologist has improved the production of milk and meat per unit of feed consumed. With only ten percent more cows than fifteen years ago, we are securing 30 percent more milk, according to Dr. Baker. With no more hogs, we are securing 30 percent more pork, through better breeding and feeding methods. The agro-biologist is steering crops from the less productive to the more productive varieties, and meat animals from the less productive per unit of feed consumed, like beef, to the more productive, like swine and poultry. "When a sufficient number of farmers reach an efficiency equal to 70 percent of that of our best farmers, 47,000,000 acres will supply the same quantity of product as we now obtain from 241,000,000 acres. And 2,500,000 men will be able to do the work now done by 12,500,000." [12] This is, of course, another of those *reductio ad absurdum* estimates, like Polakov's arithmetical mean where one factory worker can theoretically displace forty, cited in Chapter XIII. Such estimates are useful in showing a trend, highly improbable of actual attainment.

These calculations, furthermore, are based on agriculture *controlled, industrialized and collectivized.*

[12] Henry K. Norton: *New Outlook,* October, 1933.

Farming as a way of life finds no place in the picture. Mass production in agriculture follows close behind mass production in industry. Wheat growing and harvesting become a job for a few skilled technicians and mechanics, operating batteries of powerful machines. All crops technically susceptible—some, like truck farming, perhaps are not—will be brought under quantity production methods. The fact that many medium-sized farms resist the ravages of a depression better than giant, mechanized units (like those of Campbell in wheat), is not conclusive in the long run. Small factories, too, tend to resist depression better than mass production units.

Back to the land

In the face of these facts and figures, the "back to the land" movement, unsteadily under way since 1930, meets a high, blank wall. The Economy of Abundance forbids you to go back to the land. You may scratch out a few potatoes, perhaps, but there will be no market for vendible crops except at ruinous prices. There are too many farmers on the land already, armed with ever more efficient machines and methods.

"Back to the land" is again a confusion of serviceability with vendibility. As a matter of physical reality and common observation, the land ought to provide one with food and a measure of economic security. It did so provide throughout the ages of scarcity. A generation ago it was so providing for most American farmers. Today self-subsistence, in that it means no appreciable cash income, means no tractor, no car, no telephone, no radio, no electric light or power, no pump, no modern tools, no coffee, tea, sugar, oranges, tobacco (in most areas), no higher education for the children. The farmer is permanently caught in the web of specialization. He will have to accept the industrial discipline, even as the factory worker and the rest of us. He is like a man on a cliff who has climbed too far to dare a descent, and must either go up or fall off.

Homesteads are not farms, but are homes and gardens on plots of one to ten acres of good land, located near a city or center of employment where families can live and produce primarily for their own use such of the food and other commodities they need or desire to grow or make, in the amateur spirit. A homesteader is one who occupies a homestead, and has some source of income from industrial, professional or other work. . . . Hobby labor is done in the play spirit; it develops skill, releases latent talents and trains children in useful pursuits; it furnishes a means of self expression. . . . Homesteading differs from the pioneer life of the farm a few generations ago in that less time and strength is needed owing to the availability of new materials, tools, machinery, power, roads, and transportation and communication facilities. It is therefore an old method of living modernized by the creations of science and engineering—a new way of living.[13]

In this resolution, Ralph Borsodi and his friends point the way to that decentralization which cheap electric power is beginning to demand. It warms the heart; God speed the day. But observe that there is no economic security worth mentioning in homesteading of this nature, *unless* the homesteader has enough cash income from outside sources to pay for the "new materials, tools, machinery, power, roads and transportation and communication facilities." If the community outside does not keep these supplies streaming in to him, all he has is a roof, and a fraction of his

---

[13] Report to the Resolutions Committee, National Conference on Subsistence Homesteading. Dayton, Ohio. December 10, 1933.

food supply. Furthermore, as homesteads are to be electrified, the snapping of power lines cuts off heat, light, water, cooking facilities, refrigeration. It is fantastic to hope for economic security here, apart from the whole community—clear back to the central power station and its requirements of coal, oil, metals and supplies from all over the world.

Again, admirable as this arrangement may be for the homesteader with a source of cash income—as a clerk, or a doctor or a factory technician—the care that he, as an amateur, lavishes upon leeks and cabbages takes just that amount of business away from professional leek and cabbage farmers. Homesteading will add reason number eleven to the ten recited earlier in this chapter for the failure of American agriculture as a business. It is only too clear that decentralized homesteading, agriculture, power supply, manufacturing, must all be elements of one master plan. None can proceed alone without disaster.

It is time that we ceased to regard the farmer as a distinct species. Broadly speaking, his problems are now identical with those of the day laborer, the mechanic, the clerk, the small business man, the professional man. He is just one more poor devil drowning in economic insecurity. Let us welcome him into the brotherhood of insecure poor devils. We are all in the cauldron together and together we must crawl out.

CHAPTER XVI

THE STATE

The best public servant is the worst one. . . . A thoroughly first rate man in public service is corrosive. He eats holes in our liberties. The better he is and the longer he stays, the greater the danger.[1]

THIS politico-philosophical observation, delivered by the then president of the United States Chamber of Commerce, should be hewn in granite beneath the statue of a pioneer. It is the swan song of a dying age.

The rise of the technical arts has shifted the center of gravity of the political state. While the United States has retained the letter of the constitution and political forms promulgated by the Fathers in a pure scarcity economy, it has been forced within this generation to make drastic *de facto* adjustments to modern conditions. We note immediately three major adjustments:

First, technology has demanded a great increase in government services. Automobiles cannot run without surfaced roads and intricate traffic control; the great city cannot operate an hour without extensive water systems, elaborate fire protection, extensive sanitation works; modern trade and industry cannot be staffed without a high level of literacy, necessitating a mammoth educational plant.

---

[1] Homer Ferguson in *The Nation's Business.* November, 1928.

Second, the political framework of this country was laid down when it took a man on horseback one full day to traverse the average county, thus setting the geographical limit of the political subdivision. It was laid down when there were only five cities with more than 20,000 inhabitants. It was laid down when the thirteen colonies were more remote from each other than China is from us today. Counties are now largely functionless relics of the past; most states and their precious constitutional rights are little more than geographical expressions in the face of the web of specialization; Megalopolis has completely outgrown the political framework, and forms a *de facto* city-state above and beyond the constitution. The rural, sectional politics of George Washington, and even Abraham Lincoln, are obsolete in a nation where sections are utterly interdependent, where almost 60 percent of the population live in towns and cities.

Third, technology has created an acute problem of overproduction in every industrial nation. The disposal of this surplus has been too much for business men profitably to handle unaided. They have turned to the government for help. The results have been tariffs, imposts, embargoes, subsidies, imperialist adventures, and even wars. Today, autarchy, or economic nationalism, is the direct culmination of the problem of the surplus in a vendibility system.

As a result of these three developments, the central government has been pushed—despite the outcries of chambers of commerce—into a dominating rôle. Specialization, interdependence, growing insecurity, have forced the agents of the whole community to attempt controls which were never contemplated under earlier conditions, and which were anathema to the individualistic spirit of those times. Even as I write, the Chamber of Commerce, the Chicago *Tribune,* impressive organizations of bankers, frozen with horror at Mr. Roosevelt's appraisal of technological realities, are crying: "Back, back to the good old days!" And how, pray, are they crying? Through printing presses controlled by photoelectric cells; through a telephone network covering 20,000,000 unit instruments; through the ether, whose waves must be counted and allocated; through a telegraph system which spans the globe; through . . . But what is the use? These gentlemen have their legs in a live world and their heads in a dead one. They apparently want to retreat to stagecoach institutions yet fly about in airplanes.

More government in business

No man was more devoted to stagecoach institutions than President Hoover; to none were the encroachments of government more bitterly suspect. Yet despite his deep convictions, and the convictions of the party which elected him, the four years of his presidency exhibited an increase in federal government activity unparalleled in any peacetime administration up to that date. We need only to recall the Federal Farm Board, the Reconstruction Finance Corporation, Boulder Dam, the new power and radio authorities, to realize to what extent economic realities were pushing Mr. Hoover against his innermost beliefs.

Technology was dictating to the State. The State had no choice but to obey, whatever the philosophies of its agents. Mr. Hoover obeyed grudgingly, while Mr. Roosevelt seems to be obeying with alacrity. Mr. Hoover scowled; Mr. Roosevelt smiles. The difference in facial expression is not altogether due to temperament. It is better for the hormones to work with technological imperatives than against them. If the imperatives outrun Mr. Roosevelt's philosophical limits—as they may—the rotogravures will find him scowling too.

Federal government activities have fallen under six main heads, according to Dr. Charles E. Merriam:[2]

1. Services to business, agriculture and labor. (I find no fault with the order in which he reports them.)
2. Public welfare—education, health, recreation, relief.
3. Highways and communication.
4. War.
5. Regulation of morals—gambling, liquor, vice, censorship, crime.
6. Centralized control of industrial functions—the Interstate Commerce Commission, the Shipping Board, the Federal Trade Commission, etc.

On top of this, state and city governments have added their quotas, especially in numbers two, three and five. Total expenditures for all forms of government have climbed from a little under a billion in 1890, to fourteen billions in 1930.

When technology produced twenty-five million motor cars and trucks, somebody had to provide roads for them to run on, traffic rules to guide them, ambulances to gather up the dead and wounded. When it produced sixteen million radio sets, somebody had to sort the waves and police the air; otherwise no listener could have heard anything but competitive roars and static. (Some say that such is about all the listener hears now.) When technology made possible Megalopolis, somebody had to see that it had

[2] *Recent Social Trends.*

water, street transportation, fire protection, and that its wastes and refuse did not collect to kill its inhabitants in epidemics. When the pace of industry resulted in a rate of accidents and occupational diseases hitherto unknown, somebody had to provide for workmen's compensation. When women were worked brutally long hours amid evil conditions, somebody had to come to their protection. When children were deprived of sun and exercise in city canyons, somebody had to give them playgrounds.

The somebody was always the government. You cannot blindly loose a forty-fold increase in energy per capita into a social organism without hurting some people, and confusing many more. A community agent there must be to keep an eye on them, and try as well as he can to minimize the damage. Anyone who does this honestly and conscientiously bites holes in our liberties, according to Mr. Ferguson—but Mr. Ferguson has never, perhaps, felt tears of welcome come into his eyes at the sight of a municipal ambulance, after a motor accident, when people have been badly injured.

If you plot the curve of inanimate energy, and beside it the curve of manpower employed in government service, you will find the second following the first, step by step, but at a slower rate of growth. Think of it as an ambulance squad; it may help as you contemplate your next tax bill.

Recent Social Trends looks below the surface, and finds that the government is being driven into an unprecedented rôle because of technological progress, the growing helplessness of the individual, and the growing tension between urban and rural areas. "Modern science and invention," says Merriam, "have obliged the government to seek the aid of the chemist, the sanitarian, the engineer, the physicist in the performance of services now demanded by the community under the new conditions. . . . Recent social trends in America and elsewhere drive us inexorably toward a still closer relationship between education, science and government." In 1928, there were 34,000 professional and scientific workers in the federal government alone. The "brain trust" is thus nothing extraordinary in American political life.

It is not to be denied that this process costs money, and money in a vendibility system is relatively scarce. Well-to-do taxpayers are now up in arms against what they term the wastes and extravagance of government. They are closing down schools, halving health services, shutting laboratories, chopping off fire protection and welfare work. It will get them precisely nowhere, except downhill. By reducing the purchasing power of government employees, they further cripple business activity. By reducing essential services, they weaken the whole fabric of civilization and invite an even grander catastrophe. We are not discussing the petty grafts which cling to all large organizations, corporate as well as governmental. These can be trimmed with benefit to all but the grafter. By and large the services which the government performs today, in that they are *protective,* are more important than any business service. It is more important to build schools for the 4,000,000 illiterates still at large in the nation than to build radio factories with the industry operating at 20 percent of its capacity.

I am not prepared to deny, further, that if the depression continues, we cannot build schools because the taxpayers will have no money, either to pay taxes or to buy bonds. With vendibility dominant, an end is theoretically discernible where everybody starves to death in a land in which there is no money but plenty of energy, food, factories, labor power, technical direction, and scientific knowledge. I do not propose to waste my time arguing economy with well-to-do taxpayers. The State is vested, in the last analysis, with the control of money. In a desperate emergency it must override any private understanding it has had hitherto with bankers, and make purchasing power relatively abundant.[3] This will summon idle energy, materials, labor and technical skill to build school-houses, roads, sewer systems, and provide such other public works and government services as circumstances demand. The program will take the breath out of well-to-do taxpayers, granted, but I fail to see how by itself it can bring ruin upon them. In any case, their rules are subject to change when serviceability replaces vendibility. What one "cannot afford" under the latter, becomes perfectly feasible and straight-forward under the former.

Specifically, Mr. Well-to-do Taxpayer, this means the financing of government activity by government money, without benefit of the merry-go-round of bankers, capital goods sector, debt and compound interest. The federal government, let us say, lends $1,000,000 to the City of Cincinnati to destroy slums and build decent houses for working people. The city gives the United States Treasury $1,000,000 worth of *non-interest-bearing* bonds maturing over a twenty-year period, $50,000 a year. The Treasury creates the money precisely as bankers create check money, save

[3] Mr. Roosevelt is moving in this direction by distributing purchasing power through the Public and Civil Works Administrations.

that no discount is charged. Back of the credit stand the bonds of the city, the revenues of the new houses, and the physical buildings themselves. No private banker or investor receives anything. As annual payments are made, they go into the Treasury revolving fund for other advances, if necessary. At present, when the community borrows a dollar it pays back at least two dollars, due to compound interest. Under the plan proposed above, the community borrows a dollar and pays back a dollar. Gravy for bankers and absentee owners is eliminated. The community uses its own credit, thank you.

Any such program will be called inflation by bankers, but it is not inflation. Credit is issued without interest, against tangible wealth. Inflation, properly defined, is the issue of money or credit for nothing. If needed housing developments, electric light plants, sewer systems, playgrounds, forest projects, are not wealth, the term has no meaning. In this case, however, they are non-profit-making wealth; serviceable but not vendible. Any instant the State desires to finance the unemployed consumer directly, while providing more real wealth for the nation, this method—and there are other good methods—stands ready for use; its only defect that it is outside the rules of capitalism. Before we all starve to death through the inability to provide for our wants under the rules, I suspect the State will come to it.

Another method does away with the self-liquidating feature altogether. The State advances credit for public works, and subsequently retires the credit through income and inheritance taxes. The credit is created, not borrowed. This obviates all debt, while redistributing national income.

Battered constitutions

In 1930, J. Paul Goode of the University of Chicago presented a plan for fifty states to replace the present forty-eight in the union. Thirty-one old states were to be retained as having some regional significance, the remaining seventeen were to be converted into eight. That made thirty-nine. To these were added eleven new city-states, comprising respectively the metropolitan areas of our eleven greatest cities.[4] The plan, whatever its merit in specific detail, is in accord with technological progress, provided that the new states entertain no notions of exclusive sovereignty.

Telephone, radio, high speed transportation, make for centralization of control; make it easier to direct and coördinate at a distance. President Roosevelt talks to you in your home from time to time; to all of you. If he had something that he was particularly anxious to make clear, he could talk to you every night until it became clear. Your ward boss cannot talk to you every night—for one thing it would bore you to death—nor can your village selectman. The President, in Washington, can be, if he chooses, closer to you than your neighbors.

Our government was designed for thirteen small, agrarian, jealous colonies, each largely self-subsistent. The very notion of a central government was abhorrent. When Hamilton finally forced federalization through, it was made as weak as possible, with a three-point system of checks and balances—Congress checked the President, and the Supreme Court checked both. Towns were often as jealous of their state government as the state was of the federal government.[5] Re-

[4] *Recent Social Trends.*
[5] Following A. N. Holcombe: *The New Party Politics.*

member that this government was set up in an era when Connecticut was larger, in the time it required to travel from one end to the other, than is the whole United States today. Yet the *form* of government remains substantially unchanged: we have the same old county units, the same theory of states' rights, the same elective system, the same checks and balances, and the same rural and sectional party organization, controlling Congress, according to Dr. Holcombe, in the same old way.[6]

Such is the theory, and to a very hampering extent the practice. The modern facts, as we have seen, are quite otherwise. Sixty percent of us do not live under rural conditions; local economic autonomy has disappeared in the network of specialization; more than 90 percent of our goods are produced by corporations doing an interstate business; highways, airways, railroads, bus lines, pipe lines, super-power, air waves, the fixing of minimum wages, maximum hours, relief of unemployment, cut across state boundaries.

The regulation of public utilities by the states has become a dreary farce. As David Lilienthal points out, "the utilities have regulated the regulators." The farce was recognized in the case of the railroads, and the Interstate Commerce Commission was the result. It is about to be recognized in the case of electric power, radio, telephone and telegraph, which, like the railroad, are national, not state functions. Day by day, technological realities demand the federal incorporation of all interstate business. There is no rhyme nor reason in New Jersey's mothering a corporation with

[6] True, we managed to secure the popular election of the President, which the constitution did not contemplate.

a head office in Pittsburgh, and branches in every state in the union.

The *de facto* government, operating under the restrictions imposed by the *de jure* government, has sought desperately, if clumsily, to adjust itself to modern realities. It has been forced to centralize, to override states' rights, to take cognizance of the peculiar problems of Megalopolis—witness the New York Port Authority—to hail scientists into government service, to regulate interstate business, and lately, as Dr. Merriam points out, to circumvent the old doctrine of checks and balances, by setting up boards and commissions which, like the Federal Trade Commission, combine legislative, judicial and administrative powers.

There is as yet no serious demand for bringing the *de jure* government into line with the *de facto;* in short, for a thoroughgoing revision of the constitution. But the old forms are visibly cracking. President Roosevelt has a battery of pile drivers at work as I write.

"America," says Merriam, "has come to the parting of the ways in the field of public relations. The heavy pressure of powerful social, economic and technical forces threatens to crush the shell of a government which becomes more and more important in the social and economic situation. . . . If we have a weak government, its retreats will be routs, and its advances meaningless muddles."

The Economy of Abundance is crushing the *de jure* shell. Presently we shall have to get a new one. What new measures would fit the modern situation? I am no politician, but I will venture a few suggestions.

The calling of a Constitutional Convention, for

example, would open the way for modernization and for more effective federal control. The steady drift in the latter direction indicates with reasonable clarity that sooner or later Washington must become permanently responsible for local public school education; for the coördination of public works with unemployment relief and the creation of jobs for the unemployed; for the fixing of maximum hours of labor. It may be forced, sooner than we suppose, into the direct control of the issue of credit, money and new investment, superseding the private banker, in whole or in part. It cannot drop its already extensive control of agriculture, particularly if it is to encourage decentralization and homesteading, for, as we saw in the last chapter, these problems are tied tightly together. Already one central taxing authority for the nation is being suggested, with allocations of the levy to local units. Already a federal monopoly of exports and imports is seriously proposed, for a world going autarchist.

Finally, it may be that the community, as symbolized in the federal government, will be driven to adopt the rule of taking over any essential industry *if and when it loses a status of genuine scarcity,* due to the rise of the technical arts. The instant its costs begin to be padded with waste in an attempt to maintain price levels, the community may have to step in to insure that the benefits of technology be passed on. Not only will the consumer benefit; the industry itself, by operating at substantial capacity, will become a healthy industry, rather than one dosed, as heretofore, with habit-forming drugs like super-salesmanship, private monopoly and over-seas dumping.

A concrete example is the power industry. It is now in a position where, technically, it can furnish power to the nation at rates far below present levels. The habit-forming drug in the industry as it stands is the holding company, brewed with incantations at midnight by Mr. Insull and his friends. If the drug could be poured down the sewer, the scarcity status would collapse, and power come to the nation like water from a city reservoir. It may be that the Tennessee Valley Authority is destined to become the agent which will bring electrical energy out of artificial scarcity into genuine abundance.

CHAPTER XVII

THE UNHAPPY FAMILY OF NATIONS

EVERY nation on earth today is drifting, nay flying, towards economic nationalism. This is not a result of greed, selfishness, narrow ideals, fascist oratory or failure to regard benevolently the brotherhood of man. It is the result of the technical arts, operating in a pecuniary framework.

In no domain has confusion between serviceability and vendibility been more pronounced. The good, old-fashioned liberal is as bewildered as a rabbit in a maze. Modern technical methods demand raw materials and supplies from all over the world, as we noted in Chapter VIII. Areas adapted to the production of necessary materials, especially tropical plantations and remote mining areas, are glad to add to their standard of living by receiving cheap manufactured goods in exchange. They are glad to receive the services of technicians to build railroads, power lines, refrigerating units, highways. Meanwhile cable, radio, airplane, ocean liner, *turismo,* postal service, international scientific congress, Olympic games—link all areas in ever closer bonds of communication and mutual understanding. Observe, however, that this pretty picture is to be seen only when one looks through the glasses of serviceability. When one regards the world *as if* this motive were dominant, he sees science plying a magic shuttle which is fast weaving the completed fabric of international goodwill. Such is the view the liberal thinks he sees when he argues for world free trade.

Now let us pick up the glasses of vendibility. The jolly nations are not exchanging goods and services for the welfare of their citizens. On the contrary; most alarmingly on the contrary. A handful of their nationals are engaged in a series of piratical expeditions to make money by selling dear and buying cheap. The jolly national governments are engaged in abetting this traffic by the jolliest possible aggregation of battle cruisers, tanks, submarines, bombing planes, siege guns, and diplomatic mendacity. I would not hold that war was unheard of before capitalism. I do hold that the technical arts would long since have rendered war obsolete if it had not been for the money-making possibilities of foreign trade. As serviceability compresses the world, vendibility bursts it asunder. "War," says Raymond L. Buell, "is an economic dispute which has gone too far." World trade—for profit—as contrasted with the exchange of essential supplies between various geographical areas, is potential nitroglycerine.

Autarchy is a direct answer to the conflict between technological advance and the motive of vendibility. It looks like a step backward and it may be so. But its direction is more complicated than appears at first blush. The liberals should look closer. Autarchy might just prove a transition to world serviceability.

With the invaluable aid of John Strachey, let us briefly outline the history of international trade under capitalism.[1] In the culmination of the French Revolution, the middle class won its last major encounter with

[1] *The Coming Struggle for Power.*

feudalism, and capitalism came into its own. It was the way of the trader, the merchant, the entrepreneur, the man with goods to sell and capital to invest. The traditions, duties, responsibilities, of noble, peasant, churchman, guildman, were broken down into a vast free market, and all economic relationships began to turn upon a pecuniary wheel. Restrictions were lifted from the ready and profitable exchange of all forms of property. Labor became a commodity to be bought and sold on the open market. Capital was exported from creditor nations to build railroads, sink mines, establish plantations and presently rear factories, in the so-called backward countries.

As European states—and in due time the United States—industrialized themselves, one and all learned to produce a plethora of textiles, machines, manufactured articles, which could not be sold at home. Between the inordinate productivity of the mounting energy curve, and the limited purchasing power of the home market—crawling crabwise through the capital goods sector—new outlets had to be found if profits were to be maintained. From time to time, when profitable foreign outlets were not obtainable, the surplus was "dumped" abroad—at less than cost—to insure scarcity levels for domestic prices.

For many years England, the mother of the industrial revolution, had a virtual monopoly in the disposal of her surplus, but one by one competitors appeared—France, Belgium, America, Germany, Japan. Competition for foreign markets led to the development of colonial empires, where competitors would have less profitable pickings than mother-country business men. The brute fact that "trade follows the flag" was rationalized by the nobler con-

ception of "the white man's burden." From 1884 to
1900, the British Empire added 3.7 million square
miles and fifty-seven million population; the French
Empire 3.5 million square miles and thirty-six million
population; the German Empire one million square
miles and seventeen million population; the American
Empire swallowed the Philippines and Porto Rico,
and tucked Cuba under its wing. Clashes among
competitors were inevitable, and frequently sanguinary.
Finally, the efficient imperialism of Germany threatened too many British markets, and the War followed,
as a by-product of the struggle for world trade.

By 1914, this rough-and-ready traders' internationalism had covered the planet. With a universal gold
standard, goods could be bought and sold, capital
exported and imported, contractual obligations entered
into, anywhere and everywhere. But the War demonstrated the folly of trying to build the brotherhood
of man on profitable peddling. The free market and
the gold standard collapsed, as every warring nation
turned to arbitrary state control of its manpower and
material resources. The treaty of Versailles then
released a swarm of new competitive states, each with
a surplus to export.[2]

Meanwhile, due to diligent merchandising by machine manufacturers and the exporters of capital, the
backward countries were being rapidly equipped with
capital goods of their own. From 1914 to 1928, Japan
increased cotton manufacturing 530 percent, paper

[2] "The great criticism of the Peace of Versailles . . . is that it
completed the nationalist movement in Europe and established a
number of new nations, like Czechoslovakia and Poland, each as
intent as Germany and Italy had been in the last quarter of the
nineteenth century, and even more so, on organizing themselves for
industrial competence in the markets of the world." Lord Eustace
Percy in *The Modern State*.

manufacturing 500 percent, steel 570 percent. In the three years ended in 1927, Brazil added 20 percent to her spindle capacity. India now has 8.2 million spindles; China 3.6 million. From 1911 to 1928, New Zealand increased the manufacture of clothing 340 percent, agricultural machinery 175 percent, furniture 180 percent. Between 1910 and 1928, employment in manufacturing establishments in South Africa doubled. Russia, in the last fifteen years, has completely withdrawn from the world market in the old sense. She has bought and sold as one hardboiled national unit.

"America," says M. J. Bonn, "has in many cases organized the industrialization of new countries or the reorganization of old industrial areas, and financed not only customers, but also rivals . . . The best example of this policy is perhaps the financing of Poland, which has made it possible for the Poles, by constructing a coal port and a coal railway, both superfluous from the point of view of world economy, to dump coal and so depress the world market price."

The decade from 1919 to 1929 witnessed an attempt on the part of all earnest believers in international vendibility to rebuild the free market which had been badly shaken by War controls in 1914. The United States, by lending ten billion dollars abroad, kept the tottering edifice together for a time. When, in 1928, America wearied of loaning her neighbors the interest with which to validate her earlier loans, the international free market fell headlong into the abyss. Compound interest had again marched beyond physical realities.[3] Into this abyss we are privileged to peer

[3] Sir Arthur Salter demonstrated that world capitalism must break down unless a perpetual flow of foreign lending was maintained. For 1927, he found a gap so to be filled of $2,000,000,000.

and view its shattered remains today. On the brink stand Sir Arthur Salter and his friends, stout, liberal, free marketers all, wringing their hands for a golden age—well, golden for some—which has gone. International conference after conference meets, hoping against hope to get Humpty Dumpty together again. But Humpty Dumpty is smashed. He was an egg, you know. . . . Mr. MacDonald, Mr. Herriot, Mr. Salter; he was an egg, and he is smashed.

Even if governments agreed to reverse their steadfast policy of recent years, to obliterate every tariff wall and export bounty, peg their currencies to a single gold standard as in 1913—they could not get Humpty Dumpty together again. While industrial capacity grows, spurred by the power age, foreign markets shrink, due to new competitors, and the equipment of areas no longer backward. Such nations as are still under-equipped and undersupplied have little or nothing wherewith to pay. Surpluses are great beyond absorption, save at ruinously low prices. The world market, particularly under the pressure of a "favorable balance of trade," is all sellers and no buyers—to put it in its crudest form. What kind of market is that? Ask any broker.

World vendibility worked for a hundred years and more, so long as a few industrialized nations had a lush, virgin planet to exploit. Now the virgin forest is cut-over land, and the few industrialized nations have grown to many. The only way the surplus can be coped with is to distribute it at home. And that means some kind of economic nationalism.

Two major problems arise from the wreckage of the free market. If factories are to be kept in operation, their output must find a home market. There are the factories; there is the home population, glad to receive the output in terms of higher living standards. But there too is the formula of capitalism, which positively cannot allow any such distribution. So if the several governments *are* to distribute the surplus, they must first disallow the formula. They must take the control of money away from bankers, cherished scarcity concepts away from manufacturers, the control of industrial property away from the corporate "control." They must somehow provide the home consumer with sufficient purchasing power to engorge the surplus.

No nation except Russia would now admit that such was its program. No nation knows clearly that such *is* its program. But if the surplus can no longer be profitably sold abroad, and economic nationalism is as epidemic as it seems, I submit that no less drastic program is conceivable. I submit, further, that long steps in this direction are being taken by the United States since March 4, 1933, by Sweden, New Zealand, Denmark, Germany, Italy; and steps of assorted lengths by every industrial nation. Currencies are being "managed," gold standards abandoned, industries regulated, public works promoted, extraordinary attempts made to stimulate popular purchasing power. Economic nationalism, then, is forcing an extensive modification of private capitalism in the direction of State capitalism or outright socialization.

The second problem which arises from the wreckage of the world free market, is more remote but sufficiently impressive. There are only three industrial political units on earth which have the soils and minerals and energy resources to institute economic nationalism on a comprehensive scale. The United

States, the British Empire and Russia are, or could be made, perhaps 90 percent self-sufficient in respect to essential raw materials. All other nations—save a few happy nature peoples—are utterly dependent on their neighbors for a vital fraction of their necessary supplies. If they tried to become completely self-supporting, they would very soon find their factories without supplies, or their power lines without energy, or their hospitals without drugs, or their railroads without coal, or their people without food. Delete the "or" for most European countries. Continental Europe *as a whole,* not including Russia, is perhaps as self-sufficient as the United States, but no single European nation is so.

Economic nationalism, then, must bend if not break traditional capitalism, but only three political areas can carry the principle to its logical conclusion. This is as far as I have any right to go. I am tempted, however, to make a prophecy.

Technology, having smashed the free market and fostered the retreat to nationalism, will not, cannot, stop there. It leaves a world without equilibrium. Perhaps, after having forced a modicum of central planning and socialization upon the several nations, and so corrupted their loyalty to the principles of vendibility, it may drive them into adopting service-ability in international exchange. The technique would be a state monopoly of exports and imports; followed by a series of gigantic barter exchanges for essential goods. Again, technological imperatives might force a United States of Europe. They might force the World State. The end of the international peddler does not necessarily mean the end of internationalism. It may mark the beginning of a sounder internationalism whose cornerstone is human need, not trader's profit.

War in the power age

The alternative, of course, is war; a particularly bitter kind of war. It will be waged not to protect the profits of citizens abroad—because such profits are increasingly negligible—but for life itself. It will be waged to insure the supply of desperately needed raw materials; and so will be a goods war; not a money war. Science is ready to produce a variety of new and devastating weapons, true; but there is just a chance that it may do more. It may end war forever. Major General J. F. C. Fuller of England is my authority.[4] Here, he says, are 200 airplanes attacking a great city. The defense is excellent, and the pilots dare not come too close. "Why not send forward over that city 200 unmanned and partially armored planes wirelessly controlled by ten occupied ones flying at a distance from them, or at a high altitude above them? Each of these 200 machines would be nothing more than a flying projectile—a true, aërial torpedo—which will explode on impact with the ground, or be exploded by a wireless wave released by the airmen directing it. . . . What is the answer to this form of attack? Frankly, I do not know. . . . Whilst in mechanical and chemical science I see possible fertilizers of war, in electrical science I see its possible end. If an electrical wave can direct an unmanned airplane—as we know it can—it can direct and control an unmanned gun, or tank or submarine or any other weapon, static or mobile.[5] The result of

[4] *What Would Be the Character of a New War?*
[5] The British navy has just perfected high speed manless motor boats, equipped with torpedoes and directed by radio.

being able to move weapons at a distance, and yet continue to direct their course, cuts out, not completely, but very largely, the weak link in all past warfare—the human element." The power age, advancing into warfare, makes it automatic, remotely controlled, and manless. There will be no more use for soldiers than there is for manual workers in automatic factories. . . . A few technicians watching dials and pressing buttons.

Coal power produced the *Monitor* and the *Merrimac,* changed navies from wood to iron, greatly increased the size of armies by putting railroads behind them, enhanced the effectiveness of weapons. The interdependence of nations, begotten by steam, converted great wars into world wars.

Oil power produced airplanes, tanks, motorized armies; war in three dimensions. It leads to the stalemate of the trenches, as in the Great War. We are still largely in the oil power stage.

Electric power is dawning in warfare. It will produce battlefields without soldiers, naval engagements without sailors, and aërial bombardments without pilots. Most of the casualties accordingly will be in the ranks of the civilians. Wreaths will be laid on the tomb of the Unknown Pedestrian—unfortunate enough to be one of two hundred at Broadway and 48th street on the night of the second aërial attack. Is it too much to hope that then—if only then—the civilian population will flatly refuse to support any government which declares war? This argument, I know, has been raised with each improvement in offensive technique. "War will become too horrible; it will end war." But electrified warfare shows a qualitative difference. Instead of a minority actively fighting while a comparatively safe majority applauds, we shall have a still smaller minority fighting with remote controls, and so comparatively safe, while a still larger majority is gassed, bombed and horrendously butchered.

General Fuller looks at the quarter deck of the *Victory,* then at the burnished dials in the control room of the *Hood,* and sees no reason why the curve of invention will not presently reduce war to an impossibility. It will be a race, of course, between the diplomats and the engineers.

CHAPTER XVIII

CONSUMER KINGS—AND QUEENS

CONSUMERS are, of course, not a class apart, but you and I and everybody in our daily function of demolishing wealth. As consumers, we destroy what as farmers, workers, managers, inventors, we have helped to create. This is as it should be, for there is no other conceivable purpose in the creation of wealth, save to keep life in its rhythm. Consumption measures the standard of living, social wellbeing, civilization itself.

The rise of technology has given all classes somewhat more to consume, by weight, than in the days of scarcity; has greatly increased the variety of possible choices—one can still take his wheat straight, or get it puffed, pulverized, flaked, or shot from guns; has added thousands of products and services unknown and undreamed of a century ago—television, for instance, and zippers. Indeed, so profuse has been the menu, and so devious the ways in which old products have been metamorphosed and new products publicized, that a specific term had to be coined to cover the bewilderment of the modern consumer when he or she goes to market. Robert Lynd supplied the phrase and it has grown familiar: *the new illiteracy.* We are all, in this sense, illiterates.[1]

The effects of an abundance economy on the volume, quality, utility and value of consumers' goods are very

[1] See Robert and Helen Lynd: *Middletown.*

important. More important still is the fact that consumption has been torn loose from its moral base. By what right hitherto have we dipped our hands into the stream of consumers' goods and services, and drawn out an allotment? By the sanction of work. The assumption has been that before drawing something out we have toiled to put something in. Only robbers stand on the bank and take. Eating without working was declared a crime by Captain John Smith, and civilized society generally has so held, although the interpretation has been broad.

Absentee owners appear to confound this rule: they toil not but their scoop is large and deep. An elaborate justification explains away this appearance. Absentee owners are now scooping the reward of abstinence. Working like so many beavers in the past, they chose to consume frugally, and to *save* the bulk of their productive activity. The classicists assure us that, like day laborers, absentee owners are eating by virtue of work done, the only difference being the time factor. The day laborer accomplished his stint yesterday; the retired capitalist ten or twenty years ago. The fact that the latter's claim to consumption often grows at a compound interest rate is equally open to exegesis. The investment, it is assumed, was well chosen and stimulating to progress and production. Any increment clearly belongs to him who has aided his country's upward march.

The logic is so sweet and persuasive that the generality of modern men have no more questioned it than the generality of scholars in the middle ages ques-

[2] An admirable example of the profit-pleasure labor-pain calculus of the economic classicists, is found in John Bates Clark's *Essentials of Economic Theory*. Clark said flatly: "Each man is paid an amount that equals the total product he personally creates."

tioned the logic of Aristotle, when he proved that heavy stones fell faster than light ones. But Abundance is a rude Galileo, climbing the tower of Pisa burdened with cannonballs. Under modern conditions of production, no measurable relation can be found between work contributed and goods consumed; while the abstinence theory of right to consumption, duly increased by compound interest, has little more foundation in the world of economic reality. A whole moral fabric is thus rent and torn, with the most alarming and far-reaching consequences.

To the Sheltons of Stratford in 1760, work and consumption were the reverse sides of the same medal. One plowed and harvested and ate the product, which gave one the energy to plow and harvest again. Consumption was unthinkable without work, and the intensity of the work normally fixed the volume to be consumed. A century later, when the machine age and capitalism were in full swing, fortunes were often made by hard productive work. In his earlier years, the ambitious capitalist did deny himself, and invested what he might have spent. In both periods, economic facts and moral sanction roughly coincided.

Where is that coincidence in the power age, with physical production steadily growing, and employment in productive industries steadily shrinking? What becomes of one of the most ancient of work-consumption equations, when no more farmers will be needed to feed a nation of 140 million in 1950 than were required to feed it in 1850, when it numbered twenty-five millions?

Absentee owners are no longer to be described as a class who have worked hard, saved against their declining years, now to reap the rewards of thrift.

Thousands can still be so described, perhaps, but they are the small fry. The resplendent, powerful absentee owner is more typically a lucky speculator who has never done a productive day's work in acquiring his fortune. Windfall profits—so named by Keynes—have given title, in recent years, to the most luxurious consumption any nation ever knew. Again, when the formula of capitalism sags, due to excess plant capacity—saving, hoarding, thrift, operate to freeze economic activity, forcing it to ever lower levels. What was once a virtue becomes in these circumstances a vice. The moral duty rests with the spender, not with the hoarder; turning traditional doctrine upside down.

While there is hope for a steady increase in consumers' goods for many years to come, there is no hope for an increase in the labor required to produce them. Leisure is destined constantly to grow under power age conditions. If it cannot take the form of shorter working hours for all, it will take the form of total unemployment for some. Even without conscious planning, working hours have declined steadily since 1890. "The new powers," says Fred Henderson, "do not merely offer us leisure and abundance, they *force* leisure and abundance upon us." If we do not accept them intelligently and gracefully, we get them anyway—leisure in the breadline, and abundance in a mile-long pile of rotting oranges.

As for measuring output in terms of work, specialization alone, irrespective of the power age, makes such measurement impossible. When a million persons, more or less, coöperate to produce the book you are reading, how shall we measure the value of their services in terms of books produced?

What becomes, then, of an ethic which says that only workers may consume in proportion to their work; or even of a broader ethic which says that only those who do *some* work shall consume—when no work of any kind is available? Apparently we must either renounce specialization and quantity production, or renounce the ethic.

Again, let us assume that the claims of absentee owners are fully justified on the theory of abstinence; that not a windfall profiteer nor a finance capital manipulator is to be found in their ranks. Their claims to consumption are good, however, only so long as the formula of capitalism is good. As we saw in Chapter IX, the formula is no longer good; it is unworkable, due to the decline in the growth rate of expansion. If the debt structure is scaled down or collapses, the claims, in whole or in part, are uncollectible. The abstemious absentee owner cannot reclaim the work values which he earlier laid by. Of what use to owners, pray, is an ethic without the means to cash in on it? Capitalists may have the best of legal and moral claims, but if their formula runs out and their debts cannot be serviced, they are in precisely the same boat as the unemployed who want to work.

Therefore, from whatever angle you view it, hard work and thrift, admirable as they may be in themselves, and admirable as may be the titles to consumption they furnished in the Economy of Scarcity, have all but lost their utility under modern conditions. When economic individualism still had play, the industrious and thrifty really could construct, each for himself and his family, a little tower of economic security, into which he could retire, safe from storms and alarms. From our cradles onward, these towers, and the sturdy virtues which built them, were held shining and golden before our eyes. The entire generation of Americans now in their middle years were so instructed, and most of them so conditioned. Millions erected a life plan on this basis: hard work for so many years; save such and such a percentage of one's income; invest it with the soundest of advice from one's banker; never touch the principal; retire at fifty-five or sixty— then, travel, golf, a place in the country, sunny-haired grandchildren, good books, concerts . . .[3]

Too many little towers, my friends; the terrain will not support them. Specialization saps their foundations; the ebbing of capitalism cuts off their supplies. Security can no longer be found that way, but only by building one big fortress for all—possibly with turrets thereon for the industrious and able.

With this alarming and wholesale denial of claims to consume based on productive labor—present or past —and with power age industry roaring and straining to produce goods, titles to consumption must be found elsewhere, and speedily. All citizens, in their capacity as consumers, move to the center of the stage. For the first time in history, eating becomes more important in the economic calculus than working.

Even the advocates of vendibility recognized the problem. Installment selling was a clumsy attempt to finance the consumer directly. The difficulty was that he paid some 15 percent per annum, on the average, for the privilege of being financed. Such a gorgeous

---

[3] A mine mule, the story goes, was turned loose to enjoy life above ground in his old age. Every morning at seven when the tipple whistle blew, the poor creature took up his position by an old stump and wobbled in painful circles about that stump until the whistle blew at night.

rate of usury inevitably defeated itself. A philosophy appeared in business circles which has been characterized as the "Consumer King" principle. ("Consumer Queen" would be more apt. Women buy three-quarters of all goods for ultimate consumption.) Paul Mazur well summarized the point of view:

An economic age 150 years old has come to an end. The consequences of industrial evolution have made necessary a new economic philosophy, a new business point of view, and practically a new social system. Production can and will develop, but its power of development will from now on be dependent upon the growth of consumer demands as these are stimulated by new techniques, financed by new methods, and increased by a more effective distribution of purchasing power.[4]

The president of the Sun Oil Company in a recent annual report held that "even before the depression it was plain that continued prosperity demanded the maintenance of a broad-based buying power such as could be arrived at only by a general program of liberal wages and salaries. If a larger share of prosperity's profits had gone to wages, there would have been more consumption and less speculation."

Such observations bear witness to the goodwill and intelligence of a section of the business community. They must remain largely academic, however, in any system devoted to vendibility. Absentee owners as a class can hardly be expected voluntarily to forego interest, rents and dividends, in order that wages may be increased, and the national income redistributed in favor of mass purchasing power. Comparatively farsighted business men like Mr. Mazur are not quite farsighted enough to realize that the national income can be redistributed only by force—the force

[4] New York *Times*, November 29, 1931.

of blind circumstances or the force of government control. The depression supplied a modicum of the former, and Mr. Roosevelt is now supplying a modicum of the latter. It is safe to conclude that the consumer can never be adequately financed under vendibility.

"The conservative banker," says E. A. Filene, "simply has not studied mass credit. It has not been any part of his training to study the mases at all. He has learned his banking from another age—an age in which it was absolutely necessary, if there ever was to be a machine civilization, that the people generally should consume much less than they were producing, and that the resulting surplus be employed in the financing of more production." [5]

Now that the productive plant is substantially built, the time has come to consume far more of its potential output, and to save far less for its future extension. Technology demands that consumers now consume, and technology, being thoroughly amoral, does not care a fig whether they work or not, beyond the essential manpower requirements of power age conditions. Traditional ethics, however, continues to demand that work be done before consumption is permitted. A financial token must first be presented, and the token can theoretically be secured by the consumer only in exchange for work—present or past. This brings us to a full stop.

If mass production is to have its way, its imperatives will dissolve traditional ethics. This is all very sad, but what is to be done about it? "In the last resort," said Veblen, "the economic moralities wait on the economic necessities." If one cannot eat bread in the sweat of

[5] *Successful Living in this Machine Age.*

one's brow, one must still have bread to eat. Nevertheless an excellent moral case can be made out for the right of the consumer to consume. Modern production rests on six fundamental factors:

1. Natural resources available.
2. Inanimate energy.
3. Skilled and unskilled labor (a declining factor but still important).
4. Technical management (an increasingly important factor).
5. The cultural heritage of the technical arts.
6. The productive plant.

Natural resources and inanimate energy, while monopolized by private persons and corporations to a large degree, are increasingly regarded as affected with a public interest, and as property sooner or later to vest in the whole community. Certainly they were left by God or geology to mankind and not to the Standard Oil Company of California. If this is not sound moral doctrine, I do not know what is.

Even clearer is the title of the whole community to the cultural heritage of the technical arts. The findings of science and the applications of the scientific method, from Galileo to date, belong to all of us. The patent law recognizes this by allowing title to new inventions to revert to the public after twenty-one years. The whole technique of Abundance is thus the rightful possession of the community. It is more important than the tangible plant, for if the plant were destroyed the technique would remain to rebuild it—and rebuild it more efficiently.

Labor, both of worker and of management, continues as a contribution of the individual. We remember, however, that hard work, in power age processes, in no wise affects the output; it is the process which sets the pace.

Thus in three of the six chief factors in production, the community has extensive moral claims by virtue of being the heir to natural resources, inanimate energy and the technical arts. In a fourth factor, the claims of the individual worker are decreasingly important as inanimate energy takes over his job. In the fifth factor, management, one would not expect 100,000 technicians, more or less, to claim exclusive rights in the output of American industry. Factor number six, the physical plant, is now the property of absentee owners. The claims of such owners to income, however, are valueless, as we have already seen in great detail, unless the plant is briskly operating. Modern plants cannot so operate without mass volume—leaving the consumer again paramount in the situation.

I submit, then, that the consumer has a good moral claim and title to the usufruct of his property, whether he works or not. If he gets a chance to work, either as laborer or as technician, the claim is obviously strengthened by so much. It might or might not be good ethics to assume strict equality in the division of output, by virtue of membership in the community alone. George Bernard Shaw, for one, is prepared to defend equal division on any and all grounds.

"The discharge of a thousand debts," says R. G. Tugwell, "is contingent upon the consumer's purchase. . . . It is quite clear that he must be both willing and able to pay the price, or the whole scheme will go wrong. All along the different owners of the good have had this in mind. Not only their costs are important; this willingness and ability of consumers is equally important. . . . The consumer's approval of productive effort is not registered until *after* the good is completed; after countless expenses have been incurred, after numerous bargains have taken place, even after enormous commitments to overhead expense have been made. If the consumer should refuse, the whole structure will collapse." [6]

Here is the economic apparatus, drawing raw supplies from all over the world, great ships bearing this material, locomotives straining at it, vast mechanical operations grinding and processing it, jobbers, wholesalers, retailers bargaining for it, bookkeepers recording it, long distance calls hastening it, bankers financing it, trucks delivering it—all into a gigantic hopper with a little valve in the bottom. The consumer has his—or her—finger on that valve. If he pulls it open the hopper discharges, to fill again. If he fails to pull it, or pulls it only halfway, the hopper chokes; the ships, the locomotives, the mine hoists, the processing machines, the trucks, the jobbers, the banks, the very telephone girls, must bring their operations to a halt.

He opens the valve if he is willing and able. By and large he is willing enough, though stupid salesmen have grossly overestimated his saturation point in certain departments. So long as the capitalistic formula worked, he was able to buy—not to the extent of his willingness, God knows, but enough to keep the hopper reasonably clear. With the collapse of expansion and the capital-goods sector in 1930, he was no longer able to buy in sufficient volume. The hopper choked; is choked today, four years later; and will remain choked until he is able to buy again.

From 1929 to 1932, the national income dropped from eighty-five billion dollars to thirty-seven billion,

[6] *The Industrial Discipline.*

a decline of forty-eight billions. The fifteen million unemployed in that year lost approximately sixteen billion dollars in wages. Thus for every dollar industry saved in payroll, it lost three dollars in volume of turnover. The strategic importance of the consumer could not be better illustrated. The withdrawal of one dollar in mass purchasing power resulted in damage thrice as great—due, of course, to panic, fear, hoarding, losses, refusal of banks to loan, and so forth—in other sectors of the economic front.[7]

Note also the importance of the mass man and woman, as calculated by Robert R. Doane for the year 1929:[8]

67 percent of all spending (including savings) in the nation was done by persons with incomes of less than $3,000 per year.

78 percent was done by persons with less than $5,000 a year.

Only eight percent of all spending was done by persons with more than $25,000 a year.

Income group	Percent of total income for food, shelter and clothing
Under $ 1,000	64%
$ 2,000 to 3,000	48
5,000 to 10,000	41
25,000 to 50,000	26
Over 1,000,000	2

The rich furnish no market for mass production. They can absorb only a tiny fraction of the output. The power age can get along with very few workers, but it cannot reach first base without consumers.

Despite an ethic which has been undermined but not formally renounced, citizens already receive a surprising amount of goods and services simply by virtue of membership in the community. They may or may not contribute something in return in the shape of

[7] See editorial in *American Federationist,* May, 1933.
[8] *The Measurement of American Wealth.*

work, crystallized into tax payments. Certainly the work and taxes contributed, if any, bear no measurable relationship to the goods received. In some cases, the ratio appears to be inverse. Here are some of the goods distributed:

Public schools	Playgrounds
Roads	Vacation reservations
Municipal water	Police protection
Sewer systems	Fire protection
Garbage and waste disposal	Building inspection
Public health services	Elevator service
Parks	Museums
Municipal clinics	Libraries
Public lavatories	Zoos
Milk distribution for babies	Churches (free admission)
Food, shelter, clothing and supplies for the unemployed	Public concerts
	Street lighting

Thus a considerable breach has already been driven in the doctrine of *quid pro quo*. In western civilization today, probably 100 million persons are consuming at the expense of their communities—the unemployed and their families. It is likely that most of them will never go back to their old occupations. This is especially true of hundreds of thousands of miners, both in England and in the United States. Under no conceivable circumstances can they enter the pits again; technology has displaced them forever. If these people are to work it will have to be under a different system than vendibility. If they are not to work, they must either starve or be given the right to consume. The American government has paid out some 300 millions of dollars to farmers in recent months, the only recompense being an agreement to restrict agricultural production. Here we find the principle of *quid pro quo* in full reverse. Farmers are being paid not for working if you please, but for *ceasing to work*.

It is only another step, and not a great one, to the establishment of guaranteed subsistence to every citizen from birth to death. The productive mechanism can readily stand it, even if the moral sensibilities of our best people cannot. Listen to Secretary Wallace of the Department of Agriculture:

> The new policy stipulates that the federal government shall buy surplus raw materials and give them to the unemployed. . . . Farmers resent the idea of reducing production of the necessaries of life so long as people in the cities are in need. I share that feeling. I wish it might be extended beyond such necessaries as food to other necessaries like clothing and fuel and light and housing.[9]

The Tennessee Valley Authority is now proposing to finance consumers in the purchase of electrical equipment—heaters, washing machines, stoves, refrigerators. This is not an outright dividend, but still a significant step in the direction of making purchasing power available to many consumers by government action.

Dividends to consumers in money and in kind are already established practice. Under power age conditions, the principle may readily grow until it applies to every citizen, rich or poor, and whether he works or not. In return for this fundamental guarantee, the citizen must be prepared to work whenever and wherever circumstances demand it. If he demurs, the wise community will instantly, and in all justice,

[9] Article in New York *Evening Post,* October 12, 1933.

sever the guarantee. Here, however, we hover on the techniques of future control, which it is no part of this survey to describe. The point I seek to drive home is that the hopper must be cleared if modern industry is to function, and that only consumers in the mass can clear it.

CHAPTER XIX

PROLETARIANS AND PLUTOCRATS

AN unexpected repercussion, not considered at length in the foregoing chapters, but worthy of brief note here, is that of the power age upon the historic doctrine of the class struggle. The march of the technical arts provides an unparalleled example of economic determinism as it smashes ancient and revered institutions. The ultimate decay of capitalism, prophesied by Marx, is now going on before our eyes. The clean outlines of the struggle between manual worker and capitalist, however, so manifest in Europe when Marx wrote his immortal treatise, have been blurred. Technology is slowly obliterating the proletariat. The displaced manual worker, if he secures a job, drifts into the service trades, which are primarily middle class activities.

Already the middle class in America, not including farmers, outnumbers the working class. "If two-thirds of the white-collar workers and one-third of the other skilled workers," says Dr. A. N. Holcombe, "be transferred from the proletariat to the middle class, the proletariat would lose its superiority of numbers, even in the non-agricultural part of the population." [1] I think this is a fair allocation. American farmers are not proletarians. The majority are small business men, and all are devotees of use property.

[1] *The New Party Politics.*

Adding them to the middle class, the majority in sheer numbers is large. Marx, surrounded with the exhausting labor of mid-machine-age conditions, could not quite envisage the power age. His interpreters, living within gunshot of automatic factories, apparently do not know that conditions have changed, but continue an interpretation based upon Manchester and Birmingham in 1850. America still has a proletariat, but every automatic process, every battery of photoelectric cells, diminishes its numbers and its political importance. The greater the pressure of workers through organization and trade unions, the more promptly the employer installs labor-saving machinery.

It is probable that the impotence of the official labor movement in Germany in the face of the Nazi coup was due in considerable part to power age techniques instituted by the rationalization movement after the War. These techniques had developed a chronic oversupply of labor, shattering its bargaining power and cohesiveness. The worker, as such, lost his old economic importance as rationalization gained.

In the United States, a strong machine age proletariat was never developed because of the expanding west, which provided the safety valve of free land to the exploited. We jumped from Stratford to the power age in respect to labor problems. The workers never had a chance to develop class consciousness in the period of expansion, and as expansion ceased, they found themselves in an industrial milieu where collective bargaining and militant organization were no longer effective weapons. Why have mass production industries never been well organized? Is it because of the power of the bosses? No. The bosses tended to be either incompetent and dispersed absentee owners, or a finance capital control bent on the juggling of prospective future earnings. The mass production industries were never organized *because labor was not a sufficiently important function*. A declining quota was needed, but, save for the technician, it was not strategic. Workers could be rapidly trained, and many were at the gates.

"The new middle class," says G. D. H. Cole, "dependent upon the development of modern machine production, is not, like the *petite bourgeoisie* of Marx's day, a spent force. It has behind it a creative power of its own; for it largely organizes the productive work of the modern world. It is a power to be reckoned with in all policies appropriate to the twentieth century; and it is undoubtedly destined to play an important part either in the preservation or reconstruction of capitalism or its supervision by an alternative economic system." [2]

A class struggle we may have, but the lines must re-form to accord with modern industrial conditions, cutting across the received simplicities of the Marxians, with a spear point quite possibly in the technician group. If the rallying cry is economic security, to the proletariat will be added most of the white collar workers, professional people, farmers and small business men. Even the modest investor, so deftly stripped by finance capital, may struggle to get aboard. He has nothing to lose but his barrel; his shirt is already gone.

Corporate development has been such that a wedge has been driven between two sections of the capitalist class. Absentee owners are at swords' points with finance capital "control." Every large merger, every

[2] *A Guide through World Chaos.*

holding company pyramid, every pool operation by insiders, splits deeper the ranks of the capitalists. Technology, meanwhile, is busily dynamiting the formula which has hitherto sustained both wayfaring investor and high finance.

The realist must ask where in America is a strong and waxing proletariat, and where a united, belligerent capitalist class? Technological unemployment has done to the labor market what overproduction and excess capacity did to the stock market.

Marxism is essentially a scarcity philosophy, predicated on the belief that the rich will always rob the poor of a strictly limited total supply of wealth, and that only a proletarian dictatorship can insure a just division. The mistrust is well founded, but the supply of wealth in an abundance economy is more than ample.

Marx himself was, of course, more of a realist than the Marxians. He recognized that all nations did not run to one rigid pattern. Speaking at Amsterdam in 1872 he said:

Of course I must not be supposed to imply that the means to this end [the revolution] will be everywhere the same. We know that special regard must be paid to the institutions, customs and traditions of various lands, and we do not deny that there are certain countries, such as the United States and England, in which the workers may hope to secure their ends by peaceful means.[3]

A NOTE ON PLUTOCRATS

One of the curious impacts of Abundance is the difficulty it presents the rich in maintaining the gulf between themselves and the rest of us by conspicuous consumption. Heretofore the man on the top of the

[3] Sidney Hook: *Towards an Understanding of Carl Marx.*

heap and his women have been marked by palaces, horses, coaches, resplendent personal upholstery, jewels, plate, paintings, vintages, viands, costly sports, libraries, higher education, and retinue. With such chattels he has at once awed the multitude and stirred its envy. A young and vigorous capitalism adopted these consumptive insignia and added new—steam yachts, solid silver bathroom fixtures, private railroad cars, heated swimming pools, Holmes electric protection, and capacious safe-deposit vaults. Presently its heirs and assigns were to be seen in low, lumbering horseless carriages, gleaming with brass lanterns, handmade in France and England. They drove in solid clouds, part petrol and part road dust, to the stupefaction of the peasantry and its unhappy live stock.

Where are these glories now? Quantity production has all but stripped them away. Conspicuous consumption is no longer conspicuous. Consider the items one by one. The laborer—if he has a job—may have delicate food from afar—for instance, the juice of oranges brought to him by refrigerated car from California. For $7.98 any smart shop girl can outdress a duchess, to the satisfaction of the camera, if not the skilled appraiser of textiles. At Playland, the masses can enjoy a more costly swimming pool than a millionaire can afford. There were in 1929, some 10,000 golf courses in the country, overrun and shellmarked by no less than 1,000,000 citizens in white knickers. Mass production jewelry has put real jewels into safe deposit boxes. The gold hunter watch of the squire is matched by Ingersolls for everybody—more, you can have one on your wrist for an additional few cents.

Many of the middle class are far better educated than the rich, while manual laborers as a class send more children to college than the very wealthy. Plumbing is no treat to most of us. When the United Order of Steamfitters gives a dinner to its retiring president, it may be in the Statler with the brothers in tails and white waistcoat—rented, perhaps, but authentic. Where is to be found a gentleman's art gallery as good as the Metropolitan; or a gentleman's library as well stocked as hundreds of free public libraries; or a gentleman's park as fine as the Yellowstone or the Yosemite; or a gentleman's tennis court better than thousands on municipal playgrounds? The gentleman may still have his valet and his butler, but millions of persons in the new service trades are now catering to all of us as waiters, bell hops, cleaners and dyers, movie ushers in stupendous livery, lifeguards at public beaches, taxi drivers, beauty shoppe employees. In California we sit in our automobiles to be served hot meals on trays by roadside restaurant attendants. As for the gentleman's car, he has surrendered completely and taken to Ford station wagons.

Even the naked fact of being rich was put at naught during the New Era by the mass production of paper profit millionaires. Those upstarts, many of dubious literacy, all but wrecked New York Society; the class lines of our best people were brutally trampled down. One's partner at dinner might even pronounce oil to rhyme with pearl.

True, the mass cannot duplicate the quality of much of the rich man's budget, but it takes a practised eye to tell the difference between a custom-made shirt and an Arrow shirt, while for some articles, like motor cars, no craftsman's model can begin to approach the fine tolerances made possible by mass production.

The above observations emphatically do not mean that we are all rich, but only that an abundance economy, stifled as it has been by vendibility, has still operated to give to millions at least the approximation of goods and services which were once the exclusive hall marks of the few. The scarcity value of the rich man's equipment has been seriously depleted. He still hides behind superior quality, but it is a fragile shield. The thunder of his cavalcades has gone.

The rich are not important in a high energy culture, but that fact is of great importance. It cannot fail in due time to deflect the traditional course of social emulation. What do rich families gain by conspicuous consumption, when a good garage mechanic and his wife can throw almost an equal amount of dog? Superiority will have to be found in other things than material possessions; the margin is no longer worth the effort. In what other things? I don't know; but I know what I hope for: superiority in statesmanship, administration, scientific research and the arts. Abundance *must* stimulate some group of alternatives, and perhaps it will be these.

Another favorite picture demolished by technology is that the rich load their bill for luxuries on the backs of the poor. They do nothing of the kind. Times have changed since the reign of Marie Antoinette. Under the formula of capitalism the *poor would be much better off if the rich spent their entire income for luxuries,* or even, as my friend Joseph Wood Krutch suggests, for building each a monstrous stone pyramid like Pharaoh. Unfortunately they save most of their income for reinvestment at compound interest. In due time this chokes the capital goods sector with excess plant capacity, as we have seen, resulting in widespread unemployment. Here is the point at which the modern rich oppress the poor. But an Olympian justice waits. Simultaneously, the rich undermine the sources of their own income. In high energy societies, when the poor lose their livelihood in great numbers, the rich must presently lose theirs, for it is the spending power of the masses, even more than their working power, which keeps the financial system turning over.

Brooks Adams, in his *Theory of Social Revolutions,* has described the impact of technology on the propertied classes from the broad historical point of view:

In America, in 1770, a well-defined aristocracy held control. As an effect of the industrial revolution upon industry and commerce, the Revolutionary War occurred, the colonial aristocracy misjudged the environment, adhered to Great Britain, were exiled, lost their property, and perished.

Immediately after the American Revolution and also as a part of the industrial revolution, the cotton gin was invented, and the cotton gin created in the south another aristocracy, the cotton planters, who flourished until 1860. At this point the changing of the environment, caused largely by the railway, brought a pressure upon the slave-owners against which they, also failing to comprehend their situation, rebelled. They were conquered, suffered confiscation of their property, and perished.

Furthermore, the rebellion of the aristocracy at the south was caused, or at all events was accompanied by, the rise of a new dominant class at the north, whose power rested upon the development of steam in transportation and industry. This is the class which has won high fortune by the acceleration of the social movement, and the consequent urban growth of the nineteenth century, and which has now for about two generations dominated in the land.

If this class, like its predecessors, has in its turn mistaken its environment, a redistribution of property must occur, distressing, as previous redistributions have been, in proportion to the inflexibility of the sufferers.

With the liquidation of official capitalism, it looks as though the third redistribution were now upon us. The sufferers will be inflexible, and the results distressing.

To maintain the rich in the style to which they are accustomed requires only a tiny fraction of total productive effort. We could pension the whole class for life and hardly feel it. What technology cannot tolerate is compounding reinvestment. Some reformers hold that the industrial properties owned *in absentia* by the rich should be purchased by the community at fair values. I agree with them. If income falls to zero, fair value falls to zero. By all means let the community take them over at this figure.

Use property can be confiscated, giving the term its full, sinister connotation. Such a procedure always has, and probably always will, partake of outrage; "a tearing, weeping matter." Industrial property, when not operated by the legal owner, is in an entirely different category. If it provides no income, the owner does not want it. To take property away from those who do not want it is not confiscation. True, incomeless owners will be ready to put a price on their property if and when the community, or anyone else, desires it. At that instant it acquires some scarcity value. Such a price, if very, very reasonable, might be paid, even as France tenders the United States a token payment on war debts. It betrays taste and good feeling.

I have a house and a few securities. The house I live in; the securities have paid nothing for four years. I will not give up my home without a battle. The community can have the securities any time the postman wants to pick them up. I have lost all hope of their helping to provide for my old age. To hell with them. I will take the chance of the community's maintaining me in my declining years.

CHAPTER XX

THE Economy of Abundance is not a mystical force, not a genie from a bottle, despite the fact that its pressures catch us unaware. It is:

A group of buildings, mines, farms, vibrant with machines, and connected by lines of energy and transportation; founded upon

A series of scientific laws, proliferating into specific processes and inventions, and

A set of human habits.

The latter may be further divided into the habits of the scientists and technicians who control and develop the physical processes, and the habits of laymen, connoting everybody else living within the high energy orbit.

The technicians, including many thousands of mechanics without formal engineering training, carry on by a concept of cause and effect which makes them intolerant of the rule of thumb, traditional craftsmanship and common sense. Where the layman holds that a motor car can obviously go faster with a sharp snout to cleave the air, the technician takes an elfish delight in finding that a blunt nose and a sharp tail better fit the laws covering the passage of bodies through resisting mediums. No such perversity to common conceptions has ever been witnessed before; no such fidelity to mathematical equations; no such certainty as to what can happen and what cannot.

The "laws" of finance, which gave impetus to the erection of the Empire State Building, collapsed before the steel work was in place; the laws of physics will hold the structure itself foursquare and sturdy until the steel disintegrates. Banks fail but bank buildings do not. The technician has a duty, a discipline, an intellectual integrity, and a certainty which sets him in a class apart. The class is already numerous, while its appeal to youth is strong. The intelligent and able among the people of the west readily orient themselves to these disciplines. They become a kind of modern priesthood, talking a language which the laity does not comprehend; a priesthood as yet unorganized. While the laity may not understand the technique, it is mostly in sympathy with the tangible performance.

Day by day the habits of the laity have shifted to conform to the technological pattern. These mass habits now form perhaps the strongest of all the mandates imposed by the Economy of Abundance. The individual may protest that he abhors the machine, that the old days were happier, that science is a false messiah, that he is in the market for a patch of arable ground—but his acts belie the protestation. He must constantly watch clocks, consult timetables, ride on railroad trains and in subways, thrust a forefinger in telephone dials, send telegrams; dodge if not use motor cars, taxicabs and busses; be hoisted in elevators, turn the cocks of water and gas faucets, twiddle with radio knobs, switch on electric lights, trust implicitly to the complicated equations back of suspension bridges.

More important still are the habits of work to which he must submit. While he is theoretically free to choose any job which takes his fancy, all jobs, everywhere, are one small portion of a gigantic process which begins and ends beyond his purview. In a sense, we are all men on the belt, screwing one nut home. For most of us the important feature of our work is the figure on a piece of paper delivered Saturday night. We have perforce accepted specialization, and turned *en masse* to the payroll check and its promise of consumption, to right the balance. Work, particularly in its machine age phases, does not interest us much; living does. An irresistible demand is banking up for dependable payroll checks, and the chance to live with some ease of mind. As the mass realizes the age of scarcity has passed, and there is no technological reason for insecurity, this demand may be expected to take a battering, smashing political form.

Another group of mass habits, allied to the above, is that which centers around wants. Quantity production has accustomed us to certain articles and services. Even the very poor have not remained untouched. Electric lights, water supply, motor cars, talking pictures, silk or rayon stockings, frequent baths, toothbrushes, oranges the year around, tinned goods, bottled goods, rubber-soled shoes—hundreds of things are now solidly rooted in use and wont. Most of us would be miserable in the Stratford of 1760. It would take years to recondition consumption habits to that age. The compulsion is strong and belligerent to hold the line.

High energy habits have grown up, a forest, row on row, ever since the industrial revolution began. First came the great complex orienting itself about the factory, including wage work, time serving, union organization. Then the railroad habits moved in, to grip especially a nation of long distances like the

United States. From the '60's on, normal little boys confused locomotive engineers with God; lonely pioneers listened for the whistle of Number Six as she went thundering down the canyon every night at eight o'clock; the railroad station became the town meeting place when the morning mail pulled in; a rich folk lore was laid down, and

> *I've been workin' on the railroad*
> *All the livelong day*

became almost a national anthem. Presently morning and evening commuters' trains were a more cardinal part of the life of suburbia than its churches.

On the Mississippi, the Missouri and the Ohio, the flatbottomed, paddle-wheeled steamboat inaugurated a culture complex celebrated by Mark Twain: his very pseudonym a technical phrase in that culture.[1]

Bicycle habits came and went, in the lives of most of us now over forty; but the motor car provided a group which bids fair to be permanent, even if we must exchange gasoline for alcohol engines. *Recent Social Trends* notes 150 specific influences of the automobile on social life—from undermining railroad traffic to changing the habits of courtship. Literally millions of families have so organized their lives around the motor car that, deprived of it, they would be at a loss to get to their jobs, to transport children to school, to take vacations, to shop, to procure essential supplies, to carry on social life at all. Without a car, many would have to move their residence. When income fails, the automobile is not the first thing to go; it is almost the last. Americans will cut down on food before they will sacrifice gasoline.

---

[1] "Mark twain" was a measurement of the depth of the river water called from lineman to pilot.

Radio behavior is now a strong grove of branching habits. Here again, *Recent Social Trends* lists 150 specific influences. Plumbing habits, electric power habits, telephone habits are also dominant and expanding. The airplane complex is already rooted and will presently proliferate. "If the selected inventions were analyzed as was done in the case of the radio, rayon, and the X-ray, the result would be a very impressive picture of the tremendous force of inventions in producing social changes. . . . The hundreds of thousands of smaller inventions all have their effects on social change, many of them slight, but immeasurable in their total influence."

Finally, we should not forget speech habits. Our mother tongue is now thick with terms unknown a few generations ago. I give you: joy-stick, fuselage, heterodyne, hormone, adrenalin, vitamin, step on the gas, honk, mike, jitney, burn up the road, broadcast (*e.g.* a baby broadcasting all night), libido, aspirin—and numberless scientific words from physics, chemistry, biology, psychology, engineering.

Once the organic growth of technological change in human habit is grasped in all its immensity, it becomes obviously unthinkable to tear these behavior patterns out of the social fabric without a more serious revolution than that implicit in uprooting traditional attitudes towards vendible property, money, or the state. Abundance habits are a pattern based on physical realities, not on concepts more or less metaphysical. With strong inertia, with stubbornness, if necessary with ferocity, the mass of men may be expected to cling to that pattern. Its total shape they have never known or cared to analyze, but insidiously it bends all their waking hours.

Over and against the abundance complex is another complex, also strong, also belligerent, inherited from an earlier age: the cultural lag of scarcity. Most pervasive of all are the money and credit habits of an economic system founded on vendibility. This loose tangle of behavior sets buyer against seller, creditor against debtor, landlord against tenant, taxpayer against government, employer against wage earner, individual against society, and, most pitiful of all, personal integrity against financial success. The pattern assumes a fixed quantity of wealth, and a continued pressure of population upon that wealth. It assumes that the less there is for you, the more there is for me. The facts of Abundance belie this assumption. Under a free flow of energy, the more there is for you, the more there is for me. Observe I am not talking about the beautiful ideals of a coöperative society: *I am pointing out the brute fact that energy has forced us into a collective mold.*

The lesson of collective interest has already been learned in respect to disease. "This solidarity against pathogenic microörganisms," says J. B. S. Haldane, "extends beyond the boundaries of nationality, race, or even species. Every Rumanian infected with infantile paralysis, every Indian with smallpox, every rat with plague, diminishes the probable length of my life." [2] Presently we shall realize that every slum, every destitute family, every nervous breakdown due to unemployment, diminishes the probable enjoyment of wealth and comfort by all other members of the community.

Yet vendibility operates *as if* there were no collective mold, *as if* technological facts did not exist. When

[2] *Science and Human Life.*

Abundance destroys actual scarcity in goods, money, property or labor, it is a traditional money habit which necessitates the creation of artificial scarcities through monopoly and waste. Bankers, money lenders, manufacturers, mine operators and labor leaders proceed to act *as if* their several commodities were really dear. When we fall into a financial depression, although our productive power and physical wealth remain unimpaired, we proceed to act *as if* abstinence, starvation and the eating of garbage were mandatory, because of a shortage of pieces of engraved paper.

The conception of the right to consume as depending on work is, we have seen, a scarcity survival from a time when man, not energy, performed the labor. Property habits, carried over from a time when all property was for use, are becoming fantastically unreal and quite unworkable in a mass production setting. The legal title remains, but function has been stripped away. The strong habits of pecuniary thrift, saving and profitable investment, operate to clog the financial mechanism when technology has built the plant to a certain level of performance.

Political habits are also survivals of an agrarian culture. We vote; but technical problems are never decided by voting, while governmental problems become increasingly technical. In consequence they are decided ineptly or not at all. Megalopolis is not governed in any adequate sense of the word. Were it not for a few hardworking engineers on the side, the city would disintegrate. Cincinnati has begun to learn this lesson. She has scrapped old political habits and substituted a form of local government more consistent with the power age. Read Robert Taft's book thereon.

One might proceed indefinitely developing the extent and implication of the habits surviving from the days of stagecoaches. Every citizen possesses an assortment. At one moment he is driving his car to work—an abundance habit; arrived at his desk he proceeds to conference with his advertising agency as to ways and means to give scarcity value to the cigaret he manufactures—a stagecoach habit.

An impasse has been reached. The two sets of habits will no longer work in tandem. One or the other has to give way. As I write the struggle is ferocious. The stagecoach gentlemen are organizing for "sound" money—meaning, of course, scarce money; for a return to the gold standard; for less government in business; for judicial protection—especially by the Supreme Court—against federal control of hours, wages and competitive conditions. With their direction of high speed presses and broadcasting stations, they can fortify stagecoach vestiges in millions of humbler citizens. The battle, observe, is not so much between a class of citizens X and a class of citizens Y, as between X and Y impulses in the same citizen. Simultaneously he may feel that his wage in an age of plenty is abominably low, and that the gold standard must be preserved. Yet his buying power cannot be raised so long as a gold standard limits mass buying power.

The cultural laggards are noisy; but tangible events since the impasse began show net gains for dynamo behavior and losses for stagecoach behavior; not only in the United States, but all over the world. Vendibility is visibly in retreat. Nation after nation has left the gold standard, to embark on managed currency policies in which the bankers correctly find no hope for maintaining a private monopoly of credit. The State has been forced to support millions of citizens without requiring the traditional *quid pro quo* of work, because there was no work for them to do. Autarchy has all but destroyed the world free market. Dictatorships, one after another, supersede voting, parliaments, checks and balances. Centralization and government control of industry proceed at a violent pace. The end no man can foresee, but the general direction is clear enough. All industrial nations are in the turmoil of a transition period, seeking more or less blindly for stabilities which accord with technological imperatives. History is at one of her most momentous passages.

In the United States, Mr. Hoover threw billions of government dollars under tottering banks, railroads and insurance companies, all without avail, and with a curious mixture of motives. He sought to preserve economic individualism by two billion dollars worth of socialism. Mr. Roosevelt has been moved—or perhaps forced—to a direct attack upon the institutions of vendibility. His policies have obscured party lines, by giving jobs to technicians rather than to deserving Democrats; they have overridden traditional political behavior. Power has flowed out of the states to the federal government in a tidal wave. The National Recovery Administration, the Agricultural Adjustment Administration, Public Works Administration, Civil Works Administration, Civilian Conservation Corps, Tennessee Valley Authority, Alcohol Administration, railroad coördination policies, and the rest, are one and all insults to stagecoach institutions.

The case of Germany is particularly instructive.[3] Modern German industry, since its origin in the days

[3] Following Robert A. Brady, *op. cit.*

of Bismarck, has never been subjected to the extremes
of free competition found in England and the United
States. It has been closer to the technological ideal of
unification, standardization, coördination, and government control. Its scientific research has been the de-
spair of other countries. After the disaster of the War,
Germany turned to rationalization with unparalleled
eagerness—to intensified research, integration, standardization. As a result, a magnificent groundwork was
laid down, superior, as a system, to that found in any
other industrial nation. But when the depression of
1930 smote the world, Germany suffered more severely than most. Why? *Because rationalization had
gone only to a certain point;* the final and inevitable
step had not been taken. She had specialized superbly
and intelligently in this industry and that, but she had
failed to coördinate the whole machine. No dependable controls were set up to keep the power industry
articulated with the chemical industry, articulated with
agriculture, and the rest. As a result, the several
highly specialized cartels and trusts were harder hit
than would have been the case had rationalization
never been undertaken.

The program was daring, but it was not daring
enough. Again why? Because there was no steady
aim; because it was inaugurated for profit, then was
forced to accept serviceability to a degree as integration proceeded, and so wavered back and forth between the two principles. Now science was ahead,
now finance capital. For what was Germany rationalizing; why the magnificent research laboratories,
bureaus of standards, coördinating committees? Nobody knew; at least everybody had a different answer.
It was to increase the incomes of absentee owners; to

better the condition of the German people; to undersell competitors in world markets; to pay reparations;
to glorify the spirit of science; to compensate for the
inferiority suffered in 1919; for what you will.

Germany had no clear definition of aims and pur-
poses, but she went on rationalizing industry just the
same, until she finally got in so deep that she could not
turn back. The only possible direction now is forward,
to complete integration at home, followed by industrial
integration with her neighbors—for she is far from a
self-sustaining economic unit. Thus German capitalists,
looking for enlarged earnings, have put their necks into
technology's noose, and it is hanging them—as capitalists. Meanwhile the people of Germany depend
precariously on the functioning of a half completed
industrial machine. Upon the surface of these stern
realities, a gentleman by the name of Hitler seems to
be waving his arms, shouting stagecoach oratory and
dancing strange Aryan dances. Back, back from
technics, before it is too late! cries Spengler. *It is already too late for Germany.*

What is true of Germany is true of every modern
community, to the extent of its industrialization. The
United States comes close behind, with England following next in line. France is well down the list, for
her hostages to specialization have not been quite so
pronounced. Her thrifty peasants have resisted abundance habits to a degree—but not enough to save them
from the nemesis which dogs us all.

CHAPTER XXI

THE TECHNOLOGICAL IMPERATIVE

ASSUMING that the abundance pattern will prevail, what are the terms upon which it will function? Obviously in the mêlée of transition it can function only by fits and starts. From the foregoing analysis, it is possible concretely to specify the terms. An abundance economy demands:

1. Capacity operation of its plant, on the balanced load principle.

2. An unhampered flow of goods to consumers, involving the right to a minimum standard of living, regardless of work performed—*if no work is available*. Distribution must replace exchange. This imperative is practical, not idealistic, arising from the necessity of keeping the plant in operation.

3. The elimination of waste, restriction and private monopoly, as methods of maintaining prices.

4. The conservation of natural resources to the degree which, consistent with existing technical knowledge, will maintain adequate supplies of raw materials for the calculable future. Neglect of this imperative may cripple the whole productive mechanism through the failure of one resource—say copper, or oil.

5. The employment of a decreasing number of man-hours in industrial production.

6. The encouragement of research, new invention,

and a fairly high obsolescence rate for plant and processes. No more suppressed inventions; no corporate patent monopolies.

7. The capital goods sector to grow only as technological improvement, mass purchasing power, or mass demand requires it. No reliance on this sector, as heretofore, as an automatic distributor of purchasing power.

8. A one-to-one relationship between the growth of physical production and the growth of debt. In the long run, no debt can be serviced which compounds faster than physical production. This rule operates to disallow the bulk of capital claims now outstanding in the United States and in many other nations.

9. A sharp distinction between use property and industrial fixed assets. The latter must be socially controlled in that the units are no longer independent enterprises, but interlock one with another.

10. Economic decentralization; the end of Megalopolis, because it is too wasteful a unit to support. The liquidation of the distinction between city man and country man.

11. The industrialization of most agricultural staples, on a quantity production basis, and a declining number of man-hours in farming.

12. Shorter working hours for all.

13. A wide extension of social services and public works to absorb those inevitably to be displaced from industry, agriculture and the parasitic trades.

14. The continuation of industrial specialization— though decentralization may be expected to simplify it somewhat. The final form in the calculable future seems to be one flexible, far flung electrical machine.

15. No narrow economic nationalism. The plant

demands essential raw materials on a reasonable exchange basis from all over the world.

16. Revised and simplified political forms. The scrapping of outworn political boundaries, and of constitutional checks and balances, where the issues involved are technical.

17. Centralization of government; the overhead planning and control of economic activity. In North America, such planning to satisfy technology should be continental rather than national; it should, for example, let Canada distribute Niagara power over an equal radius on both sides of the border. In Europe, technology will not tolerate national boundaries indefinitely. A working dictatorship over industry is indicated, if the plant is to be efficiently operated. Technical performance cannot be subject to popular vote, but the administrative group from time to time might well be. Remember that pecuniary graft has no point with more than enough to go around; but the very human lust for power remains unimpaired.

18. Finally, and exceedingly important, Abundance demands no compromise. It will not operate at half speed. It will not allow retreat to an earlier level and stabilization there. Pharaoh did not tell the Nile what to do; the Nile told Pharaoh what to do. The industrial discipline must be accepted—all of it—or it must be renounced. The only retreat is back one hundred years to the Economy of Scarcity.

Such, substantially, are the terms upon which the Economy of Abundance will function; such the mold to which new social habits, new institutions, must conform. This is the way, and I think the only way, that a high energy culture will function in the long run.

Some of the imperatives may be subject to modification in detail; other imperatives may arise; but the basic mold is set. This is the direction in which Mr. Roosevelt is now being forced. Underneath political smokescreens, and the alarms of stagecoach champions, those of us who have eyes to see can detect the glacier advancing into Sweden, England, Italy, South America, Canada, Australasia. In Russia the march is luminous.

Do these terms violate human nature; are they inconsistent with normal behavior? Already many have been incorporated into our daily lives, as we have seen. What they do violate is a set of institutions largely developed in the eighteenth century, which in turn displaced an earlier cultural complex based on feudalism, which in turn displaced its predecessor, and so on back to Mesopotamia. Men talk as though the gold standard had been laid down by God, side by side with the law of gravitation. The universal gold standard is not so old as Mr. Roosevelt.

It is not to be gainsaid that these terms carry implications of substantial moral shock to many persons, especially to large owners of property hitherto vendible. The terms are now being bitterly fought, and will continue to be for years to come. Habit complexes do not change over night. If it requires at least a decade to modify the psychology of stolid Russian peasants, it may require twice as long to modify the psychology of Wall Street.

Technological imperative is impersonal, amoral and non-ethical. Like the Nile, it sets the boundaries within which a given culture must operate. The terms imposed by the machine age were onerous to the point of often violating human nature; the terms of the power age are more generous. Fortunate and perhaps fortuitous is the fact that the modern imperative is straight in the direction of an economic system based on serviceability. Machines do not care whom they serve, but they refuse to operate without a high volume of output; they care nothing about human leisure, but the laws of their spinning are inconsistent with the clumsy interference of the human hand. The wastes and barriers of vendibility they will not tolerate.

Any conscious plan for the new society, any revision of the structure of government, any program for social control, any valid political movement, must square with these imperatives. This is the bed we have made—it matters not how—and we must lie on it.

My book properly ends here. The good scientist would feel it unwarrantable to pursue the analysis into the uncertainties of future political or human adjustments. There the imperatives are, for us to take or to leave. I am not, however, a relentless scientist, and I cannot forbear a few words of final speculation. Can we adjust to these imperatives, and if so, how will the adjustment be made?

No one can now know whether adjustment is possible; he can only be sure of the negative: that if adjustment is not made, high energy cultures will presently stand liquidated. He can further be reasonably sure that the liquidation will not be orderly and planned, but cataclysmic. Western man, failing adjustment, will be hurled back, bloodily and painfully, to a low energy, unspecialized economy.

The timid, with the bold, will do better to push on. If we must die, let it be in the front line. The chances of dying, furthermore, are to my mind appreciably less than of capturing the line. What kind of society would fit these imperatives; would it be bleak and rigorous beyond bearing? I think it would be less bleak than that which we lived through in the later stages of capitalism. If we have been able to adjust to the years 1914 to 1918, and 1930 to 1934, a philosopher might say that we can adjust to anything.

The broad outlines of the future society stand clear in the list of imperatives. Political and economic boundaries will have to widen, not imperialistically but to accord with technological unities, especially grids of electrical power. Thus, the United States and Canada will fall into one regional frame; similarly most of Europe. Economically supreme over these frames must sit an industrial general staff with dictatorial powers covering the smooth technical operation of all the major sources of raw material and supply. Political democracy can remain if it confines itself to all but economic matters; democracy in consumption will make enormous strides as standards of living are levelled upward; industrial individualism—anarchy is a better term—in the sense of each business man for himself, each corporation for itself, must be disallowed. The principles of insurance, savings, investment, will be greatly modified in favor of a collective guarantee of adequate living standards. The margin between the relatively rich and the relatively poor will shrink enormously; conspicuous consumption and its emulation will tend to pass. The margin in the United States in 1929 between the richest family ($12,000,000 income), and the poorest family ($300 income), was 40,000 to one. I doubt if in the projected society the margin can much exceed ten to one.

Use property will be extended and protected, with

the reservation that there will probably be an increase in the rental of such property from great service companies, operated by the general staff. One may desire a washing machine, for instance, while living in the country, but on moving to town, may prefer the public laundry. Why be burdened by the ownership of the machine? Such a practice is abhorrent to vendibility, but not to serviceability. Automobiles, pre-fabricated houses, radios, electric refrigerators, television sets, uniforms, motor boats, scientific instruments, are all susceptible to the principle.

Income-producing property which one does not use will pass out of individual possession. Title will vest in the community. It will include the bulk of land, mineral deposits, forest stands, public utilities, and most of the producing and distributing plant. Banking, credit and the issue of money will be a strict government function. There will be no more private banks or stock exchanges. The interest rate will approximate zero, and the debt structure will be very modest, in no event growing faster than physical production.

Work will be carefully allocated, and what the general staff requires, citizens will have to perform. In that work is a fundamental instinct, while jobs under integrated power age conditions will be at a minimum, we may see a surprising reversal of the public attitude toward labor. Rather than being envious of the idle, citizens may become envious of those who secure an opportunity to work. Allotments might be at a premium. A great deal of thought and experiment will have to be devoted to obtaining compensation for the instinct of workmanship in the expanded leisure of that society. One would look for a revival of handicrafts on a large scale, not for sale but for amusement, gifts, and exchange.

While industrial and agricultural labor will steadily decline, we may expect a great increase in service occupations, especially doctors, dentists, nurses, hospital attendants, teachers, research workers, technicians, librarians, artists, authors, public administrators, and so on.

A society such as this would not violate the eighteen imperatives. Within it, invention and technology could continue to expand, and mass production function to a mass demand. I fail to see, furthermore, how it would violate human nature. It holds no terrors for me, in contemplation. I think I could adapt myself to it without developing Freudian complexes. It would be irksome for a time, in that it was different, but a retreat to Stratford would be even more irksome. I conclude, accordingly, that adjustment to such a society is not beyond human possibility. The administrative task of the general staff is admittedly very great. Jobs hardly smaller were done in the War, however, and are being done in Russia today.

This brings us to the second question. Granted that adjustment is conceivable, how are we to go about making it? What is the political path leading to such a society? Is it practical politics?

The eighteen imperatives must govern the platform of any political advance. Fascists, communists, technocrats, Republicans, Democrats, liberals, constitutionalists, what you will, who campaign for ends *that are not in line* with these imperatives are wasting their time and effort. Any political program now before any people anywhere, can instantly be approved or discarded, in whole or in part, by this acid test. Hitler is obviously working *against* the imperatives when he proscribes machines, hails back-to-the-land movements, the breaking up of industrial combines, the stultification of the scientific spirit. Indeed, his whole attitude is, to date, more medieval than modern. Such policies are doomed in advance; they cannot prevail. Russia is working against the imperatives when she tries to teach Marxian physics and Marxian chemistry. President Roosevelt is working against them when he plows under cotton, puts a premium on the destruction of wheat, and tries to bolster up the debt edifice with loans from the Reconstruction Finance Corporation. These are pure scarcity techniques. Mussolini is working against the imperatives when he seeks to make Italy completely self-sufficient.

We can know by this test what is a through road and what is a blind alley. We can, furthermore, come close to formulating the ideal party platform direct from the imperatives. Granted that a statesman made it his own, or that a group of new leaders espoused it, would citizens respond? Has it the proper emotional appeal? Would it sound well over the radio; could it be roared in simple words from the rostrum? Would the plain people understand and would they follow? How strong would be the opposition?

These considerations are profound. Politics, too, has a kind of technology, most of it to be developed in the laboratories of the future. I shall have to leave it to politicians and sociologists, with a solemn warning: They must apply their technique as means to an end in which technological imperatives are dominant. If they create imperatives of their own, beautiful as may be the method for leading the masses, the end of that leading will be down a steep place into the sea. All methods traceable to Aristotle, to stagecoach conditioning, to vendibility, or to a revival of the formula of capitalism, are so doomed.

Minds can direct energy and shape metal, it is true, but minds are more flexible than steel, more flexible than current tracing a copper wire. When the shaping finally crystallizes into one interlocking mechanism, the mechanism must stand or it must fall; it cannot bend. The bending will have to be done by the more flexible minds and habits of men. Stooping, a great treasure is at their feet.

SELECTED BIBLIOGRAPHY

Adams, Arthur B.: *Our Economic Revolution*. University of Oklahoma Press, 1933.

Angell, Norman: *From Chaos to Control*. The Century Company, 1933.

Angell, Norman, and Others: *What Would be the Character of a New War?* Harrison Smith and Robert Haas, 1933.

Atkins, Willard E., and Others: *Economic Behavior*. Houghton Mifflin Company, 1931.

Baker, Elizabeth Faulkner: *Displacement of Men by Machines*. Columbia University Press, 1933.

Beard, Charles A., and Others: *America Faces the Future*. Houghton Mifflin Company, 1932.

Bellamy, Edward: *Looking Backward*. Houghton Mifflin Company, New Edition, 1933.

Berle and Means: *The Modern Corporation and Private Property*. The Macmillan Company, 1933.

Bonn, M. J.: *The Crisis of Capitalism in America*. The John Day Company, 1932.

Boucke, O. F.: *Laissez Faire and After*. Thomas Y. Crowell Co., 1932.

Brady, Robert A.: *The Rationalization Movement in German Industry*. University of California Press, 1933.

Brandeis, Louis D.: *Other People's Money and How The Bankers Use It*. Frederick A. Stokes Co., 1911.

Chase, Stuart: *Men and Machines*. The Macmillan Company, 1929.

——*The Tragedy of Waste*. The Macmillan Company, 1925.

Cole, G. D. H.: *A Guide through World Chaos*. Alfred A. Knopf, 1932.

Committee on the Costs of Medical Care: *The Costs of Medical Care*. University of Chicago Press, 1933.

Coyle, David C.: *The Irrepressible Conflict.* Published by the
    Author, 1933.
Dahlberg, Arthur: *Jobs, Machines and Capitalism.* The Mac-
    millan Company, 1932.
Dennis, Lawrence: *Is Capitalism Doomed?* Harper & Brothers,
    1932.
Doane, Robert R.: *The Measurement of American Wealth.*
    Harper & Brothers, 1933.
Douglas and Director: *The Problem of Unemployment.* The
    Macmillan Company, 1931.
Editors of *Fortune: Housing America.* Harcourt, Brace and
    Company, 1932.
Epstein, Abraham: *Insecurity, A Challenge to America.* Harri-
    son Smith and Robert Haas, 1933.
Fairchild, Henry Pratt: *Profits or Prosperity?* Harper &
    Brothers, 1932.
Filene, E. A.: *Successful Living in this Machine Age.* Simon
    and Schuster, 1931.
Flanders, Ralph E.: *Taming Our Machines.* Richard R.
    Smith, Inc., 1931.
Gantt, H. L.: *Organizing for Work.* Harcourt, Brace and
    Company, 1919.
Haldane, J. B. S.: *Science and Human Life.* Harper &
    Brothers, 1933.
——*Possible Worlds.* Harper & Brothers, 1928.
Hattersley, C. M.: *This Age of Plenty.* Pitman & Sons, Ltd.,
    London, 1933.
Henderson, Fred: *The Economic Consequences of Power Pro-
    duction.* The John Day Company, 1933.
Hobson, J. A.: *Poverty in Plenty.* The Macmillan Company,
    1931.
——*Work and Wealth, A Human Valuation.* The Macmillan
    Company, 1916.
Holcombe, A. N.: *The New Party Politics.* W. W. Norton &
    Co., 1933.
Huxley, Julian, and Others: *Science in the Changing World.*
    The Century Company, 1933.

Jones, Bassett: *Debt and Production.* The John Day Company, 1933.

Laidler, Harry W.: *Concentration in American Industry.* Thomas Y. Crowell Company, 1931.

Laing, Graham A.: *Towards Technocracy.* Angelus Press (Los Angeles), 1933.

Levy, H.: *The Universe of Science.* The Century Co., 1933.

Lord, Russell: *Men of Earth.* Longmans, Green & Co., 1931.

Lowenthal, Max: *The Investor Pays.* Alfred A. Knopf, 1933.

Lynd, Robert and Helen: *Middletown.* Harcourt, Brace and Company, 1929.

Mallon, Guy W.: *Bankers vs. Consumers.* The John Day Company, 1933.

Mathewson, Stanley B.: *Restriction of Output among Unorganized Workers.* Viking Press, 1931.

Mayo, Elton: *The Human Problems of an Industrial Civilization.* The Macmillan Company, 1933.

Newman, Albert M.: *Enough for Everybody.* Bobbs-Merrill Co., 1933.

Ogburn, William F.: *Social Change.* B. W. Huebsch, 1923.

Pitkin, Walter B.: *The Consumer, His Nature and His Changing Habits.* McGraw-Hill Company, 1932.

Polakov, Walter N.: *The Power Age.* Covici Friede, 1933.

The President's Research Committee: *Recent Social Trends.* M   Company, 1933.

Rorty, James   —*Not to Praise.* The John Day Company,   34.

Rubenstein, M., and Others: *ross Roads.* Kniga (England), 1931.

Rugg, Harold: *The Great Technology.*   .ie John Day Company, 1933.

Russell, Bertrand: *The Scientific Outlook.* W. W. Norton & Co., 1931.

Salter, Arthur, and Others: *The Modern State.* The Century Company, 1933.

Scott, Howard, and Others: *Introduction to Technocracy.* The John Day Company, 1933.

Shelton, Jane de Forest: *The Salt-Box House*. Charles Scribner's Sons, 1929 (reprint).

Soddy, Frederick: *Wealth, Virtual Wealth and Debt*. E. P. Dutton & Co., 1933 (reprint).

Soule, George: *A Planned Society*. The Macmillan Company, 1932.

Spengler, Oswald: *Man and Technics*. Alfred A. Knopf, 1932.

Stocking, George Ward: *The Oil Industry and the Competitive System*. Houghton Mifflin Company, 1925.

Strachey, John: *The Coming Struggle for Power*. Covici Friede, 1933.

Tawney, R. H.: *The Acquisitive Society*. Harcourt, Brace and Company, 1920.

Taylor, Horace: *Making Goods and Making Money*. The Macmillan Company, 1928.

Taylor, Morris P.: *Common Sense about Machines and Unemployment*. John C. Winston Company, 1933.

Tugwell, Rexford Guy: *The Industrial Discipline*. Columbia University Press, 1933.

——*Industry's Coming of Age*. Harcourt, Brace and Company, 1927.

Usher, Abbott Payson: *A History of Mechanical Inventions*. McGraw-Hill Company, 1929.

Veblen, Thorstein: *The Engineers and the Price System*. The Viking Press, 1933 (reprint).

——*The Theory of Business Enterprise*. Charles Scribner's Sons, 1920 (reprint).

——*The Place of Science in Modern Civilization*. B. W. Huebsch, 1919.

Wells, H. G.: *The Shape of Things to Come*. The Macmillan Company, 1933.

Westbrook, Francis A.: *Industrial Management in this Machine Age*. Thomas Y. Crowell Company, 1932.

Wile, F. W., and Others: *A Century of Industrial Progress*. Doubleday, Doran & Co., 1928.

Zimmerman, Erich W.: *World Resources and Industries*. Harper & Brothers, 1933.

INDEX